CHIEF of POLICE

Richard CdeBaca

Praise
for
CHIEF OF POLICE

"Richard CdeBaca was dedicated to law enforcement, and he showed it by the high quality of service that he provided to the public."
—State Representative Luciano "Lucky" Varela, Chairman,
New Mexico Legislative Finance Committee

"Mr. CdeBaca has a sterling reputation statewide as a person of integrity, compassion, a strong work ethic and high moral values."
—Justice Patricio M. Serna, New Mexico Supreme Court (retired)

"Richard CdeBaca was a top administrator as well as a very honest, capable and professional police officer. He is one of the most sincere men I have ever known."
—James R. Wheeler, former Albuquerque City Police officer,
former Lincoln County magistrate judge

"Like many New Mexicans, I have read David Roybal for years because he makes us smarter. Throughout his long career as a reporter, columnist and editor, David has been able to get to the bottom of the story. More importantly, he has uncommon skill to explain to the rest of us how forces work to reshape society."
—Robert Dean, Editor (retired), *The Santa Fe New Mexican*

"Few people can tell a story better than this longtime journalist and writer. David Roybal grew up among the same landscapes and people that are the settings and players in CdeBaca's lifetime of law enforcement and knows exactly what the lawman is talking about as he remembers his adventures. David's insight and writing style will make you believe you were there, too."
—Dan Herrera, Editorial Page Editor, *Albuquerque Journal*

CHIEF of POLICE

The Career of Richard CdeBaca
During Extraordinary Times
in New Mexico 1956–1994

David Roybal

SUNSTONE
PRESS

SANTA FE

Sunstone books may be purchased for educational, business, or sales promotional use.
For information please write: Special Markets Department, Sunstone Press,
P.O. Box 2321, Santa Fe, New Mexico 87504-2321.

Book and Cover design › Vicki Ahl
Body typeface › Cambria
Printed on acid-free paper

———————————————————————————————

Library of Congress Cataloging-in-Publication Data

Roybal, David, 1952-
  Chief of police : the career of Richard CdeBaca during extraordinary times in New Mexico
(1956-1994) / by David Roybal.
    pages cm
  ISBN 978-0-86534-960-5 (softcover : alk. paper)
  1. CdeBaca, Richard. 2. Police chiefs--New Mexico--Biography. 3. Police--New Mexico--History-
-20th century. 4. New Mexico--History--20th century. I. Title.
  HV7911.C39R69 2013
  363.2092--dc23
  [B]
                    2013019520

———————————————————————————————

WWW.SUNSTONEPRESS.COM
SUNSTONE PRESS / POST OFFICE BOX 2321 / SANTA FE, NM 87504-2321 /USA
(505) 988-4418 / ORDERS ONLY (800) 243-5644 / FAX (505) 988-1025

Introduction

Richard CdeBaca as Secretary of the New Mexico Department of Public Safety in 1994.

Richard CdeBaca has history on his side when he asserts that he had an eventful career with the New Mexico State Police. He expected excitement when he joined the force in September 1956. He couldn't have imagined everything that would unfold by the time he retired from the force in February 1983. The shocking 1967 raid on the Rio Arriba County courthouse, an eruption of student unrest at the University of New Mexico in 1970 and the brutal inmate riot at the Penitentiary of New Mexico 10 years later stand out as evidence. Scathed in political battles during his very brief tenure as chief of State Police from October 1982 through February 1983, CdeBaca returned to serve as Cabinet Secretary of the Department of Public Safety, overseeing State Police, from January 1991 through December 1994.

He was a policeman when illegal drug use mushroomed around the state, when demands to sharply reduce drunken driving became inescapable and when controversial Indian gambling casinos sprouted along the Rio Grande and beyond amid piercing questions about their legality.

CdeBaca served 10 governors and six chiefs of police while assigned to postings around the state. He learned the business of policing well while rising to the highest ranks of the New Mexico State Police and the Department of Public Safety before retiring for good in 1994.

Far too often, tragedy was a companion. "I was raised in the small farming community of La Ciénega south of Santa Fe," CdeBaca said. "I grew up helping my father butcher hogs, slaughter cows and chop chicken heads off. But those were animals, not human beings. The human carnage that I came upon as a state policeman exceeded even what I witnessed while serving in the Korean War. For much of the time that I was with the State Police, the department did not provide any type of professional counseling, whether we needed it or not."

While a boy at home, CdeBaca one day was pressed into action of the sort that would later fill the career in which he was constantly being summoned for help. "It was the only tragic accident that I witnessed while growing up," he said. "I was 15 years of age at the time. A cousin of ours named Art CdeBaca showed up at our house with a .22 automatic rifle. He said he was going rabbit hunting. When he walked away from the house, he had positioned the butt of the rifle on top of his right foot and was holding the end of the barrel with his thumb. The rifle accidentally discharged and the bullet went through his thumb and shattered his jaw and blew away his lower front teeth and lodged somewhere in his head. My father took him to St. Vincent Hospital in Santa Fe, which was 15 miles away. I was sent to notify his parents who lived about one mile away, and I believe I set a record for running that distance. Art survived but the shooting left him with a deformed thumb and chin."

CdeBaca compiled more than 30 years of recollections and formal accounts from his varied experiences in law enforcement. They reflect the inner workings not just of the State Police but of local and state governments as well as private industry. So much of it is the stuff that, not surprisingly, escapes promotional materials proffered by public and private administrative offices everywhere.

Because CdeBaca worked in positions very much in the public eye, news reporters trailed him on some of his rounds. But there was a lot that escaped attention until now.

Much of what you will read between the covers of this book are CdeBaca's own words, largely unaltered. It is undeniably "police speak," lending its own flavor to the text and, perhaps, even providing insight to the career cop's personality and approach to his work. At times, as in his references to Navajos in McKinley County, entries reflect jaw-dropping generalizations that increasingly are denounced but which, arguably, remain ingrained in too much police work decades later. Even years after his retirement, CdeBaca won't be confused for a soft-treading social worker. At 79, this veteran of the Korean War has a stance and manner that would impress any general. Those who know him well say he is diligent, honest, compassionate. But he also is an opinionated man. His opinions of lawbreakers and most who test the boundaries of acceptable behavior can be largely unforgiving.

CdeBaca's writings required organization. Much of what he wrote lent itself to introductory or interpretive remarks that the career cop asked me to research and supply.

Among numerous interviews, I had more than a couple of dozen with CdeBaca. Direct quotations gleaned from those interviews appear within my own writings and are intended to add to what CdeBaca recorded in his personal entries, which are clearly set apart from the rest of the text. One of my last interviews was with Nick Sais, the state policeman who was shot during the 1967 courthouse raid in Tierra Amarilla. He didn't shrink from questions, the easiest of which was to clear up the frequent misspelling of his name. That having just been done, we can move on to entries of extraordinary times: historic, occasionally unsettling and sometimes just plain comical.

—David Roybal

1

Riding Old Wheels into a New Career

Prodded to join the New Mexico State Police by a ranking aide to Governor John Simms, young Richard CdeBaca of Santa Fe enjoyed no special treatment when in the mid-1950s he was finally sent out to begin what would be a colorful career tagged in the end by controversy ignited by two latter-day governors.

CdeBaca served the New Mexico State Police for more than 26 years, spending much of his time as a patrolman along Route 66, as busy as it is famous. He went on to become chief of the State Police and cabinet secretary for the Department of Public Safety. He was in uniform for some of New Mexico's highest-profile events of the past half century. Among them: the violent 1967 raid by land grant activists on the Rio Arriba County courthouse in Tierra Amarilla, anti-war student riots at the University of New Mexico, the brutal inmate riot at the Penitentiary of New Mexico and the unsolved case of the Santa Fe priest who was lured into the night by a dark soul requesting pastoral assistance.

Other stories offered by CdeBaca include one about a lieutenant governor who angrily demanded a restraining order and police protection against the governor with whom he had been elected; the bombastic governor visiting from another state who on a New Mexico highway denounced CdeBaca as a "Mexican bandit;" a neighbor who unapologetically asked for CdeBaca's service pistol so he could kill himself; a young man who proclaimed his innocence in a case by insisting, "I steal chickens, I don't steal cars;" and the state policeman who doubled as a preacher and admonished a robber, "God bless you son, you thieving son of a bitch."

Encouraged into service by a top gubernatorial aide, CdeBaca certainly did not appear to get preferential treatment when he eventually was assigned his first patrol car. It was the vehicle that would end up being both his office and principal tool for enforcing state laws in largely desolate expanses west of the Sacramento Mountains down to the Texas border.

CdeBaca recorded copious notes about his career of more than a quarter century with the New Mexico State Police. Many of them are quite revealing, like his writings about his first patrol car:

> "I was issued my first black and white State Police car, a 1954 Ford Fordomatic, which had 96,000 miles. The car had belonged to Captain James E. Clark. Years later Captain Clark was killed when his police car ran into a train in Clovis.
>
> "The car I was issued could only attain a certain top speed and sometimes speeding cars I was chasing would outrun my car. My police car left a trail of smoke behind when I would push it too hard, but I didn't care. I was proud of my job."

CdeBaca later had much more to say about that well-used Ford. "After receiving my commission, it took only two weeks for on-the-job training with a senior officer before I got orders to report to headquarters in Santa Fe for my first car assignment," he said. "I was elated to know that I was reporting to headquarters to get my own car which is the day that you look forward to. I didn't question the car that I was assigned. I had no choice but to accept what I was issued."

CdeBaca, having just turned 23, became the youngest member of the State Police force in September 1956. He was filled not only with joy but with pride when he picked up the keys to his first squad car. "It was only after I left headquarters that I noticed the odometer reading," he said. "I said to myself, 'This is the newest car that I've ever driven."

It's not as if he had driven many. "I didn't even own a personal car when I reported to Alamogordo for my first State Police assignment," said CdeBaca. "My sister, Alice, and I owned a car together, which was a 1950 Chevrolet, and when I went to Alamogordo, I let her keep the car. My parents, Ricardo and Agueda, took me to Alamogordo in a 1955 Chevrolet that my father had bought the previous year."

It didn't take long for CdeBaca to begin learning more about his police Fordomatic. "Little did I realize at the beginning that this 1954 Ford had the attainable speed of about 90 miles per hour on a straightaway. I would get outrun when in pursuit of other vehicles. It was frustrating and embarrassing right at about the time that you let off the gas (pedal) and this black smoke would just swirl around the rear end of that car. You were left wondering what other drivers thought of you driving a black and white that was in that kind of condition.

"Word got out among servicemen at Holloman Air Force Base, which was part of my patrol," CdeBaca said. "They knew that when I chased them, they could beat me to the gate. I visited with the base commander and told him I was tired of being outrun to the gate and I had no jurisdiction within the base. I asked for permission to pursue those vehicles inside the base where I could ticket them. To be honest about it, I was surprised that the commander granted my request.

"It only took a couple of pursuits inside the base and word got around in a hurry among the military population that you could no longer get away."

The New Mexico State Police, created in 1935, descended from the New Mexico Mounted Police. At its inception in 1905, the Mounted Police had 10 men. Headquarters were in Socorro briefly before they were moved to Santa Fe in 1906. The small organization disbanded in 1921.[1] The New Mexico Motor Patrol was created in 1933 to centralize and coordinate enforcement duties of various branches of government, including the Corporation Commission. Men patrolled not in cars but in Harley Davidson motorcycles. In 1933, they were paid $125 per month.[2]

With a need for expanded responsibilities, the New Mexico State Police Department was created and included 30 policemen plus two plain-clothes investigators. Officers worked 12-hour days with one day off every two weeks. The department to get started ordered seven 1935 Chevrolet police cars.[3]

CdeBaca had served in Korea with the U.S. Navy and when he returned, he entertained thoughts of a college education and, perhaps, a career in accounting. But while working at a transitional job at the state motor vehicles office in 1956, he was approached in the state Capitol by the chief of staff for Democratic Governor John Simms.

"I had gotten to know Everett Grantham because the governor's office was one floor above where I was employed," CdeBaca said. At 6'2", CdeBaca's size apparently had caught Grantham's eye. "Mr. Grantham asked me what I planned to do with my future. He asked if I ever thought of becoming a State Police officer. He said I have the right size for it.

"He said, 'Why don't you make an appointment to see Chief Joe Roach.' That was the turning point in my life."

In 1956, new police cruisers, like this Ford, were driven by ranking officers while rookie Richard CdeBaca and his weary 1954 unit were routinely outrun by violators.

CdeBaca made an appointment and met with Chief Roach for about 15 minutes in his office at the old Pueblo-style buildings of State Police headquarters off Cerrillos Road. CdeBaca said he was surprised that the chief did not immediately refer him to a secretary or someone under his command. "I walked in during a regular work day wearing a suit and tie because that's what I was required to wear on my job. I was nervous at the meeting. I didn't know any police officer, no one I could have consulted with before going in to see the chief."

CdeBaca got an application on his way out of the office and returned it personally. "Probably within a time period of about six weeks, I got notice that I had been accepted for training. I believe it was officer John Niles that did the background check on me, things like education, employment history, military service, character.

"Even before I was accepted, I began running in sandy arroyos around my home in La Ciénega for physical fitness training. At 6'2", I was a trim 175 pounds when I reported to the school. Before long, I was given the nickname of the White Stallion because of my running ability. There was no one in the class of 44 men who could stay with me."

CdeBaca's written recordings tell of what he found at training school on grounds that were to become the College of Santa Fe campus:

"In May 1956, I began my State Police training at the old Army Bruns Hospital facilities in Santa Fe. On July 1st, I completed my training and graduated from Recruit Class No. 10. Forty-four men started in the recruit class; 28 graduated but only 19 were hired. I was under the required age of 23 and for that reason could not get commissioned as an officer.

"Chief Joe Roach offered me a position as a radio dispatcher and was assigned to Alamogordo. My starting salary as a dispatcher was $280 per month. On September 5th, I turned 23 and received my commission as an officer. My badge number was 138. My starting salary was $330 per month. I was issued the standard State Police equipment: a .38 Smith and Wesson revolver, a shotgun, gas billy, flashlight, measuring tape, first-aid kit, stop sign, shovel, highway reflectors, and a box of 30-minute fuses. My uniforms were paid for and I was given $10 per month uniform allowance."

The newly commissioned officer from La Ciénega was known by the name DeBaca. But that didn't last long. "Increasingly, I took pride in what is derived from one of the most venerable names in New Mexico," said CdeBaca, who spells the name without spaces. "CdeBaca is shortened from Cabeza de Vaca, which originated in Spain. It was Álvar Núñez Cabeza de Vaca who was among early European explorers in New Mexico. Ezequiel C. de Baca, a distant relative, served as governor in 1917."

The six weeks of training to get commissioned was "rigid," CdeBaca said. "It reminded me of my basic training in the military: strenuous. They pushed us hard. We reported to the gym at 6 a.m. and the lights were turned out at 10 o'clock at night. We learned to acquire flashlights so that after 10 o'clock we would sit in the restroom of the old barracks and do homework and escape the attention of the instructors who patrolled the halls.

"I knew nothing about police work. I was not intimidated because I had ex-perienced the discipline with the Christian Brothers at St. Michael's High School and then experienced the same type of discipline and training in the military. I was accustomed to authority.

"On the first day of class, Chief Roach appeared before us and told us that even though the class had 44 men, only 19 would possibly be hired because of the department's budget," CdeBaca said. "Only 28 graduated from the class. On mornings, you would see a vacant chair and we were not told by the instructor under what circumstances that student left. Those that left either weren't 100 percent committed or they didn't make the grade. Those of us who remained knew that the more who left, the better our own chances of getting commissioned."

Richard CdeBaca in September 1956 became the youngest member of the New Mexico State Police at age 23.

In the end, 16 were commissioned immediately after completion of training. Two were under the required age of 23. One of them, Joe Tarazon, was commissioned a month after graduation. CdeBaca was commissioned two months after that on his 23rd birthday.

CdeBaca promptly jumped into work that was in stark contrast to his duties at the state motor vehicle office.

"Being single and ambitious, I didn't mind working 12 to 14 hours a day, six days a week with no weekends or holidays off. I enjoyed my work and never complained."

"We always patrolled by ourselves, and there was no backup within miles. We learned to take care of ourselves, knowing that at any given time, we would put our lives in harm's way. I believe my size was in my favor, being 6'2" and weighing 210 pounds. Wearing a police cap and high-heel boots made me look more like 6'6.""

If CdeBaca's size got him through some situations, it was immaterial in what he described as his "first unfortunate experience": a hanging at a private residence that he was dispatched to in his first days on the job.

"When I knocked, a young girl between the age of 11 and 12 opened the door. She told me that her brother was in the closet and she escorted me down a hallway to a bedroom. In the closet, I saw the body of her brother hanging from a rod with a belt tied around his neck, which was covered with a red neckerchief. It was obvious to me that the boy had been dead for some time.

"When I initially walked into the house, I noticed the parents sitting in the kitchen and thought it was odd that they didn't answer the door themselves. In talking to them, I got the impression that this was a dysfunctional family. The girl told me that her brother had been playing cowboys and Indians.

"The death was ruled a suicide."

Police officers routinely are reminded that their job at its core is to serve and protect. A neighbor one day asked CdeBaca to serve by helping him through his intentions. But service that day would have denied protection.

"One day I took a ride to La Ciénega, where I was born and raised. I saw one of our old neighbors walking down the dirt road near his house and I stopped to visit with him. During our conversation, he asked to borrow my gun, which I thought was an unusual request. I asked him why he wanted to borrow my gun and he replied, 'So I can shoot myself.' He told me he had been suffering from bad headaches for too long and that doctors had never been able to help him. I wished him well and went on to visit my parents.

"Weeks later, I went to the emergency room at the hospital in Santa Fe to check on the condition of a woman who had been involved in an automobile accident. While in the emergency room, I saw my neighbor being wheeled in. Part of his skull was gone and his brain was exposed. He had shot himself with a gun he had borrowed from another neighbor.

"I had known the wounded neighbor all my life and I would never have expected him to take his own life. He was a very stable man. The woman who was involved in the auto accident died in the emergency room and so did my neighbor."

CdeBaca, of course, knew going into the State Police that death rarely would be far away, including death among his peers.

"The first State Police officer to be murdered was Nash Garcia. On April 11, 1952, he was parked on old U.S. 66 a few miles west of Grants when a pickup truck sped past him at a high rate of speed. Officer Garcia pursued the pickup for several miles. He finally caught up with it inside the (Acoma) reservation and two Laguna Indians ambushed him. He was shot several times while inside his car and his car was set on fire. It was Easter and I was a senior at St. Michael's High School."

Nearly 20 years would go by before the next state policeman would be murdered in the line of duty. Like the first, this one had plenty of drama.

"On the night of November 8, 1971, officer Robert Rosenbloom, then 27, was fatally shot while making a routine stop on I-40 west of Albuquerque. The car he stopped was occupied by three men.

"Officer Rosenbloom had received a radio call instructing him to relay a witness in a trial toward Grants, where another officer would continue the relay. It was on the return trip to Albuquerque that officer Rosenbloom stopped a green Ford. The time was about 11 p.m. Six minutes later officer Rosenbloom called the dispatcher for a check on the California license number. Minutes later, the dispatcher called officer Rosenbloom with the information, but he never acknowledged the call.

"Meanwhile, a passing motorist saw the officer lying on the ground as the assailants' car raced by. The motorist was curious as to what had happened and turned around. He found officer Rosenbloom lying face down a few feet from his police car. Using the officer's police radio, the motorist called for help.

"Eighteen days later, the three males—Charles Hill, Michael Finney and Ralph Goodwin—left their Albuquerque hideout, commandeered a wrecker and forced the driver to take them to the Albuquerque airport, where they hijacked a TWA airplane and escaped to Cuba. To this day, Hill and Finney remain in Cuba. Goodwin was reported drowned in 1973.

"By strange coincidence, the murder of officer Rosenbloom took place a few miles east of where officer Nash Garcia had been killed on April 11, 1952. Deaths of other State Police officers would follow. Officer Ricardo Gomez was shot and killed during a routine traffic stop near Coyote and officer David Coker was shot and killed near Santa Rosa."

It wasn't murder but death in the service of the New Mexico State Police touched CdeBaca's own family a decade after CdeBaca joined the department.

"A cousin of mine, officer Robert Romero, was killed in a car accident while on duty at Arroyo Seco in 1967. He was returning to Santa Fe one night when a truck hauling timber crossed in front of him and he was unable to avoid it."

Then there was at least one officer's death that went without much explanation.

"Officer William Spaight's body was found under a tree off a dirt road near State Road 83 near Alamogordo on February 24, 1949. The report said he had just lay down and died. Officer Spaight had suffered from black outs caused by previous injuries.

"Years later, the exact same spot became the site of a love-torn woman's suicide. State Police Sergeant Floyd Miles in Alamogordo and a border patrolman dated women from Holloman Air Force Base. Sergeant Miles eventually married a woman from the base. The woman who dated the border patrolman was married and wanted a divorce from her husband but he refused. One day, the woman drove onto the dirt road leading to the Wolford Communications tower. She parked her car and while it was running, she attached a hose to the exhaust and climbed into the trunk, where she died."

CdeBaca said he and other state policemen were given plenty of discretion while patrolling in their districts. "Back then, you had the latitude to get out there and just do the job the best way that you could," he said. "You are assigned a patrol by the supervisor but he does not spell out the emphasis on what the priority should be while you're spending 12 to 14 hours, six days a week out there. You use your training and imagination about what you are going to put emphasis on. Every day was a learning experience on the job because you got exposed to different situations.

Richard CdeBaca was prolific at writing tickets along New Mexico roads.

"Once your supervisor compiled the statistics for the previous month, he would have a little meeting and go over all the enforcement statistics, sometimes comparing one officer to another, who was the top go-getter in the district."

Of course, policemen were pressed into action by what transpired around them, leaving little room for imagination. "You're often working in wide open spaces and people are going to speed in wide open spaces," he said. "You see a speeder go by, what do you do? You go after the speeder. Most of my stops were for speeding."

Too often, CdeBaca and other officers patrolling state highways were pressed into dealing with speeders only after it was too late.

"On July 29, 1959, my mother-in-law invited us to have dinner at their home in La Luz. I had been visiting with my father-in-law when the dispatcher called and told me he had received a report of a fatal accident south of Tularosa. For some reason, I couldn't get my police car to start. I radioed the dispatcher and told him that I was going by private vehicle and would not have any radio communications and to dispatch an ambulance and a wrecker.

"I told my father-in-law to take me to the scene of the accident. I grabbed my first-aid kit and we took off. It seemed like an eternity getting there in his old International pickup. When we arrived at the scene of the accident, we couldn't believe the tangled mess we saw.

A white car had collided with a heavy dump truck and the car was demolished into pieces.

"The ambulance arrived and we started gathering human parts and putting them in a leather bag. I found the victim's decapitated head in the wreckage. I saw my father-in-law carrying one of the victim's legs and carrying it to the ambulance. The victim's torso had been dissected when the car was ripped apart from the tremendous impact.

"I managed to find the victim's wallet in his torn clothing and used his driver's license to determine his identity. From what was left of the wreckage, I was able to determine that the victim was driving a 1958 Chevrolet. According to a witness, the Chevrolet had passed him traveling well in excess of 100 mph. The driver failed to negotiate a slight curve, lost control and the car skidded sideways into the two-ton dump truck, shredding the car to pieces. The driver of the truck escaped without injuries.

"When I located the victim's wife to notify her, she told me she had passed the scene of the accident, but due to the scattered wreckage, she did not recognize her husband's car.

"After completing my investigation and cleaning up the scene of the accident, my father-in-law and I returned home. Both of us had our hands covered with dried human blood. He refused to eat dinner and told me he wouldn't have my job for all the money in the world.

"The next day, the *Alamogordo Daily News* printed a picture of the accident on the front page and labeled it 'Most Horrible in Entire History' of Otero County. And there had been no other accident as horrible as this one that I had investigated so far."

Other times, speeders and violators of various highway laws tried what they could—or what they were familiar with—to wriggle loose of the patrolman's grasp.

"On one occasion, I stopped a 1961 Oldsmobile for speeding which was registered in the state of Illinois. When I asked the driver for his driver's license, he tried to hand me a $50 bill. I told him I could charge him with attempt to bribe an officer and he replied, 'This is the way we handle it in Chicago.' I issued him a ticket and made him turn around to go pay the fine."

CdeBaca, while chasing speeders in Southern New Mexico, eventually got much-needed help from his supervisors.

"In early January 1958, I was told to report to Santa Fe for a new car assignment. I was issued a new 1958 Chevrolet. Every officer looked forward to the day to get a new car and so did I. I spent the night with my parents in La Ciénega before returning to Alamogordo early the next day."

The '58 Chevy turned out to be CdeBaca's third patrol car. "Before getting the 1958 Chevrolet, I was issued a 1956 Ford," he said. "That was a tremendous upgrade. Like my first car, it also was a hand-me-down. Then in 1958, they gave me the brand-new Chevrolet, standard shift."

Although he drove the new car to his parents' house, CdeBaca said he did not offer his father or mother a ride. "We were not allowed to do that but my parents knew I was a very happy camper," he said.

On one unfortunate occasion, the thrill of getting a new patrol car was short lived for a state policeman close to CdeBaca.

"One evening, officer Robert E. Lee radioed me to meet him at the Wagon Wheel Café. He was returning from Santa Fe, driving a new police car and he wanted me to see it. Officer Lee and I had become good friends. He was stationed in Las Cruces, but our assigned patrols met on U.S. 70 at the Otero-Doña Ana County line. We used to meet there on many occasions and at times assist each other investigating accidents. We enjoyed a good visit that night before he departed for Las Cruces. Officer Lee was 6'4" and weighed about 160 pounds in full uniform. He used to joke that he was the only State Police officer who could hide behind a utility pole and not be seen.

"That was the last time I would visit with officer Lee. About 2 a.m., the dispatcher woke me up to tell me that officer Lee had been killed while investigating a car accident east of Las Cruces on U.S. 70. He had been run over by a car. I could not believe what I had just heard. His funeral was not only a very sad day for his family but also for every state policeman. I would miss my friend forever."

If speeders accounted for most of CdeBaca's stops as a young patrol-man, he also made it his business to be on the lookout for stolen cars. He "had a nose" for stolen cars passing through his district, wrote a police reporter for the *Alamogordo Daily News*.

The lead paragraph in a March 1958 story in the Alamogordo paper read: "State Policeman Richard DeBaca has arrested the drivers of four cars stolen or believed to have been stolen during the past two weeks, and is now looking for the fifth."

CdeBaca's supervisor at the time, Sergeant A.B. Munsey, attributed the arrests to "the alertness of a good officer."

But if CdeBaca "had a nose" for hot cars, apparently neither he nor his supervisors were overly concerned about stopping motorists without just cause.

In one such case, a reporter for the *Alamogordo Daily News* was riding along with CdeBaca and what the reporter witnessed led to the paper's unabashed praise for CdeBaca's police work. The stop led to recovery of a stolen vehicle and a lot more.

"One day, a reporter for the *Alamogordo Daily News* asked if he could ride along with me, and my supervisor approved it. I patrolled toward Bent, a tiny community, to check with justice of the peace J.T. Falls regarding a speeding ticket I had issued the day before. Before getting to Bent, I met a green Ford headed west on U.S. 70 occupied by three young men. I told the reporter that I was going to turn around and stop the car. He asked me why, and I told him that the car had Arkansas license plates and I wanted to find out if it could be a stolen car.

"When I stopped the car, I noticed several cartons of cigarettes in the back seat. I ordered the driver to step out and questioned him about the ownership of the car and the cigarettes in the back seat. He said they had bought them at a store in New Mexico but didn't remember where. I ordered him back in the car and got one of the passengers to get out. I told him I had a report of a burglary where cigarettes were taken and he admitted events of a burglary-studded trail through Arkansas, Texas and New Mexico. I arrested all three of them and took them to the State Police office for further questioning.

"The driver was 26 years old and gave his address as Tifton, Georgia, and his two passengers who were hitchhikers, ages 19 and 20, who gave addresses as Albany, Kentucky. They admitted burglarizing a café in Floyd, New Mexico. The cigarettes and $60 in cash had been taken from the cigarette machine, which they claimed to have hauled from the café and took to a remote area where they busted it to pieces. They also admitted burglarizing a store in Arkansas where they stole some tires and sold them. The car had been stolen in Georgia. All were incarcerated until they could be properly extradited.

"The next day, the reporter wrote in the *Alamogordo Daily News*: 'A nose for hot cars and dispatch in following a hunch netted the capture for CdeBaca, who first met the car on routine patrol. Alerted by what he considered possible indication of a stolen car, the patrolman turned back to investigate the car and its occupants. The arrest followed.'"

CdeBaca, in fact, would set a State Police record for recovery of stolen vehicles. En route to the accomplishment, he gained high praise from his superiors, as recorded in this notation made by CdeBaca:

"The State Police bulletin for the month of March 1958 stated: 'Officer Richard CdeBaca has run up some sort of a record at the Alamogordo Station. Within the past thirty days he has recovered seven stolen cars, none of which carried a stolen car alert. Five of the cars had drivers who were taken into custody and have pled guilty to Dyer Act charges (associated with interstate transportation of motor vehicles). This activity is extremely commendable when it is considered that during this same period, he issued 87 citations for hazardous moving violations.'"

In our conversations, CdeBaca called it all a matter of keen instincts along with wanting to do a good job. "It was just work ethics," he said. "You spend half of your day back in those years in your police car on your assigned patrol. What else is there to do besides being observant to all traffic matters, observing suspicious activity, and not just out there waiting for that one speeder to come by."

He referred specifically to the case involving the three Arkansas youths mentioned a few paragraphs earlier. "I not only noticed those out-of-state license plates, but I noticed three very young men in the car with no clothes visible hanging inside the car. I asked myself, if I had to take a second look at that car, why am I just going to ignore it and not turn around to go stop the car? Is it sufficient cause? No it is not. In those days we could get by with things that we could not get by with today."

The remark was affirmed by State Police Lieutenant Eric Garcia, who in 2009 served as the department's spokesman. Offering high praise for the reputation left by CdeBaca, Garcia said times now require probable cause for traffic stops to be made. He said officers must first conclude that evidence exists to believe that a traffic violation or a criminal act has been committed. "The way people look does not determine how an officer acts," he said.

Looking back at his tactics and those employed by other officers of the period, CdeBaca said, "It's something that you develop and become a success at it even though you don't have a legal right to stop that car other than based on something that tells you something is wrong here ... But I'll say this, too: I never made up a story, like you were weaving all over the road, to justify stopping a vehicle ... And, of course, some stops led to nothing."

The *Alamogordo Daily News* seemingly could not stop praising CdeBaca's tactics and success. The paper in July 1958 added to its own periodic praise of CdeBaca while reporting on the theft of an auto belonging to the community's chamber of commerce manager. The car was found later in La Luz where it had been abandoned after developing vapor lock.

Reported the *Daily News*: "DeBaca had been given a description of the youth who abandoned the car by La Luz residents. The officer had a pretty good idea who the people were describing and he set out to find (the boy) who was on parole from the Boys School in Springer."

The newspaper said it was the 15th stolen car that CdeBaca had recovered in the first seven months of the year. "DeBaca got statewide publicity on his 11th recovery, which was a New Mexico record at the time," the newspaper said of the milestone that CdeBaca reached earlier in the year.

CdeBaca did not seem to lack for opportunities to build on his reputation while patrolling southeastern New Mexico during the late 1950s. "In school, you're trained to look for certain things: this, that and the other, but mostly you used your own imagination," he said. Spotting suspicious activity, he'd spring into action.

"One evening, I was on my way home from Tularosa when I caught up with a 1954 Ford occupied by four juveniles. I stopped the car and discovered that the driver did not have permission to have the car. The juveniles were runaways from Kansas City, Missouri. They had in their possession a .45 automatic, a .22 rifle, a high-caliber Japanese rifle, a small blank handgun, two knives, two radios, 21 cents and very little gas in the car. The guns belonged to the driver's father. Two of the juveniles had police records. All of them were returned to Kansas City."

"One day, I was parked on the shoulder on U.S. 54-70 between Alamogordo and Tularosa when I saw a young teenager on a motor scooter traveling north. He kept looking back at my police car and that to me was a clear indication that he was up to no good. I took pursuit and when I tried to stop him, he would increase his speed. Finally, I pulled up alongside of him and gradually forced him to stop. This 13-year-old had no driver's license, had stolen the motor scooter and was armed with a .22 western-type six-shooter loaded with four live rounds.

"I arrested him and took him before the Juvenile Probation Officer, Mr. Earl Scroggins. The juvenile admitted stealing the Allstate Scooter in Alamogordo. The youngster had also switched license plates on the scooter. Mr. Scoggins called the boy's father and released him in his custody with the understanding that the boy would have a hearing on the charges at a later day. Eventually, the boy was placed on probation. This was the first time I had arrested a pistol-packing motor scooter rider."

"In December 1958, I was patrolling U.S. 54 south of Alamogordo when I met a 1955 Oldsmobile occupied by a very young boy. I turned around and stopped the car. When I asked him if he had permission to drive the car, the 15-year-old admitted stealing the car from a parking lot in El Paso. I took him into custody and turned him over to the Juvenile Probation Officer. The youngster said he passed through a Border Patrol checkpoint without being stopped. When I conducted a background check, I discovered that he had been arrested for auto theft on two previous occasions. I notified the vehicle's owner that we had recovered her car and she was very grateful to get it back."

Sometimes, it was more than hunches or very young boys behind steering wheels that led to CdeBaca recovering stolen vehicles. A tip led to the recovery of auto parts stripped from one vehicle then assembled onto another, older vehicle later. A civic-minded widow caring for her elderly mother had been left stranded.

"A Mrs. Ramona Sanchez reported her 1955 Chevrolet stolen. Mrs. Sanchez, who was a widow, ran a boarding house for handicapped trainees at the Adult Training Center for the visually handicapped and was left without transportation for herself and her aging mother.

"The 1955 Chevrolet was discovered in a secluded area on the old La Luz road just north of the intersection with State Road 83. The thieves rigged a block and tackle on a branch of a dead cottonwood tree and completely stripped the car then set it on fire. Mrs. Sanchez did not have theft insurance on her car.

"Two weeks later, following up on a local tip, I arrested two suspects, ages 17, driving a 1950 Chevrolet equipped with all the car parts stolen from Mrs. Sanchez's car. These two young men pleaded guilty to car theft and arson. Both were sentenced to serve time at the Springer Boys School. Judge Allan Walker awarded the 1950 Chevrolet to Mrs. Sanchez."

The *Alamogordo Daily News* ran a story complete with photos that showed the old cottonwood that was used while stripping the widow's stolen car and quoted CdeBaca as referring to the two youths as the "meanest thieves."

Stolen cars also turned up after CdeBaca stopped motorists with justifiable cause even without suspecting thievery, or when he simply showed up at a scene with other duties in mind.

"On the night of May 28, 1958, I stopped a 1955 Oldsmobile on U.S. 54-70 north of Alamogordo. I told the driver that I had stopped him for speeding and asked him for his driver's license and car registration, but he could not produce the registration.

"I ran a check on the car license and it had been reported stolen in Albuquerque. I arrested the driver and booked him in the Otero County jail. When I searched him, I found a ticket in his possession for speeding which had been issued to him by a State Police officer in Socorro. The driver told me he was planning to take the car across the border into Mexico and sell it. When I called the owner of the car in Albuquerque, he was delighted to hear from me."

"On January 27, 1959, at 11 p.m., the dispatcher woke me up and told me he had received a telephone call about a State Police officer killed in a car accident on U.S. 54 south of Carrizozo. When I arrived at the scene, there were a handful of people standing around close to the victim. Someone had placed a cover over the body. I uncovered the body and recognized the State Police jacket, however, that was the only part of the uniform the victim was wearing.

"I took his wallet and checked his identification but I didn't recognize the name of any State Police officer. Nevertheless, I called the dispatcher and had him call headquarters in Santa Fe to determine if we had an officer by the name that was found in the wallet. The call came back that there was no State Police officer by that name.

"The next day, I had the dispatcher put out an APB to ascertain if any State Police offer had his leather jacket stolen. Officer Jim Clayton, stationed in Vaughn, replied that his car had been broken into the previous night and his leather jacket had been stolen. The deceased had also stolen the car he had been driving. I concluded that he had fallen asleep and the car ran off the road and rolled over ejecting the driver and crushing him."

And in matters of theft, there was the case of a Southern New Mexico man driving down the road when he recognized his own truck coming at him with a stranger behind the wheel. Oddities did not end there.

"A resident of Laborcita Canyon was driving a school bus and returning home after dropping the kids at school when he met his own pickup approaching from the opposite direction. Mr. Paul Klopfer had not loaned his pickup to anyone and realized it had been stolen from his property.

"He turned the school bus around and gave chase but couldn't catch up to his pickup. He stopped to use a telephone to call the State Police to report his pickup stolen. The dispatcher put out an APB on the stolen pickup, but we never found it.

"When Mr. Klopfer returned home, he found a 1954 Chevrolet car on his property, which turned out to be stolen from El Paso. I sent the wrecker to pick up the stolen Chevrolet. On the way to the wrecking yard, the car broke loose from the wrecker and sustained heavy damage. I notified the owner of the car in El Paso and advised him that we had recovered his car, however, it had been involved in a freak accident while being towed and it was not drivable. The owner came to look at it and report it to the insurance company."

Recovering stolen vehicles also could create scenes worthy of some of that era's best television crime shows.

"One day, the Texas Highway Patrol radioed that they were in pursuit of a stolen car traveling north on U.S. 54 in the direction of Alamogordo, and I positioned my police car at an angle on the side of the highway. I took my shotgun out of the car and loaded a live round into the chamber and waited for the speeding car to approach. I realized I was positioning myself in harm's way but in those days, we did not have any spike belts to lay across the road.

"As the speeding car approached, I knelt down to make myself a small target and took aim. I knew I only had time for one shot before the car would go by or run over me. I focused the shotgun barrel on the front grill of the car and fired. I saw sparks fly and the car just kept on going.

"A few miles down the road, the Texas Highway Patrol were arresting the driver as I arrived. The one shot I had fired had put holes in the radiator and the car lost all its water and overheated.

"In any given situation, you used your own judgment, right or wrong. If you were wrong, you had to answer for it. You only had a few seconds to make a decision and act. The driver was taken into custody and charged with interstate transportation of a stolen motor vehicle."

And then there were the traffic stops made by CdeBaca when he seemingly suspected car theft but came upon thievery of a different sort.

"On Sunday, March 1, 1958, I was on stationary patrol on U.S. 70 south of Tularosa when an APB (all-points bulletin) came over the police radio that the home of State Police officer Bob Journey stationed in Hondo had been burglarized. Among the personal property taken were a small filing cabinet and a bag of banana candy . . . About one hour after the APB, I observed a black Ford traveling towards Alamogordo; the car displayed out-of-state license plates. As the car went by, the driver looked in my direction. I caught up to the car and pulled it over.

"When I asked the driver for his driver's license and car registration, I noticed an open bag of banana candy on the front seat. In making small conversation with the driver, an airman from Holloman Air Force Base, I mentioned that banana candy was my favorite but that I could never find it at the grocery store, and I asked him where he bought his. He said he didn't remember the name of the store where he bought it in Roswell . . . I asked him if I could get his permission to look in the trunk of his car, which he refused. I told him I had probable cause to get a search warrant because I had reason to believe he had stolen the banana candy from officer Journey's house.

"I ordered him to get out of the car for questioning and when he got out, he opened the trunk to the car. Inside, was all the loot he had taken, including the small filing cabinet. While waiting for a wrecker to come pick up his car, the airman confessed in detail how he had burglarized Officer Journey's house. Officer Journey not only served as a state policeman but he also served as a preacher in the local church in the small community of Hondo.

"I'll never forget what Preacher Bob told the airman when he saw him: 'God bless you son, you thieving son-of-a-bitch.' Officer Journey took the airman into custody and incarcerated him in the Lincoln County jail. The next day, officer Journey declined to file charges against the airman, stating that he did not want to ruin the young man's career. Our supervisor went along with it. I transferred the airman to Holloman Air Force Base, where he would face AWOL charges. He had to pay for the towing and storage of his car."

CdeBaca temporarily got help for his patrolling of southeastern New Mexico highways from an unexpected friend of the four-legged kind, a companion that CdeBaca described as his best partner ever.

"An Air Force sergeant who had become friends with me received orders to be transferred to Germany. He owned a trained dog named Stormy and the sergeant gave him to me. Stormy was a German Shepherd and in no time, he became accustomed to his new master.

"My supervisor had no problem with Stormy riding in the police car with me. Every time I would stop a car, Stormy would get out and sit by my side until I started to go back to my car. I got used to having the dog by my side as he was the best partner I could have.

"Stormy was with me one night when I observed a 1954 Pontiac crowding the center line several times. I pulled it over and told the driver to get out for a sobriety test. The driver got out but so did the passenger. I ordered the passenger to get back in the car but he refused. He had been drinking and I could tell I was going to have trouble with both occupants of the car.

"I grabbed Stormy by the collar and walked him up to the passenger and gave Stormy the command to 'get him.' Once Stormy stood up and snapped his teeth at him, the passenger backed up and got in the car. The driver passed the sobriety test. Maybe the presence of Stormy sobered him up."

CdeBaca acknowledged later that Stormy could have been trouble for the state if he had injured someone while accompanying the patrolman on his rounds. "No other State Police officer had a police dog riding with him at the time," CdeBaca said. "Yes, he could have been a liability issue. But he was a trained German police dog when I got him. He took to me as his new master and rode in the police car with me and became the best partner I have ever had."

Stormy's companionship was short-lived, however. Orders came down months later prohibiting dogs from riding with officers.

CdeBaca's notations show that with or without dogs, trouble on New Mexico's highways can be both sudden and severe.

"In March 1958, I was called to investigate a 17-car pileup 25 miles west of Alamogordo on U.S. 70. A car rear-ended an 18-wheeler that had stopped on the highway due to a blinding sand storm. The driver of the car, a liquor salesman, was killed instantly. The car he was driving was ripped apart, spilling cases of miniatures all over the highway.

"That same month, during another blinding sand storm, I parked my police car a short distance away from the wall of dust and placed reflectors on the roadway to warn motorists of a serious accident ahead. My eyes and mouth were pasted with a layer of mud and my uniform had turned brown from all the dirt and dust. When I returned to my car, all the reflectors had been run over. These sand storms have been the cause of many fatal accidents over the years and drivers still continue to push their luck driving through them."

"About 1 a.m. on March 2, 1959, the dispatcher called me and told me he had received a telephone call about an accident with injuries west of Carrizozo. I asked the dispatcher why he didn't call the officer stationed in Carrizozo and he said he was on vacation. The distance between my house and the accident was about 50 miles. I told the dispatcher to send an ambulance.

"When I arrived at the scene, I noticed a white car resting on its top. The driver was on the ground and a motorist standing there told me that's the way he had found him. The victim had been thrown out and was complaining about chest and back pain and had suffered multiple contusions and abrasions. The ambulance arrived and I told Al Ferguson, the driver, to keep an eye on the victim because he was having trouble breathing.

"Once the wrecker arrived and picked up the car, I headed back to Alamogordo to check on the victim. On the way there, the dispatcher radioed and told me that the ambulance had broadsided a car at an intersection in downtown Alamogordo and the patient was declared DOA at the hospital. The city police investigated the accident and their investigation determined that the car struck by the ambulance had failed to yield."

In May 1961, having already recovered many stolen vehicles, CdeBaca recovered his first stolen car that was being driven by a fugitive wanted by the FBI.

"I was patrolling U.S. 66 west of Gallup when a 1958 Ford caught up with me but wouldn't pass. I slowed down but he still wouldn't pass. Finally, I pulled off the road and fell in behind him. When I stopped the car, I discovered that the 33-year-old driver had stolen the car in Cleveland, Ohio, and was on his way to Reno, Nevada.

"He had served time in Terre Haute, Indiana, for car theft. He also had in his possession a stolen credit card. I incarcerated him and referred him to the FBI."

If highway incidents routinely place police officers at risk, so too can domestic violence situations. Officers say they are among calls that they dread most. Three of CdeBaca's notations tell of contrasting situations.

"One day while writing a ticket to a violator, I heard the Tularosa police officer calling for help. When I got to him, he was out of the car and appeared to be in a state of shock. He told me, 'Something terrible has happened, a terrible murder.'

"He led me to the house nearby where I found the body of a pregnant woman and a man in bed dead from gunshot wounds. The woman was on her back under the sheets with one arm exposed on top of her stomach and her other arm folded under her head. The man, who was fully clothed, was slumped on top of the bed with both legs hanging over the edge of the bed and a .22 rifle cradled across his lap. He had a bullet hole that had entered the right side of his head, behind his right ear. The woman also had been shot in the head.

"There was no sign of a struggle. The woman appeared to have been shot in her sleep. It was clear to me that her husband had sat on the bed and smoked cigarettes before he shot himself. There was an ashtray full of cigarette butts lying on the end of the bed.

"There were no witnesses to interview. The deaths were termed murder-suicide. I questioned the neighbor who discovered the bodies and she told me that she had never heard of any domestic problems with the couple.

"Officer Trujillo, age 69, was distraught. He said he had known the couple all their lives and couldn't believe that the dead husband was capable of committing such a thing."

"One day I was dispatched to answer a domestic call in Cloudcroft that involved an argument between a man and his common law wife. The man returned home from work and got into a verbal confrontation with his wife. The man picked up a piece of firewood and struck the woman. She, in turn, picked up a butcher knife and swung at her husband, cutting his hand. The man grabbed a small axe and struck his wife in the face with it, knocking out a bunch of teeth and thus ending the physical confrontation.

"I arrested the man on charges of assault and battery with a deadly weapon. Justice of the Peace R.W. Zimmerle sentenced the man to 30 days in jail but suspended the sentence with the stipulation that the two no longer live together. Several days later, I stopped to check on the couple but they had moved."

"Sometimes, domestic situations aren't of such a serious nature. I had made friends with a couple named Clyde and Hattie Mattock who operated a small filling station north of Alamogordo on U.S. 54-70. I stopped there regularly to purchase gas and enjoyed visiting with them. Clyde and Hattie were an odd couple, in size, that is. Clyde was about 5'6" and weighed approximately 145 pounds. Hattie, on the other end of the scale, was 6'2" and weighed 210 pounds and always wore coveralls.

"Hattie fixed flat tires of all sizes and Clyde serviced vehicles. Only one problem with Clyde: He liked to drink. On a couple of occasions, he called me to complain about Hattie. I would show up at their place of business, only to find Clyde sporting real 'shiners.' I would advise Clyde not to drink; that Hattie obviously did not approve of it. I told him to stop drinking before she cripples you. One day, I passed by and noticed a sign posted on the door that read: 'OUT OF BUSINESS.' I never knew where they moved to and never saw them again."

Notations by CdeBaca also tell of time that he thought could have been better spent by State Police officers, who already were spread thin while tending to law enforcement.

"In the 1950s, the State Police had to provide escort for the Highway Department paint trucks that striped the highways, and also provide escort for oversized loads, especially houses being moved from one location to another. Every year during the month of August we had to inspect all the school buses in the state. We were not specifically trained for this; it was just a perfunctory inspection we performed, checking brakes, steering, lights and tires. These special services took up a lot of our time providing non-essential police services."

And then there was time spent enforcing laws in areas where results, arguably, were of questionable value.

"During the hunting season one year, the Game and Fish warden, Roy Owens, requested our assistance manning roadblocks checking for illegal game. At one of these roadblocks, I was helping Warden Owens when I noticed part of a bird feather sticking out of a truck hubcap. I brought it to the attention of Warden Owens and he asked the driver if he had been hunting and he said he had not.

"I ordered the driver to park on the shoulder and said that I was getting the tire tool from the car and I was going to remove the hubcaps from the wheels of his truck. When I removed the two rear hubcaps, two quail fell out from each one. Warden Owens cited him to court and confiscated the birds."

Variety never seemed to be missing from CdeBaca's notations about what he encountered in his daily rounds.

"I was walking into the State Police office one day to work on reports. A car drove up and the driver got out and appeared to be excited. I asked him if I could be of help. He told me that while he was traveling west on U.S. 83 approaching the junction of U.S. 54-70, two low-flying jets came by and sucked the windshield out of his car. His passenger confirmed his story. I had never heard of such a thing and didn't know if it was possible. I explained to them that all I could do was write an incident report based on what they said. I then referred them to the Safety Officer at Holloman Air

Force Base and wished them luck."

"One day, I was patrolling U.S. 70 north of Alamogordo when I observed a Packard parked on the shoulder of the road. As I passed by, I noticed that the rear license plate was folded in half. The driver appeared to be reading a map. I turned around and parked my car right behind the Packard.

"I knocked on the window and got the driver's attention. When I ordered him to step out of the car, I noticed a handgun on the front seat. I un-holstered my service revolver to protect myself in the event he reached for the weapon. I placed him under arrest for being in possession of a firearm, handcuffed him and escorted him to the back seat of my car.

"I confiscated his handgun and locked it in the trunk of my police car. I searched his car and found a suicide letter he had just finished writing to his mother. In the letter to his mother, he wrote: 'Strange, but as I sit here knowing in a few minutes I shall attempt to take my own life, I feel very little, please do not allow anything I have done to grieve you too deeply, I am not worthy.'"

"A master sergeant whom I had met during one of my regular traffic safety talks at Holloman Air Force Base invited me to go see the special training program he was involved with. He trained chimpanzees for all types of military purposes, but primarily there were a handful of chimps being trained for part of an experimental program to prepare them for the first sub-orbital flight into space. One of them would be chosen for the maiden flight.

"Their training consisted of subjecting them to stressful circumstances, such as putting them on a sled and propelling them down a track at great speeds and then suddenly bringing the sled to a stop. The sergeant showed me the chimp that likely would be chosen for the first flight, favored be-cause of his disposition.

"The sergeant took me to the restricted area where they kept the chimps caged. I never saw so many chimps in one place. I was introduced to the chimp that eventually would be named Ham. He was isolated from the others. I told the chimp, 'Pleased to meet you,' and he returned the greeting by spitting on my uniform. I don't know if my uniform turned him off but I stayed away from him. The sergeant had warned me to keep my distance.

"Later on, the chimp made history when he became the first hominid launched into outer space. His flight lasted just over 16 minutes. The name, Ham, came from the lab where he was trained and prepared, the Holloman Aerospace Medical Center. I never had the opportunity to get Ham's autograph, but I did get his spit."

"I was at a service station one day when a Cadillac with Texas license plates pulled up to the pump next to me. This little boy of about six years of age got out of the car and asked me with a straight face: 'What are pennies made of?' I looked at him and answered, 'Copper.' His grandfather, overhearing the conversation, came over and made the boy apologize to me, telling him, 'You know, your grandfather was a policeman.'"

Early during his first State Police assignment to Alamogordo, CdeBaca was quietly encouraged to think about a career outside of the department.

"On occasion we would set up roadblocks and invite the Border Patrol to assist us. While we checked for drivers' licenses, the Border Patrol would check for illegal immigrants. One day one of the border patrolmen showed me his paycheck, which was quite a bit more than mine, and he told me to apply for a job with the Border Patrol. I explained to him that regardless of the pay, I knew I would never be transferred out of the state as long as I remained with the New Mexico State Police. But in all honesty, I didn't find the Border Patrol job very challenging."

But as CdeBaca was nearing completion of his first five years with the State Police, he found himself with what he called "mixed emotions about spending the next 25 years doing the same thing." Citing an extraordinary situation at home, CdeBaca already had successfully convinced a supervisor to rescind orders that would have transferred CdeBaca out of Alamogordo down the Mesilla Valley and into Anthony straddling the Texas border. Suddenly, he was wondering if he might find better conditions outside of the State Police.

"I must admit, up to that point, my work was my passion. However, working long hours every day, six days a week, never off on weekends or holidays was taking its toll. My regular day off had never changed in five years, and I had been under the supervision of four different supervisors.

"I always thought I was making a difference saving lives by taking drunk and reckless drivers off the highways, writing speeding tickets, and giving public safety lectures. But there seemed to be no end to the human carnage on the highways and the human suffering. I don't believe for one moment that my feelings weren't shared by other officers.

"The attrition rate in the department occurred within the first few years of service. Already, there had been two officers from my recruit school who had left: one of his own volition, the other one was terminated for pistol whipping a drunk driver who would not get out of his car and then accidentally discharging his firearm and putting a bullet hole through the roof of the car. This officer was so mean spirited that when Chief A.P. Winston called him to terminate him, Chief Winston called the two largest officers in the department—Sergeant Dwight Marable, 6'8", and Bill Driggers, 6'4", 260 pounds, to stand guard outside the chief's office."

An unexpected opportunity to explore other avenues suddenly presented itself right in CdeBaca's front yard. It occurred just as CdeBaca had been informed that he was to be transferred to the State Police district based in Gallup.

"Early in 1961, the chief of police of Alamogordo, Clarence Walker, announced his retirement and Mayor Richard Stanley was advertising for his replacement. My wife's brother-in-law, Mr. Gus Najera, was a member of the city council and he put the idea in my head if I would be interested in applying. I discussed the idea with my wife and she left the decision up to me. I must admit, it was a turning point in my life. As a matter of fact, I discussed it with Lieutenant Wimberly and he told me, 'You do what you think is right, but I know you have a bright future with the State Police.

"I went ahead and applied for the position and was interviewed by Mayor Stanley. Within three days, Mayor Stanley called me and offered me the position, which I accepted. I submitted my letter of resignation to Chief Winston. I would be Alamogordo's youngest chief replacing the oldest chief.

"Chief Winston got word of my resignation and the new job I had accepted. He called me to tell me that I was making a mistake and he would not accept my resignation, which I was flattered to hear. But I told him I couldn't live with myself if I told Mayor Stanley that I was changing my mind. Chief Winston then asked me when this appointment was to become effective and I told him not until March 15th. He said in a stern voice, 'You are still a state policeman. I'm flying to Alamogordo tomorrow to discuss this with you.'

"The following day Chief Winston flew to Alamogordo just like he said he would. He told me in the presence of Lieutenant Wimberly that I was an outstanding officer and why throw my career away. Chief Winston was too familiar with my work ethics. He was my first district commander. One night, when he was still my captain, I had chased him for speeding in his unmarked car. When I caught up to him and turned the red light on, I heard his voice come over the radio, saying, 'Is that you, CdeBaca?' I immediately turned the red light off and told him to drive safely. He told me, 'You're doing a good job.'

"I told Chief Winston that I sincerely appreciated everything he was doing on my behalf, but how was I going to face Mayor Stanley? He is a man of honor and I made a commitment. Chief Winston was a very articulate man. He said, 'Let's approach the mayor and get his reaction to this whole thing. I want to do everything I can to convince you to stay with the State Police.'

"On the way to the mayor's office, I thought to myself that Chief Winston had a lot of class to come down here and talk to me. He could very well have accepted my resignation. Mayor Stanley listened to Chief Winston. He spoke eloquently, telling the mayor that he had picked a good cop, but that my future belonged with the New Mexico State Police. Mayor Stanley told Chief Winston that I had a good reputation in the community and 'I just want what's best for him.' Everything was handled in a very professional manner.

"Before Chief Winston left, I told him I would talk to my wife and make a final decision. That evening, I apprised my wife of what had transpired and I told her I respected Chief Winston for his visit to Alamogordo and trying to convince me to stay with the State Police. I told her I should accept the transfer to Gallup that I felt I had a secure future staying with the State Police.

"The next day, I informed Mayor Stanley that I was declining the appointment. He wished me the best of luck. I called Chief Winston and told him I would accept my transfer to Gallup, and he assured me I wouldn't regret it."

2

Patrolling Along Busy Route 66

State Policeman Richard CdeBaca packed up his belongings and moved to Gallup just as the region's annual snow blizzards were letting up early in 1961. He looked at the transfer, at least in part, as a step necessary to advance his career.

> "My orders transferring me to Gallup read that my potential could be better used on highway 66. It was probably a standard line used for all those who got transfer orders. When we got commissioned, we signed agreeing to transfer at the discretion of the department. I knew that we were all subject to transfer, however, a few officers never did and spent their entire careers in the same place, but only a few of them climbed the career ladder."

Soon after CdeBaca's own change in assignment, change was announced at the top of his state agency. Republican Edwin Mechem, just elected to his fourth term as governor, asked State Police Chief A.P. Winston to step aside. Winston was replaced by Captain K.K. Miller, who had served as communications director for the department. CdeBaca was on good terms with Miller, who during trips to Alamogordo would stop to visit with CdeBaca if the two crossed paths on a highway.

It took time for both men to settle into their new assignments.

> "I had spent five years in a warm climate and now I had to get used to one of the coldest places in the state. I also had to get used to the amount of traffic on U.S. 66 compared to what I was accustomed to in Alamogordo."

CdeBaca also had to adjust to sharp contrasts in populations of the two regions. "You do approach a transfer like that with some apprehension simply because you're being moved from one location that you have become comfortable with, and you have made friends there, and you know that you're leaving all that behind," he said.

One of CdeBaca's superiors in Gallup told him he should brace himself for the change.

"Sergeant Edward Jaramillo in Gallup informed me that I was in for a culture shock because of the drinking problem among Navajos. One piece of advice he gave me, 'When you stop a Navajo for whatever reason, especially for drinking, keep a close watch, or you will spend your time chasing them.'"

CdeBaca said he did not consider the remark bigoted. "It did not influence me in that manner," he said. "I only took it as advice to look after myself because of the alcoholic problem there."

The advice from Sergeant Jaramillo was framed in a manner not uncommon among police officers, particularly during the time in which CdeBaca served. It has come to be known as racial or ethnic profiling, and it has been outlawed in just about all applications. Still, certainly among themselves, police might always speak in the most descriptive of terms—whether referring to automobiles, clothing or people—because they have found the approach to be important while carrying out their assignments and protecting their surroundings.

Nonetheless, an increasing number of those whom police are assigned to serve and protect frown upon and outright object not only to the conduct but the thought processes embedded among some officers, even when applied innocently. Here is an entry recorded by CdeBaca while still at his post in Alamogordo:

"On April 13, 1957, during the Annual Spring Day event at White Sands National Monument, a seven-year-old black boy got separated from his parents in the picnic grounds and wandered off and got lost. When I received the radio call about the lost boy, I figured it would be no problem finding him in all that white sand."

Later in the entry, it became abundantly clear that CdeBaca was being neither derogatory nor flip when he referred to the lost boy as being black in a sea of white sand. His entry tells how, as his concern mounted, he called the commander at Holloman Air Force Base to request volunteers from the base and also phoned the local radio station to solicit other volunteers. The following afternoon an Air Force helicopter helped find young Allen Smith, who was promptly reunited with his mother and grandfather at the site from which the search was being directed. "It was a happy reunion and one I will never forget," wrote CdeBaca.

Republican David Cargo, who served two terms as New Mexico governor from 1967–1970 and has been a lifelong advocate for the state's Navajos, said CdeBaca generally treated people fairly. "Richard was a real capable guy. He was a good state policeman," Cargo said.

Conditions around Gallup were not entirely foreign to CdeBaca by the time he reported to his station there.

"In October 1958, I received orders to report to Gallup to be part of a 'wolf pack' operation, so named by Chief Joe Roach for combating chronic enforcement problems. McKinley County always topped the state in highway fatalities involving drunk drivers. This 'wolf pack' operation resulted in a record number of drunk driving arrests."

Once stationed in Gallup, CdeBaca said he soon "began to get adjusted to the fast pace of U.S. 66 and the high number of drunk drivers." His recordings tell of varied experiences, sometimes in very blunt terms.

"One day, I stopped a black Ford on U.S. 66 occupied by four Navajos: two men in the front and two women in the back. I asked the driver for his driver's license, which he didn't have. I arrested him, but didn't handcuff him and placed him in the back seat of my police car. Not cuffing him was poor judgment on my part. He had obviously been drinking. I returned to the car to determine if the passenger had a driver's license so that he could drive the car home. Before I could ascertain if he had a license, I heard the door to my police car slam shut.

"The Navajo I had arrested was already running at full speed, making his getaway. I gave chase and he jumped a barbed wire fence and kept going. By this time he had put some distance between us. I un-holstered my revolver and fired two rounds in the air. That was a mistake because he picked up his run and I could see that he was hitting nothing but the high spots on the ground. The last I saw of him is when he was disappearing over the horizon. When I turned around to return to my car, I saw that the car I had stopped was gone. There was a hitchhiker standing on the shoulder of the road taking it all in. I'm sure he thought it doesn't get any better than this, just like in the movies.

"I asked the hitchhiker if he had noticed what direction the car had gone, and he pointed to a dirt road which disappeared over a hill. I took pursuit and found the car parked next to a juniper tree with all three passengers still sitting in the car. I am sure they were going to wait for their runaway friend to come back.

"I asked the old man for his driver's license and he didn't have any. I placed him under arrest and was escorting him to my car when suddenly I felt a Navajo blanket thrown over my head. While I was removing the blanket that one of the ladies had thrown over me, the old man had galloped away. I gave the Navajo blanket to the ladies and told them to get lost. Totally frustrated, I returned to my car, empty handed and outsmarted minus two bullets in my revolver. Like the old cliché: Some days it doesn't pay to get up.

"I never told Sergeant Jaramillo. I was not about to get belittled. Besides, I remembered too well he had warned me about such antics."

"On the night of December 12, 1962, I was dispatched to investigate a two-car accident 12 miles west of Gallup on U.S. 66. A woman driving under the influence drove her car across the center line and sideswiped another car, causing extensive damage to both cars but no serious injuries to the passengers. I arrested the drunk woman and without handcuffing her, I placed her in the back seat of my police car.

"While taking statements from witnesses, I heard a man's voice say, 'Watch out, officer!' Immediately, I felt a stabbing pain between my shoulder blades. The woman had gotten out of the police car and had taken one of her high heel shoes off and used it to strike me in the back. I pinched her upper lip and marched her limping back to my car, only this time I handcuffed her with her hands behind her back. I jailed the woman and filed charges of DUI and assault on an officer.

"The following day, I took her before Justice of the Peace Edward Romero, where she pleaded guilty to both charges. She was fined $100 for DUI and another $100 for assault, plus the usual $5 court costs. She apologized to me for her abnormal behavior."

"There were so many drunks being arrested and locked up in jammed drunk tanks, that it was pathetic. I had never seen so much misery in my life, and I felt sorry and helpless for their lifestyle. Since the Gallup city jail could not accommodate every drunk, the city built a detention center that could accommodate several hundred. This was not a jail facility. It was just a place to keep drunks overnight for detoxification.

"During the Annual Inter-Tribal Ceremonies held in August, we were assigned multiple duties: traffic and crowd control. In those days, U.S. 66 passed right through the heart of Gallup. It was a nightmare trying to control traffic and hundreds of Indians and tourists who stormed Gallup for this colorful event. The detention center would be filled to capacity during this three-day event."

"Liquor was the scourge of the Navajo people. It kept us busy arresting drunk drivers along with their drunk passengers. The State Police district had a suburban, which was referred to as the patty wagon. It was equipped with a metal divider separating the driver from the passengers, and it had no seats in the back.

"The purpose for the patty wagon was to prevent officers from getting attacked and injured by drunks who otherwise would be riding in the back seats of police cars. In those days, police cars were not equipped with protective screens. One officer had suffered an injured neck and another officer had suffered a broken finger. On weekends, our supervisor rotated assignments to drive the patty wagon."

"One night, I arrested a drunk man and on the way to the city jail, he spit on the back of my head. From then on, every time I would arrest a drunk, I would put a pair of panty hose over his head."

"We always carried a can of aerosol spray in our patrol cars. It helped some."

"One morning I was getting in my police car at Earl's Restaurant when a Navajo man approached me and asked for 50 cents to buy a cup of coffee. He looked like he had slept in the bushes all night. I offered to take him in the restaurant and buy him coffee but he declined. Fifty cents would have bought a half pint of wine."

"I dealt with drunks around Gallup more than I care to remember. One morning my wife was getting in the car to go to work when I heard her scream. I ran outside to her aid. She found a drunk passed out in the back seat of her car."

"Sunday liquor sales were illegal in McKinley County and bootleggers spawned all over selling from their houses and some brazen enough to sell out of their trucks. These unscrupulous people were scalping those who were buying the liquor with what they charged for it. One Sunday, a friend of mine by the name of Frank Mora called me and said he knew of a man who was selling beer from his pickup on a dirt road outside of Gamerco. He gave me the man's name and description of the pickup.

"After getting directions from Frank how to get there, I found the green pickup and another pickup occupied by Navajos parked next to it. I arrested the man who was selling the alcohol and confiscated 10 cases of beer. I incarcerated him in the McKinley jail and he posted a $500 cash bond and was released. When he appeared before Justice of the Peace Edward Romero, he was fined $300."

"Captain E.A. "Tuffy" Tafoya had received information that a black couple was selling liquor from their house. He assigned me and with the help of a city police officer by the name of Stanley Deniyazzie we went to the house in question. We were in civilian clothes and wearing Navajo hats.

"When we knocked on the door, a black woman answered. Stanley, acting like he was drunk, asked for a bottle of wine and a six-pack of beer. The woman disappeared for a minute and returned with a bottle of wine and a six-pack of beer. After handing her the money, I identified myself and told her she was under arrest.

"She called out to her common-law husband, 'Lordy Lord, Mr. Moore, the do-rights are here.' When Mr. Moore came to the door to see what she was talking about, we arrested him. Mr. Moore was fined $100."

"During a snowstorm on the night of January 7, 1962, a drunk Navajo asked a family living in a hogan if they would put him up for the night, which they refused. In retaliation, the drunk got into his Chevrolet, backed it up, then drove forward head on into the hogan. The husband and wife suffered contusions and abrasions but their 13-year-old daughter had to be hospitalized at the Indian hospital with a broken arm. The driver managed to drive away.

"The family hogan, built with railroad ties, was destroyed from the impact. A few days after the incident, I returned to the scene and there was no trace of the hogan."

"One Saturday afternoon, on a summer day, the dispatcher radioed me and advised me there was a report of an accident south of the Gallup city limits on the road to Zuni. When I arrived at the scene, I couldn't believe the number of women scattered all over the place. A pickup was loaded with nine women in the bed. They were thrown out when the pickup ran off the road and rolled over on its right side. Four men were also riding inside the pickup. None of them required hospitalization. The pickup was traveling very slow. I arrested the driver for DUI."

The vast expanse of the Navajo reservation and isolation of homes within it posed extraordinary problems for CdeBaca and other officers there. To try to reduce the number of drunk drivers, officers took to enforcing so-called suspension orders issued by the state motor vehicle office. "The orders allowed us to confiscate the drivers' licenses, the license plates and vehicle registrations from those who had been convicted of drunk driving," CdeBaca said.

"We usually just wasted our time looking for individuals on the reservation. There are no street signs. They're all dirt roads or trails. The thing I noticed about the Navajos living there was they were astonished to see you show up in that vast reservation asking for someone. Eventually the State Police got out of the business of serving suspension orders issued by the motor vehicle department."

CdeBaca made this notation:

"We would waste an enormous amount of time going from hogan to hogan trying to locate a person to no avail. If we were looking for a Navajo by the name of Billy Joe, we would find someone in a hogan that would say, 'I know a Joe Billy but I don't know a Billy Joe.'"

And there were other challenges that came with patrolling around Gallup.

"The port of entry was just outside the west city limits of Gallup and I was forever getting radio calls that a commercial truck had evaded the port. I would intercept the truck, issue the driver a ticket and escort him back to the port. He then would have to appear before the justice of the peace and pay a fine. Most trucks that skipped the port either had overweight loads or were bootlegging illegal goods."

Problems posed by stolen cars were not left behind with CdeBaca's move from Alamogordo to Gallup.

"On the night of November 22, 1962, we received a radio call to assist an officer who was in pursuit of a stolen car west of Grants and traveling in the direction of Gallup. We set up roadblocks in different locations east of Gallup waiting for the stolen car to show up. Traffic was very light and it was very cold so we took turns checking cars as they approached the roadblock.

"A city officer and I were checking cars when a red Buick that was heading west stopped. The driver lowered the window and pointed a gun at me and warned, 'If you want to arrest me, you have to kill me.' Without firing a shot, he stepped on the accelerator and sped off. We engaged in pursuit and alerted the officers at the second roadblock to be prepared to stop a red Buick being driven by a man who was armed.

"The Buick went through the roadblock at a high rate of speed and none of the officers fired their weapons and the pursuit continued. I was driving and I instructed the city officer riding with me to attempt to shoot the rear tires. I would try to maneuver my car alongside the Buick but the driver would cut me off.

"Finally, officer Griswold, who was ahead of the Buick, managed to force the Buick to slow down. By this time, other officers had pulled up alongside the Buick and started shooting. It didn't take long before both rear tires were shot, which caused the driver to lose control and the car came to a stop in the median. The driver turned the gun on himself but didn't fire. I busted the window with the butt of my shotgun and took the gun away from the driver. The man had stolen the Buick from a parking lot in Las Vegas, Nevada. The FBI took him into custody."

CdeBaca said it was the only time in his entire career that someone pointed a gun at him. "It is hard to believe," he said. "I arrested many individuals whether they were fugitives or not, who were armed to the teeth and not one ever pointed a gun at me or threatened to shoot me except for that one individual in Gallup at a roadblock."

Nor, said CdeBaca, did he ever have to shoot anyone. But it didn't mean that guns were hard to come upon in his work.

"On the night of September 17, 1962, the dispatcher radioed me and told me he had received a telephone call about a shooting. When I arrived at the house where the shooting took place, there were about a half dozen people outside the house. A young man in his twenties was bleeding from his abdomen. He had been shot in the stomach, and when he turned to run, he was shot in the buttocks.

"The ambulance arrived and rushed him to the hospital. After taking statements from witnesses, I concluded that a jealous boyfriend had gotten into an argument over a girlfriend and a fight ensued. The jealous boyfriend then shot the victim with a .32 caliber pistol. The city officers at the scene knew the man responsible for the shooting."

That incident led to an extraordinary development and also to what CdeBaca acknowledged later might not have been the best use of his time.

"I went to St. Mary's Hospital to check on the shooting victim. Dr. Keney, who was our family doctor, was on call. To my surprise, Dr. Keney invited me to witness the surgery. He told me to remove my uniform and get into surgical garments. Dr. Kettle and Dr. Keney would perform the surgery. Dr. Keney got me a step stool to stand and watch the surgery.

"The victim had been X-rayed and they showed that the bullet which entered the stomach had lodged close to the spinal cord. The other bullet had traveled down the victim's right leg. Both doctors agreed not to remove the bullets, but they would do surgery to repair the intestines which had been perforated by the bullet.

"As Dr. Keney was making an incision below the sternum, Dr. Kettle was pinching the blood vessels. When Dr. Keney had the victim open to below the navel, he reached in with both hands and pulled a pile of intestines and set them on the side. He began the tedious task of stretching one by one to stitch the holes. This procedure took a long time. Finally, he was satisfied that all the intestines had been repaired. The stitching of the cavity was left to the intern."

CdeBaca told me later, "This doctor liked State Police officers. It was not the best use of my time but it was already late at night when this shooting took place. I went to the hospital to check on the victim and ended up viewing the surgery." CdeBaca would connect with Dr. Keney again.

"When Dr. Keney removed my tonsils, he asked me if it would be possible for him to ride in my police car with me some Sunday. I got permission for him to ride with me, and he would get all excited when I would be chasing a speeder."

Paths of the two men would cross yet again.

"Late one night in February 1963, I was on patrol on U.S. 66 west of Gallup when I suffered a mild heart attack. Officer Joe Cotton took me to St. Mary's Hospital. Dr. Keney attended to me and kept me in the hospital until test results were completed. I was diagnosed with acute angina and Dr. Keney referred me to Dr. Richard Streeper in Santa Fe, a renowned heart specialist.

"Dr. Streeper recommended to Chief K.K. Miller that I be relieved of patrol duties and be assigned to administrative work until my condition improved. Chief Miller accepted the advice of the doctor and transferred me to Santa Fe."

"Assigned to administrative duty in Santa Fe for health reasons in March

1963, I signed up for Dale Carnegie classes on public speaking. After I received my certificate of completion, I was asked to serve as student assistant during the next session of classes.

"Soon I was assigned by Chief Miller to teach criminal law, New Mexico history, testifying in court and report writing at the Recruit Classes and in-service schools."

"On January 14, 1964, I had an operation on my back at Lovelace in Albuquerque. Somehow I had separated one of the fusions done as part of a 1958 surgery to correct a congenital defect on the lower part of my back. In two weeks, I was back to work and Chief Miller assigned me to security at the Legislature."

In 1965, CdeBaca was among 10 officers promoted to sergeant. He was promptly assigned to yet another new district: Las Vegas.

"Chief John Bradford said I would be in charge of officers stationed in Santa Rosa, Fort Sumner and Vaughn, and I would answer to Captain Frank Lucero, the district commander."

"My first official action was to visit the captain in Las Vegas to get my orders as to what he expected of me. While in Las Vegas, I visited with the district attorney, Donaldo 'Tiny' Martinez. He thanked me for visiting him and wished me well. His mother and my father were related."

The new posting exposed CdeBaca to new thieves and more stolen cars.

"While stationed in Santa Rosa, there were many tiny communities that required our attention: Anton Chico, Puerto de Luna, Pastura, La Loma, Colonias and Cuervo among them. One day, a man called from Anton Chico to report that his 1954 Chevrolet had been stolen. Later, his car was found abandoned in an arroyo.

"When I met with the caller, I asked him if he suspected anyone in the community who might have stolen his car. He said he had heard that a young man there had a reputation for stealing and told me where I could find him, but the man told me not to mention his name. When I located the youth, I asked him if he had stolen the Chevrolet or if he knew anyone who did. When I told him that I had heard that he had a reputation for stealing, he replied, 'I steal chickens but I don't steal cars.'"

If the incident reflected a peculiar kind of innocence to CdeBaca, he came upon an innocence of yet a different sort one night while stopping an elderly couple headed home.

"I was returning from Las Vegas one evening when I caught up to an old green Chevrolet pickup without taillights. The pickup was traveling slow and when I tried to pull it over, the driver just ignored me. No matter what maneuver I attempted, the driver would not pull over and stop.

"When we turned onto I-40, I called officers Urioste and Dodgin to come and help me intercept the pickup. With their assistance, the driver of the pickup stopped in the middle of the road. When I asked the driver why he wouldn't stop, he told me with a straight face, 'I thought you were robbers trying to hold me up.' Mr. Pablo Flores had not been drinking and I was convinced he had never been stopped by a police officer during his lifetime. He and his wife were returning home to Puerto de Luna."

CdeBaca, recalling the incident later, said he did not cite the elderly man for driving with defective equipment. "Learning that he was just a farmer from Puerto de Luna, I wasn't about to give him a ticket," he said.

Though it was a minor infraction that caught his attention, CdeBaca said he felt justified in calling for backup from not one, but two other officers. "I didn't know who this driver was who was avoiding being stopped," he said. "He probably got shook up. He and his wife were not a young couple. I don't think he was deliberately trying to evade me. He may have been sincere about fearing I was going to rob him. Keep in mind that police cars in those days were not equipped with all these fancy lights. The lights in those days were small and were referred to as bubble gum machine lights."

Well-acquainted with Route 66 west of Interstate-25 while stationed in Gallup, CdeBaca found that the busy thoroughfare was demanding on the east side, as well.

"Time and again we would get calls from gas station operators complaining about people filling their cars with gas and driving off without paying. Some managed to get away, but most of them weren't so lucky. On the other hand, we used to get complaints from motorists about greedy gas station attendants who slashed their fan belts or tried to sell new tires when they were not needed. Some of these complaints were legitimate. U.S. 66 was an invitation to all kinds of problems."

Later, CdeBaca referred to them as more than problems. "There were many atrocities at service stations along Highway 66," he said. "The alleged cutting of fan belts was a common complaint, but I don't remember ever citing anyone for cutting fan belts. The reason for not filing charges against these unscrupulous people is that we did not witness the offense. The burden of proof was on the complainant, the tourist. We'd offer to take the complainant before a judge to file a formal complaint but they were not about to disrupt their vacation."

CdeBaca, like other state policemen, learned to take relief where he could find it.

"I formed a basketball team while stationed in Santa Rosa to keep us in shape. We played anyone that wanted to play, including the Catholic priest, Father Raymond Aragon's team. It was all for a good cause: to raise funds for the athletic fund."

And, then, there were the occasional pleasantries that couldn't help but remind CdeBaca of home.

"My favorite restaurant in Santa Rosa was the Spanish Inn. I ate lunch there almost every day. Bill and Nora Carpenter owned it but it was Nora who did the cooking. One day, I asked Nora if she would fix me pan-fried potatoes, beans, red chile and sopaipillas. I told her, 'It's not on the menu but it would be nice if you would fix it for me.'

"Nora fixed it for me and what she prepared reminded me of my mother's cooking. Thereafter, I used to order the same thing over and over again. One day, Nora called me at the office and invited me to come eat. She said that it was 'on the house.' When I arrived, she proudly gave me a copy of her new menu. In it was a dish named 'Sergeant CdeBaca's Special.'"

The restaurant's special cost $1.25. There was nothing unusual about the modest price. A bowl of posole sold for 55 cents; a plate of green chile and beans, $1; three tacos, $1.25; a rib steak ranchero style, $3. Coffee was a dime.

CdeBaca made it a point of saying farewell to the restaurant's owners when his next posting took him away from Santa Rosa.

3

A System of "Disgraceful" Justice

Like so many others, Richard CdeBaca displays little restraint when asked about the controversial justice of the peace system that he relied upon so often as a state policeman in the late 1950s and early 1960s. "One of the most-embarrassing forms of justice was the justice of the peace court system," he said.

The justice of the peace system was the precursor to today's county magistrate court system, which was created after state voters in 1966 approved an amendment to the state constitution by a vote of 81,055 - 26,317.[1]

Prior to that, each political precinct in New Mexico was allowed to have a JP. Several hundred existed statewide when in 1959 a newly impaneled state legislative committee set out to reform the old system.[2]

Much criticized was what came to be known as the JP fee system. Along with assessing fines for highway violations, JPs would impose a $5 fee for court costs if people brought before them were found guilty. If declared innocent, there would be no fee for the JP. Far more often than not, JPs found guilt. Some JPs raked in $25,000 to $40,000 a year.[3]

"At that time, that kind of money was unheard of," said former Santa Fe County Magistrate Eugene Romero.[4]

Information collected by the State Judicial System Study Committee and its staff documented how JPs held court in cafes, gas stations, living rooms, kitchens, basements, abandoned schoolhouses, even a coal mine.[5]

CdeBaca said he couldn't help but notice how people whom he cited often responded to conditions that they were required to report to. "The violators were often surprised by the lack of decorum," he said.

The state reform committee reported that few JPs had a college degree and it was probable that a JP presiding over a case did not even graduate from high school.[6]

JPs out to boost their earnings were known to actively encourage police officers to cite violators into their courts in return for kickbacks or other favors. One JP in the late 1950s admitted that he could not recall dismissing a single case out of 570 over which he had presided.[7]

Busy Route 66 used by motorists traveling across the country was a nest for the corruption of the JPs. "On old Route 66, which is now I-40, there was a fellow who had a deal going on with the police. Everything that got cited east of Albuquerque would go to him, and the JP would get money back to the police," said former Santa Fe Magistrate Romero.[8]

The newly impaneled state reform committee said in its report to the Legislature: "The justice of the peace system in New Mexico is administered in a manner that varies between the incompetent and the ridiculous."[9]

The committee's first chairman, influential Democrat Fabián Chávez Jr. of Santa Fe, said simply, "My God, what a disgrace."[10]

And the corrupt JP system stained more than poorly prepared judges. The reform committee said, "When the JP system reaches to the police, many odd and unhappy things begin to happen. No matter how brilliant the policeman's star of law enforcement may be, the mud of the JP system begins to splatter it."[11]

One JP, under questioning, told the state committee of gifts he gave to state policemen:

Q. "Did you ever give them a set of silver and turquoise gun handles?"

A. "No, sir, I never have. I have given them a set of Mexican silver and gold but not turquoise."[12]

CdeBaca said he never was offered a bribe, although he acknowledged getting what he considered to be simple gifts offered by friends. "On Thanksgiving holidays, Justice of the Peace Howard Beacham in Alamogordo used to give us all a turkey; on Christmas a bagful of apples and oranges and candy. That was customary for Judge Beacham to do with State Police. Anyone who wants to say that is no different from a bribe, so shall it be." CdeBaca said this of Beacham in one of his entries:

> "You would have to know what type of a person Judge Beacham was. He was a very well-respected man in the community. He gave us gifts out of compassion. He did not expect anything in return. He never asked me to give him more business or anything like that.

"In Alamogordo, Judge Beacham was the only judge who presided over cases in a formal office in the Otero County Courthouse. Judge Beacham at one time had served as a federal officer during the Prohibition days. He got to meet the notorious Al Capone, the mafia 'king pin' from Chicago."

CdeBaca tells how other JPs with whom he came into contact around Alamogordo used makeshift courtrooms.

"Justice of the Peace John Harding owned a small motel in Tularosa and he held court in one of the motel rooms. Justice of the Peace J.R. Falls, who lived in Bent, held court cases in the dining room of his house. He handled very few cases.

"Judge Falls and his wife spent time hunting arrow heads and owned one of the largest collections I have ever seen. He was also a master at using the so-called water witch and was relied upon to locate potential sources of water for well drillers. He demonstrated his talent to me one day. It worked for him but I couldn't get it to work."

JP Nelson Naylor, working in Orogrande, had at least a slightly more pronounced profile, according to CdeBaca's notations.

"When I was assigned to patrol U.S. 54 south of Alamogordo to the Texas state line, I cited most of the traffic violators to Justice of the Peace Naylor in Orogrande. Orogrande is a small community located halfway between Alamogordo and El Paso, Texas.

"Judge Naylor owned a filling station, which is what they were commonly called in those days. There were no qualifications for these judges in those days and no requirements where they held court. Judge Naylor had no formal office to conduct court. He held court over an old desk at his filling station. There were shelves in the room that were stocked, mostly with oil cans. He had a habit of carrying a shop rag over his left shoulder to wipe his hands.

"When a violator would appear with a ticket, Judge Naylor would have him wait until he finished servicing a car: checking the oil, water, tires and cleaning the windshield. When Judge Naylor was finished, he would identify himself as the judge and summon the violator inside the filling station.

When he banged his gavel on the top of his desk, his sleeping cat would jump off the desk and land on top of one of the shelves.

"Judge Naylor would then recite his standard line: 'The justice of the peace court in and for the County of Otero is now in session. You have been cited for speeding. How do you wish to plea: guilty or not guilty? If you plead not guilty, I will have to set bond and you will have to return for a hearing at a later day. If you plead guilty, you will have to pay a fine as set by the court and you will be assessed $5 court costs.'

"Violators seldom pleaded not guilty. They just paid their fines and left. On occasion, a violator would not only challenge the ticket but also the validity of the court. A violator who refused to pay the fine would be arrested and taken to jail in Alamogordo and his car would be impounded. The fine collected by the judge went to the state, but the $5 court cost was kept by the judge. The judge would always issue the defendant an official receipt. If the judge dismissed a case, he lost out on $5. This happened once in a blue moon.

"On one occasion, a defendant did not have the $30 to pay the fine and he offered Judge Naylor $15. However, the judge told him that the court could not accept a partial payment. The defendant, who lived in El Paso, was told by the judge to leave the spare tire to his car as collateral and when he returned to pay the fine, he could get his spare tire back. The defendant agreed and the following day, he returned to pay the fine and claim his spare tire. While this was not common practice and certainly not legal, some judges went out of their way to accommodate violators on minor traffic violations."

Naylor and his wife, like Judge Beacham, were known to be kind toward State Police officers. "After we cited numerous speeders while working the radar, Judge Naylor's wife would invite us over for pie and coffee," CdeBaca said. "It was just a good gesture on her part. We never looked at it as anything other than her being a kind woman. I remember her telling us, 'You probably don't get to have fresh pies too often when you are working late at night.'"

One such visit came after multiple speeders had been cited and after CdeBaca had been engaged in a prank that could have had a far-more serious ending.

"One evening, officers Felix Work and Allen Whitehouse radioed me to meet them at Orogrande, 35 miles south of Alamogordo to assist them with a radar operation. They instructed me to pick up the radar at the office and bring it to Judge Naylor's service station.

"When I arrived, both officers were waiting for me inside the local gas station. Officer Work asked me in an irate voice how come I was late, and before I could answer, both officers un-holstered their service revolvers and began firing in the direction of my feet. I could see the fire coming out of the revolver barrels. They had me tap dancing, trying to dodge the bullets. I was unaware that their revolvers were loaded with blanks.

"Judge Nelson Naylor, who owned the gas station and lived next door, heard the shots and came to see what was going on. The officers had their good laughs. I told them they should consider themselves lucky that I didn't fire live bullets back and then gave them a few chosen expletives.

"After we finished with the radar operation and Judge Naylor finished fining the last of the speeders, Mrs. Naylor treated us to fresh home-baked apple pie."

CdeBaca said the shooting stunt that unfolded at Naylor's service station surely would have drawn reprimands during later years. Just as likely, the state Legislature's judicial reform committee would have at least looked askance at police officers citing speeders into a particular JP's court then sitting down for fresh pie at his table once court costs had been collected from all the violators.

Judge Naylor on one occasion found himself in a serious dispute that involved much more than home-baked pies. CdeBaca tells of it in his notations.

"An Attorney from Alamogordo, Albert Rivera, who was married to Pat CdeBaca, a distant cousin of mine, requested security through the chief's office due to threats he was getting while defending a murder trial. Chief Martin Vigil assigned me to provide the security.

"When I arrived at the Rivera's house in Alamogordo, I saw a man on top of their house armed with a gun. I got out of the car and un-holstered my revolver and ordered the man to come down. He told me that he had been hired by Mr. Rivera to guard the house. Mr. Rivera confirmed that and I told him to get rid of him, that I would provide the security. I instructed Mr.

Rivera that I would answer the door and their telephone. They provided me with a room.

"Mr. Rivera was representing Justice of the Peace Nelson Naylor in a murder trial. Judge Naylor had shot and killed Ricardo Falcon at his service station in Orogrande. Ricardo Falcon and his friends were traveling from Colorado when they stopped at the service station and got into a confrontation with Judge Naylor. Judge Naylor feared for his life and shot Falcon.

"At the trial, Judge Naylor was acquitted. Mr. Rivera was called a 'white lover' and a 'vendido' by the Chicano activists from Colorado."

At alternate times, CdeBaca as a state policeman worked busy Route 66 on both its east and west ends all the while well aware of reported transgressions by justices of the peace as well as by police. "Before I was transferred to Gallup, there were reports of judges handing envelopes to State Police officers. This got out and there were major changes made with personnel before I arrived."

Tourists traveling along Route 66 often felt that police officers and JPs were in cahoots.[13] "Particularly around Gallup, you're dealing mostly with out-of-state traffic," said CdeBaca. "The motorists always had the impression that the State Police were picking on tourists. I already had a pat reply. I'd ask them to observe the license plates on the cars going by. By the time I returned with the ticket for the driver to sign, I'd ask the violator to tell me how many cars went by with New Mexico plates.

"Very few of them did."

None of that consoled every driver. CDeBaca tells this account of an incident outside of Gallup:

"Sometime in November 1962, I stopped a Cadillac for speeding and the driver was from Texas. The driver refused to sign the ticket. I explained to him that refusal was automatic arrest and I would have to take him directly before the judge. He replied, 'I'll follow you,' and I told him that that was not an option and placed him under arrest.

"I took him before Justice of the Peace George Bradley in Gallup who had a reputation for having a short fuse. After Judge Bradley explained the court procedures, he asked the driver how he wanted to plea and he replied, 'Not guilty.'

"Judge Bradley told us to raise our right hands and he put us under oath. The judge asked me to explain to the court the circumstances of the arrest. I testified I had stopped the defendant for speeding and before I could say anything else, the defendant accused the judge of running a 'kangaroo court.' Judge Bradley warned the defendant to refrain from criticizing the court. Once again, the defendant stated that he was being 'railroaded.'

"At this time, Judge Bradley got up from his chair, walked around the bench and grabbed the defendant by the collar and forced him down on the chair. Judge Bradley got back behind his desk and told the defendant, 'I find you guilty of contempt of court and sentence you to one day in jail.'

"The judge told me, 'Arrest this man and book him in jail and bring him before the court tomorrow afternoon.' As I was escorting him out of the courtroom, he told the judge, 'I demand to see an attorney.' The judge totally ignored him. The next afternoon, I took the defendant before Judge Bradley. He entered a plea of guilty, paid a $25 fine and $5 court costs.

"Apparently the defendant did not enjoy his stay in jail with all those drunks. In addition to the fine, he had to pay for the towing and storage of his car. The last thing he said is that he would never travel through New Mexico again."

After Gallup, CdeBaca was posted at the Las Vegas State Police district, where he worked as a sergeant. Despite his own harsh criticism for the JP system, CdeBaca insisted that not only was he never offered a bribe by a judge, he was not personally aware of any other officer getting such an offer.

"I was a first-line supervisor in Santa Rosa. Nothing like that was ever brought to my attention. And with something like that, sooner or later it would have leaked out," he said.

4

Raiders, Cops and a Storied Courthouse

Routine work in the auto theft unit at New Mexico State Police Headquarters was interrupted on a warm afternoon as spring prepared to give way to summer during a decade that forever will be remembered across the country for unrest. Sergeant Richard CdeBaca recalls how his attention to auto theft was unexpectedly redirected to a situation that did anything but polish the image of the State Police.

"On Monday, June 5th, 1967, about 3:30 p.m., Lieutenant Colonel Steve Lagomarsino called me, Captain Monroe Alexander and Sergeant David Kingsbury to his office to inform us that a group of armed men had raided the Rio Arriba County Courthouse in Tierra Amarilla and ordered us to patrol up there ASAP to be of assistance. We got our shotguns from our cars and took off to Tierra Amarilla in State Police unit #64, an unmarked car assigned to Captain Alexander."

Land grant activists led by charismatic, volatile Reies Lopez Tijerina had stormed the old courthouse in Tierra Amarilla on the day that nearly a dozen of their compatriots were to have been arraigned on charges that activists considered bogus. The band of 20 raiders were among Northern New Mexico residents who believed that Tijerina could help them reclaim hundreds of thousands of acres in land grant property, much of which had been taken over as forest lands by the U.S. government.

Tijerina, who had moved to New Mexico years earlier from Arizona, considered the land grant battle in New Mexico to be only a start. He envisioned reclaiming millions of acres stretching from Texas to the Pacific Ocean.

Few openly opposed Tijerina's movement as aggressively as 1st Judicial District Attorney Alfonso Sanchez of Santa Fe. It was on Sanchez's orders that 11 of Tijerina's followers had been arrested June 2nd near the community of Coyote. And it was Sanchez who was to have represented the state during arraignment of the prisoners on June 5th.

Tijerina said he wanted to make a citizen's arrest of Sanchez, who he accused of terrorism and civil rights violations. CdeBaca was among State Police officers who came to suspect otherwise.

"We heard that Tijerina and his people were going to grab District Attorney Alfonso Sanchez and take him to Canjilón. There, they supposedly would give him a 'fair' trial then hang him," CdeBaca said.

Tijerina and the other raiders escaped from the courthouse after their assault.

There was no particular reason that CdeBaca, Alexander and Kingsbury left Santa Fe toward Tierra Amarilla in an unmarked car late in the afternoon of June 5th as Tijerina and others were scattering in multiple directions. Alexander decided to drive so it was his car that was taken, CdeBaca said. "We had very little information other than that there had been an armed raid on the courthouse," he said. "We did not have any more to go on. We were not yet aware that this was the work of Reies Lopez Tijerina, and we didn't yet know that the raid had been directed primarily at District Attorney Alfonso Sanchez."

The three officers—Alexander, Kingsbury and CdeBaca—had been instructed only to drive in the direction of Tierra Amarilla, the Rio Arriba County seat. Their orders did not include a specific destination. Just south of Abiquiú, approaching the colorful sandstone hills of Georgia O'Keeffe country, an unsettling message was transmitted through the car's police radio.

"We heard over the police radio that State Police officer Nick Sais and Deputy Sheriff Eulogio Salazar had been shot during the raid. We had no idea who was involved in the raid and how many ... Approaching Abiquiu, we met the ambulance transporting officer Sais to the hospital."

CdeBaca said he and other officers in the car promptly realized that they likely would confront armed, angry citizens who seemingly wouldn't be reticent to fire upon them. "All kinds of things go through your mind," he said. "At that time we had no orders informing us to approach the situation in a cautious manner.

We didn't know if we were going to the courthouse. We were assigned to head in the direction of the courthouse and then, after learning that the two officers had been shot, we were given instructions to proceed to the little community of Canjilón, which is south of Tierra Amarilla."

Chief Joe Black and Captain T.J. Chaves were in a police car a few miles ahead of Alexander's vehicle and it was Black who ordered that Alexander's unit go directly to Canjilón.

> "By the time we arrived, other State Police officers had assembled there. These officers had been alerted to keep a pink house under close surveillance. Information was given that some of the people involved in the raid were hiding in the vicinity of the pink house.
>
> "Shortly after we arrived in Canjilón, about 5:30 p.m., we received word that a 1966 Pontiac GTO belonging to Deputy Sheriff Pete Jaramillo was on its way to Canjilón with two hostages. Chief Black dispatched two State Police cars to intercept the Pontiac, but they had no luck doing it."

The hostages were Jaramillo, who was driving, and UPI reporter Larry Calloway who was at the courthouse when the raid unfolded. Two of the courthouse raiders, a young Baltazar Martinez wearing a green beret and his uncle, 72-year-old Baltazar Apodaca, held weapons on the hostages.

CdeBaca said the officers pursuing the GTO opted for caution rather than attempting to force the car off the road. "They were aware that there was a contingent of officers stationed at Canjilón. I assume that the officers who were in pursuit of the GTO concluded that the car would come to a roadblock, and eventually that is what happened. We had sealed the road there in Canjilón by the church."

Drama in the tiny community was about to intensify.

> "We were positioned about one block east of Baldonado's Shell Service Station. Within a few minutes, the black/green Pontiac GTO approached the service station. The Pontiac traveled a few yards east of the Shell station and stopped. There were four men in the car, two of them armed with weapons, one in the front and one in the back.
>
> "One officer shouted at the men in the car to throw out their weapons and step out, but they ignored him. At the same time an elderly lady unexpectedly broke through the group of officers lining the road and walked in

the direction of the Pontiac. I ordered her to stop but she kept walking and finally stopped alongside the car and engaged in conversation with one of the occupants of the car."

The officers didn't seem to know how to respond when their orders went disregarded. "We had the GTO surrounded. We all were standing by with un-holstered weapons, either handguns or shotguns," CdeBaca said. "I was standing in front of the car at an angle to the right about 150 feet away. Chief Black was at about the same distance standing at an angle to the left."

The standard weapons issued to State Police officers in those days were .38 Smith & Wessons.

"I had my handgun on top of a fence post aimed at the GTO, at no one in particular. All four people were still in the car. I told Chief Black that I could see a weapon pointed at Jaramillo's head. We learned later that the old man, Baltazar Apodaca, also had a carbine pointed at Larry Calloway where they were seated in the back seat.

"The woman who walked up to the car acted as if she didn't even hear my order to stop. It turned out she was Baltazar Martinez's mother," CdeBaca said. "She was standing beside the GTO and she caused problems for us. Chief Black was in control of the situation and with this woman standing there, he was not going to give orders to shoot. So we waited patiently to see who was going to make the first move."

It didn't take long. CdeBaca said all four men within a few minutes got out of the car with one weapon pointed at Calloway's back and another aimed at Jaramillo's head. The hostages were forced to walk toward the church nearby. CdeBaca wrote this in his entries:

"I shouted at the armed men to surrender and the young man wearing the beret shouted back in Spanish, '*Mata me si quieres*,' (kill me if you want to). The four men walked through a small opening in the fence and into the churchyard. At this time the hostage wearing the sport coat, later identified as UPI reporter Larry Calloway, pushed the elderly man, Baltazar Apodaca, and grabbed the carbine and threw it on the ground. Captain Alexander grabbed Mr. Baltazar Apodaca and another officer picked up the carbine.

"Meanwhile, the man wearing the green beret, Baltazar Martinez, escort-ed Deputy Jaramillo around the front of the church. He then commandeered a car from a couple and took off with Deputy Jaramillo. We gave chase on a dirt road leading into the forest. After a short chase, Baltazar Martinez stopped the car and ran into the forest, shooting at us as he disappeared into the woods.

"Back in Canjilón, the National Guard began to arrive in great numbers in Jeeps, trucks and even a tank, without any coordination. We were then given orders to move out in the direction of the pink house on the hill to search homes even though we didn't have search warrants and didn't specifically know who we were looking for, other than Reies Lopez Tijerina. In a few minutes, a group of men, women and children had been gathered and were being escorted by officers out of a campsite. These people were held inside cow pens while being questioned."

A lawsuit would be filed later alleging that authorities violated civil rights of those who had been led into livestock corrals. "Under the circumstances, not knowing what we were going to be confronted with, I thought that it was the right thing to do to be able to identify these people," CdeBaca said. "I did not do any questioning of the people in those pens. There were a handful of investigators from the New Mexico State Police that did question these individuals."

Some of the people who ended up in the pens had been rounded up by CdeBaca and several other State Police officers while searching nearby homes in Canjilón. "Once things were put together there, we branched out with the National Guard and other officers to search for these people who had raided the courthouse," he said. "People had assembled in Canjilón expecting Reies Lopez Tijerina and his followers to show up there after the raid. People who were waiting had assembled in an open field, picnic style.

"When we began our searches later, there was no hesitation on our part, going and knocking on doors. If they were not opened, we'd kick doors open. The searches, I might add, were done without warrants. Many of the people who we came upon were taken to these corrals."

A Canjilón land owner identified only as Juan C. had harsh words for how State Police officers conducted themselves. He spoke to historian Rubén Sálas Márquez. "The camp where the June 5th picnic was taking place is private property ... But when the State Police arrived they pulled up as if it was their own private playground," he said. "They drove in a cloud of dust. Those on foot jumped fences, they pointed guns and rifles as if they were in the jungles of Vietnam.

"The police commenced to ask questions, put gun barrels in our faces. They searched all the buildings and especially my house where they moved beds, looked underneath, searched closets, pantries, chests of drawers, the whole works. They impounded some of the cars and trucks that had been left on my property. I don't remember what reason they gave ... fact is I don't even remember if they gave a reason, everything was happening so fast.

"I feel the State Police showed nothing but scorn and disdain ... But there wasn't anything I could do about it. They had all the guns."[1]

Joe Black, State Police chief at the time of it all, died in September 1981.

CdeBaca insisted that State Police officers acted responsibly in Canjilón. "There was not any excessive force being displayed by the State Police," he said. "There were no shoot-to-kill orders, nothing like that. I never saw any police officer act out of line, certainly not with the chief of State Police being present there."

CdeBaca offered that judgment even after acknowledging that Canjilón homes were searched without warrants, some of them after their doors had been busted open.

Chief Black eventually pulled CdeBaca and Alexander aside and gave them another assignment.

"After some of the detainees had been identified, Chief Black assigned myself and Captain Alexander to transport Mrs. Patsy Tijerina and her 7-month-old baby to Santa Fe. We were advised by District Attorney Alfonso Sanchez to book Mrs. Tijerina on conspiracy charges. We arrived at the Santa Fe City jail at approximately 10:30 p.m. Mrs. Tijerina's young daughter was left in the care of a welfare worker. We reported to Lieutenant Colonel Lagomarsino at State Police headquarters for further orders."

CdeBaca said the drive of about 75 miles in the dark was mostly quiet. "We did not interrogate her. We did not question her," he said of Mrs. Tijerina. "Captain Alexander and I were in no position to question her because we were not well informed about the situation ourselves. We tried to make her feel comfortable, respecting the presence of her child.

"I do recall that she made a comment, expressing that she did not know what all the fuss was about, that she and others in Canjilón had just gotten together for a picnic."

CdeBaca said that in retrospect, Patsy Tijerina had good cause to wonder why she had been arrested. "Why we were ordered to take her to the Santa Fe City Jail is beyond me. She hadn't done anything," he said.

Having left Mrs. Tijerina at the Santa Fe jail, CdeBaca and Alexander were sent back into the Northern New Mexico night with all its uncertainty and tension.

"We were assigned to patrol State Road 96 from Abiquiú Dam to Gallina, looking for fugitives from the raid. About 2 a.m. Tuesday, June 6, we were assigned to man a roadblock at the turn-off to Abiquiú Dam to prevent people from traveling north to Tierra Amarilla. We were being assisted by a member of the National Guard. At 7 p.m., we were ordered to relieve Sergeant Kingsbury at the ranger station in Canjilón, which had been set up as the communications center for police activity. All activities were being coordinated at the ranger station.

"That night, officer Louis McEwen radioed to inform us that he had an individual by the name of Alfonso Martinez in custody who claimed that he was a Tijerina lieutenant. We instructed officers McEwen and Doug Davis to bring Mr. Martinez to the ranger station for questioning. I introduced myself to Mr. Martinez. He spoke in Spanish only. Mr. Martinez was 3'10" tall and weighed 80 pounds. Not knowing if he had been involved in the courthouse raid, I informed him of his rights. Mr. Martinez told us he was a member of the Federal Alliance of Land Grants, but he had not partici-pated in the raid. He could not furnish any information on the whereabouts of Reies Lopez Tijerina or his followers, and he denied being related to Baltazar Martinez, the 'Green Beret.' We instructed the officers to return Mr. Martinez to Tierra Amarilla."

CdeBaca said he and Alexander encountered little resistance from motor-ists who were stopped at the roadblock near Abiquiú Dam on June 6th. "To begin with, there was very little traffic at that hour. I remember we stopped a Seven-Up truck. We asked for a couple of cans of Seven-Up and the driver gave them to us at no charge.

"The negative reaction we got was mostly from news reporters, not the traveling public. We were told that if reporters had their authorization, which in those days was issued by the State Police, they were to be let through."

State Police officers, national guardsmen and others—several hundred—posted at the Canjilón ranger station were poorly prepared for the extended stay. Snacks initially at their disposal did not last long.

"The Shell Station sold out of everything. Some women started making bean burritos, and they were selling faster than the women could make them."

"The following morning (June 7th), we were told to get a motel room in Chama and to get some rest. We were totally fatigued. That night, I was assigned to the sheriff's office at the courthouse in Tierra Amarilla, which was Sheriff Benny Naranjo's office. The office was equipped with a radio base station and I could communicate with all the officers who had been assigned to Tierra Amarilla."

CdeBaca said there were about 10 to 12 State Police officers who remained in the Tierra Amarilla area after the National Guard had been pulled out. "From the very beginning, I remember wondering, 'How come the National Guard is here? What can the National Guard do that we can't do?'" he said. He said it must have been State Police Chief Joe Black who asked Lieutenant Governor E. Lee Francis to dispatch guardsmen. Governor David Cargo was out of state at the time, leaving Francis to serve as acting governor.

The night of June 7th threatened to be as eventful as the day of the raid, and CdeBaca remembered getting a real scare.

"At midnight, the telephone rang and when I answered it, an unidentified man said they were going to raid the courthouse and this time there was not going to be a 'screw up' and he hung up the phone. Then a second phone call came in and the caller said I was going to get visitors. I immediately radioed the State Police officers in the vicinity and instructed them to secure the courthouse and to stop any car that moved in the area. I radioed the dispatcher in Santa Fe and told him to try to trace the anonymous phone calls."

"Suddenly, I heard glass drop somewhere in the hallway. I walked out of the sheriff's office and through the secretary's office armed with my shotgun. The entire courthouse was dark and I couldn't see anything. I waited a couple of minutes before stepping into the hallway. While walking to check the front doors to the courthouse, I heard glass breaking behind me. I turned around ready to shoot but there was no one there.

"I returned to the sheriff's office and got my flashlight and discovered that glass had fallen from a vending machine which had been shot during the raid. I heard footsteps on the wooden floor and turned around to see a man walking in the hallway. I have no idea why I didn't shoot. Fortunately, I didn't because it was the jailer housed in the basement who had heard noises and had come up to find out what was going on."

CdeBaca said he had never stepped inside the Rio Arriba County courthouse prior to being sent there by Chief Black to direct the State Police presence in days following the raid. "I had never seen that courthouse in my life," he said.

He said he did not know that there was a jail in the basement of the building or that anyone was in the basement at the time. "Thank God I didn't shoot that jailer. I was really walking on eggshells when I heard that glass fall."

As time went on, fugitives from the raid were being apprehended. CdeBaca recalled one incident largely because of where it happened.

"Three men who participated in the raid were arrested in Santa Fe. The car they were in was chased on Cerrillos Road and was finally stopped near the State Police headquarters. Those arrested were identified as Vicorino D. Chaves, age 66, Santiago Anaya, age 53, and Camilo Sanchez, age, 51. They were charged with conspiracy to incite a riot. By now all those involved in the raid had been identified and law enforcement officers were continuing the manhunt."

The big catch came five days after the raid as a result of a call made out of the Jemez Mountains about 100 miles from the Tierra Amarilla courthouse.

"On June 10th, Reies Lopez Tijerina came out of hiding. He was a passenger in a car that stopped at a gas station in Jemez. He was recognized by the station attendant when Tijerina got out of the car. The attendant got the description of the car and when it left, he called the State Police. Tijerina was arrested at a roadblock near Bernalillo. Even though Tijerina was armed, he offered no resistance.

"By the end of June, only two of the wanted men remained at large:

Tijerina's brother, Cristobal, and Baltazar Martinez. Martinez, known as the Green Beret, was regarded as the most dangerous. On July 4th, he surrendered to an off-duty Albuquerque policeman. Martinez's mother negotiated the surrender, telling police officers she did not want her son hurt.

"Governor Cargo had posted a $500 reward for information leading to his arrest. Mrs. Martinez, mother of Baltazar, collected the check in a ceremony at the governor's office. When the cancelled check was returned, it had been co-signed by her son, the Green Beret.

"Cristobal Tijerina surrendered on August 2nd to district Judge Joe Angel at the Guadalupe County courthouse in Santa Rosa."

CdeBaca said Cargo clearly wanted the fugitives caught even though it was widely suspected, including within the law enforcement community, that the governor was sympathetic toward concerns that drove at least some of the activists. "I think he was sympathetic and understanding about the concerns in the North about the land grants," CdeBaca said. "And I'm sure that he understood that cause. I don't mean to say, though, that he was sympathetic to Reies Lopez Tijerina."

5

Tijerina Through a Policeman's Eye

Reies Lopez Tijerina ignited the land grant battle of the 1960s convinced that he had been sent to the mission by God himself. In the midst of the tumult, he told me that he was slowing down because he was "getting ahead of God."

He repeatedly accused the New Mexico State Police, 1st Judicial District Attorney Alfonso Sanchez, the FBI, the courts and others of waging "a campaign of terror" against him and his family. Some of his accusations seemed contrived. Others were all too real: Plate glass windows at Tijerina's headquarters in Albuquerque had been smashed twice on separate nights; an off-duty Bernalillo County sheriff's deputy had attempted to throw a bomb into the building only to have the device go off prematurely.[1]

Richard CdeBaca is well aware of Tijerina's disdain for the New Mexico State Police. He noted how Tijerina and his confederates described police as running like "scared coyotes" during the raid on the Rio Arriba County courthouse.

Members of the State Police, on the other hand, have long had their own impressions of Tijerina. Authorities had collected much information on Tijerina and his group. CdeBaca shares some of what he came to know.

"In order to learn about the events that led to the raid on June 5th, one must know about Reies Lopez Tijerina who was responsible for the armed assault on the Rio Arriba County courthouse. Reies Lopez Tijerina was born in 1927 in a migrant *campesino* camp in Texas. He did not have any formal education to speak of, but he learned from the Bible and became a minister in the Assembly of God Church. Mr. Tijerina traveled and preached and became a good orator. He finally settled in a small town in Arizona called the Valley of Peace and became the minister for a small group of *campesinos.* Mr. Tijerina later showed up in New Mexico. It is not known for sure at what time he became interested in the Treaty of Guadalupe Hidalgo of 1848. He became a land grant activist and began exploiting the land owners in northern Rio Arriba County, calling himself 'King Tiger.'

"It all began in February 1963 when Reies Lopez Tijerina formed the *Alianza Federal de Las Mercedes* (Federal Alliance of Land Grants) and later known as the political Confederation of Free City-States. It was his claim that the land in question in almost the entire Southwest was originally granted by the Spanish crown and the Republic of Mexico, and it rightfully belonged to the descendants of the grantees and should be returned to whom it belonged. He made believers out of people whose ancestors acquired the land, and soon he had a following loyal to him and his preachings. Paid membership was required to be in the Alliance and the number of members kept growing over the years.

"There were reports of criminal acts in Rio Arriba County involving burning of haystacks, destruction of barbed wire fences, and cattle killings, mostly targeting Anglo ranchers. One of those ranchers was Bill Mundy, who lived between Tierra Amarilla and Chama. Mr. Tijerina was now drawing the attention of law enforcement.

"One year, Mr. Tijerina and his followers forcibly occupied a natural wonder called Echo Amphitheater and 'arrested' a U.S. Forest Service ranger and charged him in connection ... with occupation of the site. Mr. Tijerina had established the 'Independent Nation of *Pueblo Republica de San Joaquin del Rio de Chama,*' complete with its own mayor, government officials and its own flag. He was convicted on federal charges growing out of his occupation of Echo Amphitheater.

"In May of 1967, Mr. Tijerina and his followers met and voted to re-establish the *Pueblo Republica de San Joaquin.* They declared that the revolution had started and 'all the vendidos and gringos were running scared like cornered dogs, and they are plotting how to stop the movement.' By this time, the State Police had infiltrated the Alliance through the use of informants."

CdeBaca suggested later that it was one police informant who had infiltrated Tijerina's organization. "Naturally, I don't know who the informant was. I have no idea, other than to conclude that he had to be a paid informant for these State Police investigators who were tracking down the activities of the *Alianza,*" he said. "Almost any informant that you get to work with you in law enforcement, they're not going to work for nothing. They're not going to take risks and not get paid for their services."

Referring to his assignment to the State Police auto theft unit, CdeBaca said he was "not privy" to intelligence information that was channeled to Chief Joe Black's office.

Tijerina in 1966 said his *Alianza* had 20,000 members, up from 6,000 members claimed in 1964.[2]

The occupation of Echo Amphitheater north of Abiquiu referred to by CdeBaca occurred in 1966. Following his conviction on charges growing out of the incident, he remained free pending lengthy appeals.

State Police officers considered the burning of haystacks and destruction of fences around Tierra Amarilla in the early 1960s to have been "isolated incidents," CdeBaca said. None of them was formally pinned on Tijerina or his followers, although they topped the list of suspects.

"These things had probably been going on for years. There was no intelligence information that this was going to lead to an armed raid of the county courthouse," CdeBaca said.

With at least one police informant inside Tijerina's organization, trouble leading up to the courthouse raid began to percolate.

"Word got out that the *Alianza* was going to have a meeting in Coyote to plan their strategy for June. On June 2, District Attorney Alfonso Sanchez gave orders to set up a roadblock on State Road 96 and arrest and confiscate the *Alianza's* records. We arrested 11 members of the *Alianza* on warrants signed by the district attorney, charging unlawful assembly and extortion in connection with past activities of the Federal Alliance of Land Grants. The records were confiscated along with some small firearms. Those arrested were taken to the Santa Fe City Jail, then they were transferred to the Tierra Amarilla courthouse, where they were to be arraigned on the charges."

CdeBaca said he wondered about the validity of the warrants obtained by Sanchez even while carrying out his own responsibilities to enforce the warrants. "We didn't question authority. We just followed orders. It's part of our training," he said. "But it did enter my mind: Where and how did the district attorney obtain or have sufficient information for probable cause to have these warrants executed? Obviously he had sufficient information to convince Judge Joe Angel in Las Vegas to sign off on these warrants. No judge is going to sign off on blind warrants."

The warrants and the police action they led to set off a firestorm. "It's what provoked Reies Lopez Tijerina and infuriated him to the point that he called for a plan to get back at the district attorney, Alfonso Sanchez," CdeBaca said. "And I think that when he found out that these 11 individuals that had been arrested and booked in the Santa Fe City Jail and were being taken up to the Rio Arriba County courthouse for arraignment, he put a plan into action to go up and arrest the district attorney."

CdeBaca is convinced that Tijerina planned more than an arrest.

"Mr. Tijerina had been inciting his loyal followers for some time and the incarceration of the 11 men infuriated him. The district attorney would be at the Tierra Amarilla courthouse on Monday, June 5th, to personally arraign those who had been arrested. Mr. Tijerina got word of this and he put a plan to kidnap the district attorney and take him to Canjilón, supposedly to hang him.

"Meanwhile, Chief Black received intelligence information that Mr. Tijerina would attempt to disrupt the arraignments at the Rio Arriba County courthouse and the chief assigned a handful of State Police officers to deter any overt acts by Mr. Tijerina and his followers. Because of the poorly planned security, Mr. Tijerina was able to carry out his plans with one exception: The district attorney was not there.

"At the time Mr. Tijerina and his followers arrived at the courthouse there was one State Police officer inside. Other State Police officers were on patrol. No one picked up on Mr. Tijerina and his followers headed to the courthouse. Sheriff Benny Naranjo and Deputy Eulogio Salazar were in the sheriff's office. Deputy Sheriff Pete Jaramillo was somewhere in the courthouse and Deputy Sheriff Daniel Rivera was assigned to the jury.

"Mr. Tijerina and his followers stormed the courthouse about 3 p.m., armed with weapons and the reign of terror began. State Police officer Nick Sais was standing in the hallway when they entered. He was immediately surrounded and they pointed a gun at him and ordered him to give them his gun. When he started to un-holster his gun, he was shot. Officer Sais fell to the floor wounded and the shooting began in all directions. It was complete pandemonium inside.

"County employees jumped out through windows for their safety and others scrambled for cover. One of the gunmen took officer Sais' gun and handcuffs. Hearing the shots, Deputy Eulogio Salazar stepped out of the sheriff's office and into the hallway, at which time Tijerina saw him. Deputy Salazar turned around and ran back into the sheriff's office and opened a window to jump out when he was shot in the face and shoulder while straddling the window.

"He managed to jump outside while bleeding profusely from his wounds. Sheriff Naranjo lay on the floor and Tijerina and his brother, Anselmo, stepped all over him but didn't hurt him. The gunmen were all over the courthouse shooting and looking for the district attorney. A group of armed men ran upstairs and by this time, District Judge James Scarborough and the prosecutor had hidden themselves in the judge's chambers. The jury, together with Deputy Daniel Rivera, had locked themselves in the jury room. The gunmen tried to kick down the door then fired several rounds with a carbine busting the door lock. Deputy Rivera, who was armed, was kicked and clubbed over the head with a rifle butt. None of the jurors was hurt, only left traumatized.

"Tijerina then led his followers to the courtroom upstairs and into the front office of Judge Scarborough's chambers but for some unknown reason did not enter into the judge's private office. Judge Scarborough said later that someone shot open the door to the hall that led to his chambers. He said it sounded like a machine gun.

"Deputy Eulogio Salazar stumbled around the corner of the courthouse after he jumped from the window and hid between parked cars. Mr. Solomon Luna, an employee in the county treasurer's office said he was in the office when he heard several gunshots. He and other employees bailed out the window. Mr. Luna saw Deputy Salazar staggering outside and then bent over moaning. Mr. Luna also saw a gunman ready to give it to Deputy Salazar again. The gunman fired at Deputy Salazar and shot his hat right off his head. Deputy Salazar played dead and they left him there bleeding."

Salazar would say under oath later that it was Reies Tijerina who shot him inside the courthouse. CdeBaca said Luna identified one of Tijerina's brothers as the man who shot at Salazar outside the courthouse and left him for dead. "The first shot fired inside the courthouse was by Juan Valdez when he shot State Police officer Nick Sais," CdeBaca said. "Baltazar Martinez, the so-called Green Beret, said after officer Sais was shot, 'Let me finish the son-of-a-bitch off,' pointing a carbine at Officer Sais' head but Juan Valdez, seeing officer Sais bleeding, prevented Baltazar Martinez from shooting officer Sais even though it was Juan Valdez who had shot Officer Sais."

Sais said for this book that it was both instinct and training that prompted him to move for his gun. "I had been looking at the bulletin board and then I saw these people coming in with weapons," he said. "I went for my pistol and got shot. I wasn't taught in the State Police how to surrender. The guy who shot me was so close that all I saw was a ball of fire come from that weapon."

Even though police officers purportedly did not fire a single shot, bullets were flying in all directions, CdeBaca said.

"According to Mr. Luna, there were some people in the street watching, but a gunman took a shot at them and they cleared the street. Outside the courthouse, the raiders fired shot after shot at two State Police cars, units 26 and 227. Bullet holes were everywhere. Empty cartridge cases lay on the stairway, halls, walls and offices.

"During the shooting, State Police officers Alex Quintana and George Chaves were riding together in one police car and they approached the courthouse from the south side. Some of the gunmen saw them and began to fire in their direction. The officers did not return fire. Instead, they put the car in reverse and backed up at a high rate of speed. The police car struck a concrete abutment and the front seat broke loose from its track. The car was badly damaged but the officers managed to drive away.

"Inside the courthouse, in the hallway, UPI reporter Larry Calloway was the only newsman covering the (scheduled) arraignment. He was in a telephone booth reporting events of the arraignment when the shooting began. Larry squatted down on the floor of the phone booth after he saw officer Sais shot. He remained on the floor as the gunmen ran back and forth, yelling and shooting. He raised up and saw a man shoot out a door and he ducked again. Larry said he could hear officer Sais moaning in the hallway.

"When Larry looked again, he saw Tijerina with pistol drawn and shouting orders. He described Tijerina as 'every bit a revolutionary leader.' Larry then heard footsteps coming toward the phone booth. A man with a pistol opened the door and pulled him out. One man reached in the phone booth and ripped the telephone from the wall. He was taken down the hallway and saw officer Sais lying on his back observing everything that was going on.

"Larry was pushed inside the county clerk's office, where there were several people including Sheriff Naranjo and Deputy Jaramillo. He could hear more shooting outside and for a few minutes everybody stood in silence while the gunmen held rifles on them. Larry said that a young, short man stepped into the room and ordered him and Deputy Pete Jaramillo to step outside where they were tied with cords. He was told, 'If you want to live, do as we say.'

"Larry said the gunmen fired rifle shots through a locked door. He related that the young gunman went wild when they stepped out of the courthouse and shot three times at the red light on top of a State Police car, and in the next few seconds, he must have shot 50 rounds at police cars shattering all the windows of one. Larry saw them steal weapons from the police cars.

"An attorney from Albuquerque, Carlos Sedillo, who was representing one of the defendants witnessed some of the shooting when he left the courtroom and went outside to get in his car. He heard a gunshot and saw some people getting out of a truck in front of the courthouse. According to Mr. Sedillo, he saw an old man bleeding from the face who had come around his car and hid next to a truck. Mr. Sedillo got in his car and several shots were fired at him, one bullet hitting the bumper of his car.

"After the gunmen loaded all the weapons they could get their hands on, they forced the hostages in Deputy Jaramillo's car and drove south on U.S. 84, then turned on the road to Canjilón. When they arrived in Canjilón, we were waiting for them. When Baltazar Martinez and Baltazar Apodaca ordered Larry Calloway and Deputy Jaramillo to get out of the car, Larry had worked his bindings loose and felt he could free his hands. According to Larry, the old man, Baltazar Apodaca, who had a carbine on him did not appear to want to shoot anyone. When they walked into the churchyard, Larry pulled the gun from Baltazar Apodaca and pushed the gun to the ground and that's when Mr. Apodaca was arrested.

"The gunmen had terrorized the courthouse between 3 p.m. and 5 p.m.

I don't know at what time Chief Black requested the help of the National Guard but they began to arrive in great numbers. Who knows what the Guard had in mind when they brought the tank to the small community. Governor David Cargo was out of state. That meant that Lieutenant Governor E. Lee Francis had to authorize the mobilization of the Guard.

"Reies Lopez Tijerina, who orchestrated the whole thing, his brother, Anselmo Tijerina, Juan Valdez, who shot Officer Sais, Baltazar Martinez and others who participated in the raid got away.

"The night Captain Alexander and I took Reies Lopez Tijerina's wife in custody, she said, 'I don't see what all the fuss is about. We're just up here for a picnic.' The rumor was that the reason they had assembled in the field in Canjilon was to witness the hanging of the district attorney.

"A man identifying himself as one of Reies Tijerina's followers called an Albuquerque radio station after the raid and announced, 'You think they're having trouble up north, wait until night.' He then threatened to blow up the city's military bases.

"When the arrests of the 11 men were made on Friday in Coyote, maps and organizational charts were confiscated which identified areas as prime objectives of what was apparently an Alliance plan for taking over some 600,000 acres of Northern New Mexico land.

"Those who criticized the manner in which law enforcement responded claimed that the raid could have been prevented. Having known that an attempt would be made to disrupt the proceedings at the courthouse, there should have been State Police cars on the highways leading to the courthouse and more state policemen and deputies stationed in front of the building. None of the State Police officers or deputies fired a shot. One of the gunmen stated later that the State Police 'ran like scared coyotes.' The additional State Police car parked in front of the courthouse must have been for deterrence."

CdeBaca acknowledged later that the Rio Arriba courthouse raid was not a shining hour for the New Mexico State Police. "What kind of police work was it? Not good," he said.

"I don't know that we had specific information that an attempt would be made to arrest the district attorney. I think the information that State Police had was that there were going to be problems there," he said, suggesting that Tijerina and his followers could not have been stopped and kept from approaching the courthouse based only on what was known prior to the raid.

Still, he said the police presence on the highway and in the courthouse should have been greater, knowing that Tijerina and his followers planned a disruption at the courthouse. "With the kind of intelligence information that we had, there should have been more than a handful of officers assigned," he said. "State Police should have been directed to be especially observant of traffic headed to Tierra Amarilla, specifically the courthouse."

Sais tells how he and two other officers were assigned to the courthouse that day. "We got a call that there was a wreck and the two other (officers) took the call," he said. "I was left in the courthouse alone. It was a bogus call. Things might have been different if the three of us had been in the courthouse."

Criticism of how the State Police responded once shooting started might also be justified, CdeBaca said. He referred specifically to the incident in which two officers approached the courthouse from the south side then fled in their wrecked car after being fired upon. "I think that's the reason that Reies Lopez Tijerina said later that police ran like scared coyotes," CdeBaca said. "You have to look back and say, 'What would I have done under the same circumstances?' I don't know. But why wouldn't Tijerina think that way? It's almost a true statement."

"Once word got out about the raid, why didn't all the police officers that were in that area go in and take over the courthouse?"

Nor does CdeBaca spare the Rio Arriba County Sheriff's Department of criticism. "Officer Nick Sais was caught off guard but there were opportunities by other officers there to do something," he said. "Not a single shot was fired during the raid by law enforcement there, not by a deputy, not by Sheriff Benny Naranjo, who in my opinion had an opportunity to have prevented his employee, Eulogio Salazar, from being shot. He did not take a position one way or another to defend the courthouse.

"Eulogio Salazar went out to see about the shots being fired when Officer Sais was wounded. Sheriff Naranjo took no action to shoot the assailant. They stepped all over him on the floor and to this day I wonder why he was spared. Why was Eulogio Salazar shot and not the sheriff?"

But even amid such comments, CdeBaca acknowledged that the raid might have turned out even worse if law officers had aggressively engaged the activists. "If the handful of officers that were assigned there had engaged in a shootout, innocent bystanders might have been shot," he said. "I'm not saying that I would have gone in there in a blaze of glory trying to take every armed individual down, but the whole thing was just bungled from the beginning. It was bungled in the sense that there was not adequate security there and law enforcement was ill prepared."

Martin Vigil, then a captain in charge of the State Police district in Española, took much of the public criticism after the raid but it can't end there, CdeBaca said. "Ultimately, it's the chief's responsibility," he said.

And criticism after the raid wasn't all aimed at men in uniform, CdeBaca recalled.

"No sooner did the dust settle down from the raid and Governor David Cargo and the district attorney began blaming each other. The district attorney, Alfonso Sanchez, stated publicly, 'Maybe if the governor quits holding hands with them, maybe then they will know they can't take the law into their own hands.' Governor Cargo, who was in Michigan when the raid took place, was apparently upset after the arrests were made on the Friday before the raid.

"A State Police officer who wanted to remain anonymous because he feared retaliation, told a reporter for the *Albuquerque Journal* that Cristobal Tijerina, while in jail in Santa Fe on Friday night, had made the statement, 'I'll be out of here in three hours. Your boss, the governor, will get me out. We got him 2,300 votes.' That would not be the case.

"On Tuesday, Governor Cargo made the statement that each participant in the courthouse raid would be held equally responsible. He said, 'Every person involved is going to be equally liable whether he pulled a trigger or not.' Governor Cargo emphasized that there would be no more attempts at negotiation between his office and the federal Alliance of Land Grants. He said, 'You can't sit down and negotiate with Jesse James, and that's what it amounts to.'

"Governor Cargo expressed his displeasure over the mobilization of the National Guard, and I believe this caused a strained relationship between him and Lieutenant Governor E. Lee Francis, though I thought they were never fond of each other to begin with.

"Meanwhile, both officer Nick Sais and Deputy Eulogio Salazar were recovering from their wounds in the hospital with a good prognosis for a full recovery.

"After the raid in Tierra Amarilla, District Judge James Scarborough was reporting to work in his office in Santa Fe armed with a six shooter. He was referred to as the 'gun-toting judge.'

"Reies Lopez Tijerina was a fugitive and I'm sure he was totally disappointed that his plans to kidnap the district attorney were foiled when they did not find him at the courthouse on Monday. And I am equally sure the district attorney was counting his blessings that he had not been at the courthouse."

CdeBaca said Tijerina's own intelligence from confederates who he had relied upon failed him leading up to the raid. Tijerina went into the courthouse thinking that Sanchez would be there. Reies Lopez Tijerina is an intelligent, very articulate individual but he was not well informed prior to going into the courthouse. He grew so inflamed about what had occurred a few days earlier that he bungled it."

Figuring that Tierra Amarilla and its surroundings would need watching for a while, State Police Chief Black eventually placed CdeBaca in charge of the task.

"Chief Black called me to report to his office. He told me to stay in Tierra Amarilla until all the suspects involved in the raid were arrested and the community returned to normal. I went home and packed my suitcase and returned to Tierra Amarilla. My orders were to remain at the sheriff's office and supervise the officers on special assignment. The county employees were relieved to see me in the courthouse every day. In talking to them, I was pretty much able to piece together the events of the raid. None of them had been hurt during the raid, except for a few bruised while climbing out of windows.

"A Mrs. Dabbs called the sheriff's office and told me that her husband, Dr. Dabbs, who ran the clinic in Parkview, was in Vietnam and she was worried about the security of the clinic because it was closed for business. She and a helper lived in a trailer next to the clinic and they were in fear due to recent events. She asked if I could help assign a State Police officer or a deputy to stay at the clinic.

"I had not slept more than eight hours since my assignment to Tierra Amarilla, and I didn't have a place to stay. Other officers were doubling up in whatever rooms were available in Chama. I went to visit Mrs. Dabbs. She showed me the clinic and I accepted to sleep there. She gave me a set of keys and both her and her helper thanked me for staying there. They felt comfortable with my marked police car being parked in front of the clinic. There was only one restaurant in Tierra Amarilla and if we wanted to eat anywhere else, we had to travel to Chama."

CdeBaca said that most people in and around Tierra Amarilla welcomed the police presence. "I was left to oversee about 10 officers and the citizenry appreciated the heavy number of State Police officers in the community," he said. "Though still tense, they felt secure in their houses and they welcomed us. In time, I began to get invitations to come and eat at their houses, and I did that on a couple of occasions.

"I was aware that there were several fugitives that had participated in the raid on the courthouse who were still out in Tierra Amarilla, Canjilón or other surrounding communities. We had orders to try to apprehend these individuals but I was also mindful that we were assigned there to keep the peace in the community, to calm the fear that something like the raid might happen again. There was no apparent reason for anyone to assault the courthouse anymore but officers were on the alert all the time."

In truth, they couldn't help but be on edge.

"Word got out that a State Police car would be the target of a bombing. I called a meeting of all the officers and advised them not to leave their cars open at any time and to inspect them every morning before they started them. Things were still tense in the community.

"While thoroughly inspecting the courthouse for bullet holes, I spotted one in the south side window of the building. I went outside and noticed that the door to the house next door was in direct line with the bullet hole in the window. I walked to the house and when I knocked on the door, I saw a small hole in the screen door and a hole in the entry door. A woman answered. I identified myself and explained to her why I was there. She called her husband and he invited me in. I asked them if they had been home during the raid and they replied that they had not.

"However, when they got home they noticed the hole in the door and found a bullet lodged in the wall. I asked them if any of the investigators had questioned them, and they said that no one had. I told the man of the house that I would have to confiscate the bullet for evidence and he went and got it and gave it to me."

CdeBaca said he knew little about the investigation conducted by the State Police after the raid but admitted that a thorough investigation would have turned up the bullet in the home across the road which then would have led to an interview of the occupants. "It says that certain things may have been overlooked," he said. "That was something that should not have been overlooked. It could have been an important piece of evidence in the prosecution of at least one of the individuals involved in the raid."

Although most in the community purportedly were looking to settle back into normalcy, others apparently wanted to keep public attention focused on long-simmering issues that they thought were rooted in injustice.

"On the evening of June 9th, officers Jack Johnson and Billy Taylor came into the sheriff's office and informed me that there was a gathering on the main street just a short distance from the courthouse. They reported that a man was standing in the bed of the pickup which was parked under a street lamp and he was talking to a group of men. The officers had no idea what the meeting was all about.

"I thought it was highly unusual for a meeting to be taking place in the middle of the street in the darkness. I told the officers I was going to walk over there and find out what was going on. They tried to discourage me from doing it. Officer Johnson worried that they might be planning another raid. I told him that they would not be that open about it. I instructed them to keep me under surveillance from a distance.

"When I approached the crowd, one of the men signaled to the speaker pointing in my direction. The speaker was speaking in Spanish and spreading propaganda about the State Police. I raised my hand and introduced myself in Spanish and asked him if I could say a few words. I was apprehensive and didn't know what to expect. The man in the bed of the pickup told me to speak up.

"I moved to the middle of the crowd and explained that I was the supervisor in charge and that as long as I was there we would respect the citizens and try to co-exist with the community. I told them I was raised in

La Ciénega, a community very much like theirs and I knew how I would feel seeing a dozen State Police officers every day in the community. I assured them that as long as I was in charge, I would be responsible for the officers' conduct and that they could hold me accountable for their actions.

"I said, 'It is unfortunate what happened here on Monday, otherwise we wouldn't be here. We are simply carrying out orders to be peacekeepers and that is what we intend to do.' I thanked them for the opportunity to talk to them and told them if they had any complaints they could find me in the sheriff's office.

"I learned later that the man speaking to the crowd was Pedro Archuleta, president of the *Comancheros del Norte*, an activist group."

In time, Captain Martin Vigil visited Tierra Amarilla and met with CdeBaca, who recommended that the number of officers working in Tierra Amarilla on special assignment be reduced. It was.

CdeBaca continued making friends in the area, friendships that included one with the deputy sheriff who was shot during the raid.

"Deputy Sheriff Eulogio Salazar was released from the hospital. He wrote to Governor Cargo, requesting financial assistance. He had amassed a huge debt from medical expenses. Shortly thereafter, the governor obtained a job for him with the State Game and Fish Hatchery at Park View. Deputy Salazar did not stay with the hatchery very long and returned to work at his old job. Deputy Salazar and I got to be good friends.

"I made many friends in Tierra Amarilla, hard-working farmers and sheep herders. Mr. Leo Smith, foreman of the Chama Land and Cattle Company, invited me to fish in their private lakes any time I wanted to."

Relationships developed by CdeBaca over months in and around Tierra Amarilla apparently were devoid of any contact with Rio Arriba Sheriff Benny Naranjo. "I worked out of his office in the courthouse but I never saw him come around," CdeBaca said.

Finally, the time came for CdeBaca to return home.

"In July, I wrote a letter to Captain Martin Vigil, Chief Joe Black and

Governor Cargo about the situation in northern Rio Arriba County. I mentioned that there had been no more civil disturbances and there was no reason to keep any officers on special assignment there; that the resident officers could take care of things. Chief Black took my recommendations, and we were all relieved of our duties in Tierra Amarilla."

Critical of how law enforcement officers failed to prevent the raid or stop it once it began, CdeBaca said he understood how people subjected to the State Police and other officers in the hours following the raid might have felt that law enforcement was overpowering. "It has to be a shock to a small, peaceful community like Canjilón," he said. "One day there is an overwhelming show of police force that is reinforced by the National Guard. What ensued—kicking down doors and searching for people, searching houses without search warrants—I'm sure it was very disturbing to some of those families that were subjected to all of that. They hadn't done anything. Why wouldn't they be disturbed? Some might not even have been aware of the raid at the courthouse."

CdeBaca did not back away, however, from his earlier assertion that officers acted responsibly under the circumstances.

The raid, itself, was unwarranted, said CdeBaca, even if orders issued by District Attorney Alfonso Sanchez to arrest Tijerina followers on June 2nd were questionable. "Reies Lopez Tijerina had no legitimate right to make a citizen's arrest on Alfonso Sanchez," he said. "If he felt that his rights and his followers' rights had been violated by actions of the district attorney, he had other avenues to pursue."

CdeBaca said that he was unable to address Tijerina's repeated assertions that he could not rely on law enforcement to protect his rights so he had to act on his own. Nor, CdeBaca said, was he in a position to address the assertion by state District Judge Paul Larrazolo that Tijerina and his followers did, indeed, have a right to seek Alfonso Sanchez for a citizen's arrest.

Nearly a year after the courthouse raid, residue from the assault was still falling on CdeBaca.

"On May 30, 1968, Chief Black called me into his office and apprised me of a confidential report which had been submitted by agent T.J. Richardson, stationed in Albuquerque. According to Agent Richardson, he had received a call from an informant associated with the Tijerina *Alianza*, stating that she had been at an address in Southwest Albuquerque and heard four members of the *Alianza* say 'that they did not like Sergeant Richard, or Dick, DeBaca and that they were fed up with him.' It was said that they were going to do the same thing to DeBaca as was done to the (deputy) sheriff, but this time they weren't going to make any mistakes.

"The report submitted by agent Richardson named the four *Alianza* members who were 'perturbed' with me. The informant was instructed to try to get more specific information. I was never informed of any further developments.

"We were worried about our two sons. They were enrolled at E.J. Martinez School in Santa Fe and they walked to and from school.

"The only overt act that took place late one night is when a truck pulled into the neighbor's driveway and deliberately backed into the side of my police car, which was parked on the street parallel with the curb. Our neighbors, the McCorkles came out of their house about the same time I did to find out what happened. My car sustained moderate damage on the left side. I called the city police and an officer came and made a report. I believe it was a random act and had nothing to do with the *Alianza*."

6

Drama on Both Sides of a Courtroom Door

More than a year after Reies Lopez Tijerina stormed the Rio Arriba County courthouse with a small band of well-armed followers, the "King Tiger," as he once liked to be called, would face trial in downtown Albuquerque.

He had been charged with 54 criminal counts tied to the raid after being arrested at a roadblock in Bernalillo. He would be tried on only three: assault on a jail, false imprisonment and kidnapping.[1] State District Judge Paul Larrazolo of Albuquerque was on the bench.

Tijerina had several lawyers defending him but he also did much of the work in court himself. As a poverty-saddled youth, he was known as *el abogado sin libros* because of his oratory skills.

Richard CdeBaca, by now serving as a State Police lieutenant, would get another assignment growing out of that incredible day in June 1967, this one bringing him face to face with Tijerina for the first time.

"In November 1968, Chief Black assigned me among others to provide security at the Bernalillo County Courthouse in Albuquerque for the trial of Reies Lopez Tijerina. District Judge Paul Larrazolo would preside over the selection of the jury and the trial. Attorney Jack Love had been appointed as special prosecutor. The judge had requested heavy security knowing this was a high-profile case and he wanted to have an orderly trial. Already tension was building up for the selection of the jury.

"Chief Black assigned Major Hoover Wimberly to be in charge of security and he in turn assigned us to strategic locations at the courthouse. The Bernalillo County sheriff and the Albuquerque police chief also assigned officers. Deputy Sheriff Julian Narvaiz and I were assigned to the third floor where the trial would be heard. Judge Larrazolo ruled that no cameras would be allowed on the third floor of the courthouse. This ruling did not go well with the news media. Every television and newspaper reporter wanted to take pictures. The officers assigned to the entrance to the courthouse had to screen everyone coming in."

CdeBaca said that about 12 officers from the three agencies combined worked security during the trial on any given day. CdeBaca was posted on the third floor outside the courtroom.

"The selection of the jury was a long, involved process. Prospective jurors (in panels of 35) had to be under the watchful eye of every police officer and the same applied to Tijerina's loyalists. The defense counsel made a motion early on calling for a mistrial on the grounds that we were mingling with the prospective jurors. During recess, Judge Larrazolo warned us to refrain from conversing or mingling with the jurors, which we were not. To confuse things, all the prospective jurors received telephone calls from an unidentified woman, asking each juror if he or she believed in horoscopes. The prospective jurors had been instructed to report any intimidation or harassment.

"Once the jury was selected and the trial started, we became prime targets of harassment. Among other slurs, we were called 'vendidos' and 'lambes.' Judge Larrazolo cautioned us not to overreact to verbal abuse. He did not want to see massive arrests and risk a mistrial. No matter what we did or didn't do, we were not in a comfortable situation."

CdeBaca said he had been subjected to such harassment before but not with as much intensity up close. "Only a person involved in a position like the one I was involved in at that trial would know of the tensions and racial overtones that I experienced," he said. "There was unrest all the time with shouting and verbal confrontations. It didn't let up."

Hispanics at the courthouse had land issues on their minds. At least a bit of the anger that some expressed against Anglos probably was rooted in the long-passed conduct of the Anglo-dominated Santa Fe Ring that was responsible for so much of the land theft that people at the courthouse resented, CdeBaca said.

State Police Deputy Chief Steve Lagomarsino playfully congratulates Richard CdeBaca upon his promotion to lieutenant in 1968.

"You've been a police officer for so long, you know not to take those things personal. You're being called those names because you represent the law. I knew I was assigned there for one specific purpose and that was to keep order and peace in the hallways of that courthouse."

Even before the trial, Tijerina and his followers had been widely accused of attempting to drive a wedge between Hispanics and Anglos. "Tijerina Preaches Racist Gospel," read a headline in the *Albuquerque Journal* as the paper's reporters followed Tijerina's trail.[2]

CdeBaca was well aware of the stage that had been set as he stood on duty during the trial just outside the courtroom while drama unfolded inside.

"Even though Tijerina had attorneys, he wanted to handle his own defense, declaring himself 'King Tiger.' He said, 'I stand before you like David before Goliath.' He continued, 'I am not an attorney. I'm just a man against political machinery and the press.' He denied that the raid on the Tierra Amarilla courthouse was an attempt to begin a violent revolution. He stated that he was there simply to help make a citizen's arrest.

"Wilfredo Sedillo had been instructed by one of Tijerina's attorneys to position himself in the hall outside the courtroom where he could monitor (police) conversation. He would hang around close to us. During one of the recesses, John Higgs, attorney for Tijerina, accused us of being prejudiced against his client. We ignored him. Sergeant Narvaiz and I seldom spoke to each other. We already had been falsely accused of everything.

"One day, I observed a young man in the courtroom making finger gestures, simulating pointing a gun at the jurors. During recess, Sergeant Narvaiz and I escorted the man outside the courthouse and instructed the security officers not to let him back in.

"On Thanksgiving day when Judge Larrazolo invoked the rule and ordered all the spectators to clear the courtroom, they became unruly and directed their hostility towards everyone. I heard one woman say, referring to the judge, 'That son-of-a-bitch will pay for his misdeeds. They are a ring of conspirators.' All kinds of derogatory remarks were being made. Sergeant Narvaiz said he heard one member of the Brown Berets tell a KOB reporter, Bill Leverton, 'I am going to get you, you gringo.' Inside the courtroom, attorneys were arguing over trial procedures. I overheard one woman tell a member of the Brown Berets to go out and call for more activists.

"I alerted Major Wimberly of the disturbance on the third floor and he ordered the security officers to seal the courthouse. Tijerina sympathizers were picketing on the sidewalks with signs that read, 'Justicia' and 'Viva Tijerina.' People in support of Tijerina began to arrive in vehicles and circling the courthouse. More officers were summoned to deter trouble. It was a tense moment for all officers. Some picket signs chastised District Attorney Alfonso Sanchez."

The sun would set and rise again before tension erupted anew.

"Two Albuquerque city police officers assigned to security arrested an individual in the courthouse for having a pint of whiskey in his possession. He was taken into custody and incarcerated. Word got to Tijerina during recess and he and Lieutenant Roy Beserra of the Albuquerque Police Department engaged in a verbal exchange.

"I escorted Tijerina into the courtroom just as we were beginning to get surrounded by his followers. Back in the courtroom, Judge Larrazolo admonished Tijerina and his followers and warned them that he would not tolerate any more civil disobedience. I thought Judge Larrazolo had ignored the problem too long."

CdeBaca also knew he had a potential problem standing near his side during the trial's first days.

"Deputy Sheriff Julian Narvaiz had a 'short fuse' and he wasn't about to take any abuse from anyone. He had already been involved in several verbal confrontations with Tijerina's loyalists. At one point, I told him not to take insults personal. Several times Sergeant Narvaiz escorted hecklers out the door and warned them he didn't want to see them again. Tijerina brought Sergeant Narvaiz's actions to the attention of his attorneys. Later, I heard that Tijerina's attorneys had complained to Sheriff Lester Hay. I am not sure what the sheriff was told but Deputy Narvaiz was relieved of his assignment and I never saw him again. Later, Deputy Narvaiz was shot to death after stopping a car."

Attention and tension mounted both in and out of the courthouse as the principal witness prepared to testify.

"The day that Officer Nick Sais was to testify, Chief Black called me and told me not to let Officer Sais out of my sight. That morning, the news media was represented in full force. During recess, Tijerina spotted officer Sais standing next to me and Tijerina walked right up to officer Sais' face to intimidate him. I grabbed officer Sais and escorted him to the witness waiting room. Officer Sais was the key witness in the trial and he gave damaging testimony against Tijerina.

"During the testimony of another of the state's witnesses, a man in the courtroom called him 'a damn liar.' Judge Larrazolo, hearing the remark, called the man to stand up, then under threat of contempt of court barred him from the courthouse.

"Not a day went by that I was not accused of discrimination for not allowing more people in the courtroom. They could care less about my explanation that the courtroom was filled to capacity and the judge would not allow any more inside."

Daily publicity about the trial and animosities attached to it were hard to escape and seemingly had people everywhere taking sides, CdeBaca said. An act outside the courthouse fueled Tijerina's assertions that police and other authorities would never let up on their "campaign of terror." CdeBaca took note.

> "The *Alianza* headquarters in Albuquerque was riddled with bullets in a drive-by shooting. The police were accused of being responsible. Some Albuquerque officers were blatantly warned by members of *Comancheros del Norte* not to be seen in Northern New Mexico.
> "When the case went to the jury for deliberation, Major Hoover Wimberly increased security in anticipation of trouble. When the jury declared Tijerina innocent, all hell broke loose in the hallways. It took all the police manpower to clear the courthouse."

Tijerina's acquittal was the climax to events that disillusioned prosecutors. State District Judge Joe Angel dismissed all charges against nine of the courthouse raid defendants even before Tijerina's trial.[3] Later, Judge Larrazolo's instructions to the jury prior to its deliberations in the Tijerina case arguably paved the way for the rebel's acquittal. Larrazolo told jurors: "The court instructs the jury that anyone, including a State Police officer, who intentionally interferes with a lawful attempt to make a citizen's arrest does so at his own peril, since the arresting citizens are entitled under the law to use whatever force is reasonably necessary to effect said citizen's arrest and to use whatever force is reasonably necessary to defend themselves in the process of making a said citizen's arrest."[4]

Following his acquittal, Tijerina and his followers made multiple attempts at citizen's arrests, targeting, among others, U.S. Forest Service officials, Governor Cargo and U.S. Chief Justice Warren Burger.[5]

In time, U.S. Attorney Victor Ortega, stationed in New Mexico, complained that New Mexicans had grown "quite concerned about Tijerina going around threatening citizen's arrest, which I think is a bunch of legal nonsense."

U.S. District Judge Howard Bratton concurred. "Legal nonsense is a moderate characterization," he said. "The concept of citizen's arrest does exist, but misuse and abuse can be tragic."[6]

None of the 11 *Alianza* members arrested in Coyote days prior to the courthouse raid, arrests that sparked the assault in Tierra Amarilla, were ever brought to trial.[7]

A federal lawsuit was filed on behalf of 13 *Alianza* members who alleged, among other things, that their civil rights were violated when they were detained in a Canjilón cow pasture on the night of the raid. The New Mexico State Police, the National Guard and District Attorney Alfonso Sanchez were named as defendants. A jury exonerated them all on charges of conspiring to deny plaintiffs their civil rights. However, the jury awarded $3,000 to one plaintiff who was arrested while protesting the unwarranted search of his home.[8]

A state district court jury in Albuquerque found Juan Valdez guilty of assaulting State Police officer Nick Sais in the Rio Arriba County courthouse during the June 1967 assault. Valdez also was found guilty of false imprisonment of Deputy Sheriff Pete Jaramillo. Baltazar Martinez, the so-called Green Beret, and his uncle, Baltazar Apodaca, both were declared to have been mentally incompetent at the time of the raid and were absolved of charges that they falsely imprisoned Rio Arriba deputy Pete Jaramillo and news reporter Larry Calloway.[9]

CdeBaca reacted to the fact that so many involved in the courthouse raid escaped punishment. "There was never any dissention that I heard of among those of us who followed up on all those arrests," he said. "But as an officer there's always a disappointment when so many hours have been spent investigating these cases and there is overwhelming evidence to convict an individual and then the charges are dismissed."

Sais for this book spoke about Tijerina's acquittal, first carefully then with a bit less reservation. "I just figured that's the kind of system we have. You go to court; sometimes you win and sometimes you lose," he said. "But (really) there wasn't a thorough enough investigation to convict him. They (investigators) weren't doing a good enough job. They were doing things too fast. Take your time; do it right."

Sais also was very critical of the pardon granted to his shooter, Juan Valdez, by Gov. Bruce King as memories of the courthouse raid faded. "It was a kick in the teeth right there. You're there defending our laws and the constitution, you get shot while doing your duty and then the guy who shot you gets pardoned? That's not right!"

CdeBaca, following Tijerina's Albuquerque trial, returned to State Police headquarters in Santa Fe and, at least temporarily, far less-demanding conditions. An entry in his records tells simply of the transition.

"Upon my return to my regular duties, I was again assigned to attend civil defense courses at the University of New Mexico."

For CdeBaca, the rush ignited by the Tierra Amarilla courthouse raid was over.

7

Hippies, Berets and Unsettled Times

If generalizations or profiling often drive police work, Richard CdeBaca makes no apologies for asserting that hippies and the culture that followed them through the 1960s and early 1970s were responsible for ushering in large-scale use of illegal drugs in New Mexico.

Stationed at Santa Fe headquarters, CdeBaca worked as a sergeant for the New Mexico State Police in the mid-1960s. He was assigned during most of the period to the agency's auto theft unit and to various duties in and around the state Capitol. This notation appears in his records:

> "The hippie cult moved in during the 1960s which law enforcement was not prepared for. The heavy influx of hippies added another dimension to the state's multicultural population. The hippies set up communes, trespassing on private as well as public lands and brought their drug culture with them.
>
> "With the Hippie culture, came LSD, among other drugs. College kids picked up on it and began to experiment with it."

Hippies, of course, advocated peace, love, joy, harmony. No problems there. But they also were followed by a mantra of sex, drugs and rock 'n roll. Illicit drug use did create problems. Those problems and much of what came to be associated with the hippie counterculture, to be blunt, caught the New Mexico State Police with their pants down.

"I try to phrase it in a nicer way, but there's no doubt about it. We were totally unprepared for this movement," he said. "I don't think we realized that New Mexico would be a prime location for them to set up their camps. But it turns out that we had what they wanted: wide open spaces, remote areas, forest lands."

Timothy Miller wrote in the forward to *Leaving New Buffalo Commune* that most communes were set up as "harbingers of a future society of peace and love and mutual aid" even though stereotypical images were of squalor, orgies, filth and exotic drugs. The "communal spirit," he wrote, was especially strong in New England, Northern California, Virginia and New Mexico.[1]

"The latter might have seemed an unlikely communal magnet ... New Mexico did, however, have an air of alternative culture to it," Miller wrote.[2]

The times were ripe for a counterculture to take hold, he asserted. "By mid decade, the civil rights movement had exposed grave flaws in the nation's social contract, protests against the war in Vietnam were mushrooming, psychedelic substances were newly available," he wrote.[3]

Among New Mexico communities where hippies settled were "Chamisaville," or the northern Taos County area; Pilar, Ojo Sarco, Truchas, El Rito, La Madera, Cundiyó, Placitas and Silver City. CdeBaca said he personally had an unexpected face-to-face encounter with a small band of hippies who had set up a temporary encampment south of Santa Fe on property he knew very well.

Open spaces around isolated communities, like Cundiyó in northern Santa Fe County, were popular destinations for hippies in the 1960s and 1970s.

"One day I patrolled to La Ciénega where my parents lived," he said. "My parents have about 350 acres there and a creek runs through the property. On that particular day, I saw this old school bus painted with psychedelic colors and below the creek there were about 10 hippies camped out. They had littered the banks of the creek with trash.

"There was no need for me to identify myself as I stepped toward them; the uniform identified me. I asked, 'Who gave you permission to camp here?' One of the them replied, 'We got permission from the owner.' I asked, 'Who might that owner be?' I believe I was told it was 'someone up the road.'

"That's when I said, 'This property belongs to my parents and I know they did not give you permission to camp here. I'm giving you 30 minutes to pick up the trash, pick up your belongings and move out,' which they did. They were never to be seen there again."

But for years, the hippies' presence was inescapable elsewhere, on public forest lands, on old land grant property and on private lands, too. Enmeshed in the hippie culture, Pam Hanna (Read) wrote of a situation in Northern New Mexico where a father of two stillborn babies supposedly obtained permission from the "local powers-that-be" to bury his babies himself on what he considered to be his own property. When confronted by another man later, the father purportedly said he had been given the OK to bury his babies on his land. He supposedly then heard in reply, "Ah, señor, but this is not your land."[4]

Hanna wrote of living in a commune near La Madera: "Cindy was sitting on one of the boulders—wearing—clothes! A skirt anyway—no top—and her signature beads and feathers. She was fabulously zonked on Peyote and floating through the archetypes before our very eyes ... As soon as somebody would get money, there would be beer and ice cream. The rest of the time, we lived on beans and potatoes and chiles."[5]

CdeBaca said State Police officers were in a "reactive mode" as they responded to reports of trespassing "and the drugs that came with it."

"The State Police were not receiving reports about this culture movement that was springing up elsewhere in the country," he said.

But if CdeBaca and others in his agency received nothing from official police sources, stories about the movement were common in television broadcasts and other news media, nonetheless.

"We saw those kinds of reports, yes. Maybe we just didn't think about the consequences that would come with it. It's as simple as that," CdeBaca said. "Nowadays there are means of tracking gang activity and drug trafficking but back in those days, maybe we just looked at it in a passive way. So they're going to camp out. So what?"

State Police officers might have been passive at the onset but not for long. Most in the State Police had a common response to what they suddenly faced. "We didn't like it," CdeBaca said. "One State Police officer was admonished by Chief K.K. Miller for being quoted in the newspaper for saying that hippies were dirty, unkempt, unemployed and a nuisance.

"The thing about it, it was not far from the truth. That basically described the common feeling among law enforcement but as an officer, you don't make a comment like that without it coming back to bite you. So the chief had a responsibility to admonish that kind of conduct."

The State Police department grew sufficiently concerned about the hippie culture that it had narcotics agents infiltrate communes under cover. "Once it was discovered that this hippie movement came along with their drugs, the State Police realized that something had to be done," CdeBaca said.

He said that probably no more than a handful of undercover agents worked such assignments. "They did what they could. I wouldn't say that they smoked marijuana. But they made an attempt to live with the population," he said. "As law enforcement officers, I'm sure they remained cognizant of activities other than illicit drug use. They probably were on the alert for fugitives that may have come with the hippie population."

Marijuana and LSD were among drugs that State Police most commonly associated with hippies, CdeBaca said. "If there was any use or abuse of LSD prior to the influx of the hippies, it hadn't come to our attention. I do know that shortly thereafter, there were incidents of students in colleges using and abusing LSD."

CdeBaca made this entry in his records:

"LSD was initially hailed as a wonder drug for use in psychoanalysis, particularly for gaining insights into schizophrenia. During a seminar I attended on drug abuse, I learned that the use of LSD exposes a user to a not-unpleasant intoxicated-like condition, characterized by an extremely stimulated imagination. The user can be left in a dreamlike state of fantastic pictures, extraordinary shaped with intense kaleidoscopic play of colors. After two hours or so the condition can fade away."

And then there is this entry in those records about one of CdeBaca's earliest encounters with someone on LSD:

"In Gallup, I experienced one of the most bizarre cases of illegal use of LSD ... One morning, the Gallup Police responded to a call that came from a trailer. They encountered a young man who claimed to be Hercules and attacked them with dumbbells. This lad was a weight lifter and very muscular. The officers called for backup. I went to their assistance and it took four of us to subdue him and get him handcuffed. While in jail, the man destroyed the partition that enclosed the commode. With bull-like charges, he was determined to break down the cell. After a good while, he was totally exhausted and settled down. In a subsequent search of the trailer he lived in, evidence of LSD was found, which appeared to be pieces of clear plastic."

CdeBaca tells of violent crime that grew out of illegal drug use and other activities in communes.

"A multiple murder took place at a hippie compound in Placitas, north of Albuquerque. We had a person of interest in these murders but he was never apprehended. Years later, he and his wife were found dead in a barn in Iowa."

Still, some assert, if police focused on occasional violent crimes and illegal drug use among hippies, they missed the bigger picture. Actor and frequent film narrator Peter Coyote wrote of communes, "Urban kids came together and learned cabinetry, animal husbandry, carpentry, irrigation, weaving and a host of critical survival skills to make a life based 'in place' and not predicated on exploitation."[6]

No matter one's perspective, there was much to observe from the hippie counterculture. *The Santa Fe New Mexican* referred to hippies several paragraphs into a May 2, 1968, story about increased use of illegal drugs in the state capital. Reporter Harold Cousland quoted Santa Fe police Detective Richard Rodriguez as saying that the narcotics traffic in the city was 'now practically out of hand.' There is no difficulty obtaining illegal drugs in Santa Fe anymore, the detective said. The story then reads: "(Rodriguez) said narcotics use is heavy 'not only with the so-called hippies' but with 'established citizens' of many ages."

The following day, *The New Mexican* ran a story about drug raids and nine arrests at New Mexico State University. Eight were arrested for possession and sale of marijuana; one for possession and sale of LSD. The story said two had been arrested on drug charges earlier in the week at New Mexico Highlands University.

CdeBaca's records also include entries for the period about other groups that surfaced during the 1960s, often agitating the peace that CdeBaca and others in law enforcement were expected to preserve. Groups that he cites were those that sought to advance interests of minority groups, mostly Hispanics. He wrote:

"Activist groups emerged: *La Raza Unida*, the Brown Berets, the Black Berets, the *Comancheros del Norte*, and the *Alianza*, which was led by land activist Reies Lopez Tijerina."

"One radical publication, *Veneremos, Papel Del Barrio*, published biased stories about the police labeling us *'marranos'* (pigs). The paper published accounts such as: 'Pigs violate property rights,' '*Marranos* murder chicano veteran,' '*Marranos* abuse their authority,' '*Marranos* harass Berets.' Law enforcement was in a reactive mode, not prepared to handle all the extra activities, including demonstrations at the state Capitol."

The tabloid newspaper was almost venomous toward the State Police and others in law enforcement. Along with murder, its first issue of 16 pages accused police of beatings, macing, corruption and racism in separate stories.

But CdeBaca said law enforcement generally did not feel threatened by such publications. "Those days were days of a lot of expressions but not a whole lot of attention was given to this type of publicity by the public. It was just something that was taking place and we recognized it as such," he said.

The late 1960s and early 1970s was a period marked "by individuals being rebellious against the establishment, and we were a part of it," CdeBaca said.

On the University of New Mexico campus, several days in May 1970 captured attention nationally and had the New Mexico State Police along with national guardsmen at the forefront. CdeBaca made this entry in his records:

"Confronted with the worst riot in the history of the University of New Mexico, the governor was prompted to call out the National Guard to help law enforcement keep the peace. For days, police officers and guardsmen were harassed by the demonstrators. All in all, police used every restraint possible, unlike the student riots at Kent State University in Ohio, where several demonstrators were killed."

Tensions, indeed, were high across the country. The United States' engagement in the Vietnam War was at a controversial peak, and news headlines told of escalating combat daily. Students protested the war on college and university campuses across the country.

CdeBaca's records had few entries about campus unrest in New Mexico but during interviews he recalled troubled times at the University of New Mexico and how authorities responded. First, though, a look at tensions behind it all.

The *Albuquerque Journal* on May 5, 1970, reported that four people had been killed and 11 others injured at Kent State University after national guardsmen opened fire during a disturbance on the campus of 19,000 students. The same day's paper told of national guardsmen patrolling the University of Maryland during campus disturbances. Another story told of Jane Fonda criticizing the U.S. policy in Southeast Asia.

The following day, the *Journal* in a front-page story reported of unrest at the University of Wisconsin, the University of California-Berkeley, the University of Texas and State University of Buffalo in New York.

By May 7, a front-page story in the *Journal* told that approximately 224 colleges across the country had been closed because of anti-war activities; classes were cut or cancelled at many others. In that day's newspaper, a report said that Vice President Spiro Agnew believed national guardsmen overreacted at Kent State.

Conditions at the University of New Mexico were coming to a boil as April turned to May in 1970. Governor David Cargo at the end of April asked UNM regents and administrators to "stiffen up" discipline and policies pertaining to campus speakers, the *Journal* reported. Cargo's position was prompted by the scheduled appearance of Lenore Kandel, author of the controversial "Love Lust Poem," which had been slammed in some quarters as pornographic.

"I'm getting more and more mail and telegrams which indicate to me there is a great deal of dissatisfaction with UNM. And I think that is the understatement of the year," the May 1st *Journal* quoted Cargo to have said.

The paper said Bernalillo County Commission Chairman Ed Balcomb had called upon citizens to block the entrance to Popejoy Hall on the night of Kandel's appearance. Democratic gubernatorial candidate Jack Daniels suggested Balcomb was looking to incite a riot, the paper reported.

Also that day, the *Journal* said that 1,200 national guardsmen and 200 Ohio State Police officers had battled for four hours with militant students who tossed home-made tear gas bombs, bricks and bottles at Ohio State University.

At UNM, Kandel ended up reading her "Love Lust Poem" and 26 other works to a packed house, mostly students, according to the *Journal*. Another 1,000 people waited outside, the paper said.

It reported on May 6th that students and faculty prepared ready to strike in protest of the war in Southeast Asia and the deadly shootings earlier in the week at Kent State University. Tensions mounted.

On May 7th, a banner headline on the *Journal's* front page told of an emotional explosion: "Officials Close UNM as Students Strike." Smaller headlines on the same page read: "3 Stabbed In Clash Over Flag," and "Hurt Youths Cite Opposite Strike Views."

The main story on that Thursday told that Governor Cargo and UNM President Ferrel Heady had ordered the campus closed for the rest of the week following violence that erupted during a student strike to protest the escalating war overseas and student killings at Kent State University. Four UNM students were stabbed during a dispute over the raising of the American flag. Five students were targeted for arrest on charges of aggravated battery.

Four more persons were injured when a small car was driven through a barricade and students around it were tossed to the ground.

That same day several hundred strikers forced their way into the Student Union Building with the intent of occupying it for the night. Students smashed glass of the front door after employees had barricaded it with furniture, the *Journal* reported. Campus administrators consulted with the New Mexico State Police and others before deciding that students occupying the building would not be evicted during the night.

Warrants charging aggravated battery were issued for five students. The district attorney asked that three of the five magistrates in Bernalillo County remain on duty during coming days in case of mass arrests, the *Journal* reported.

Governor Cargo, meanwhile, ordered 150 national guardsmen and 50 state policemen to remain on alert, although neither the guardsmen nor the police came onto campus that day, the *Journal* reported.

Richard CdeBaca said he is confident that State Police Chief Martin Vigil had multiple conversations with Governor Cargo during those first days of the UNM unrest. CdeBaca was a lieutenant at the time stationed at headquarters in Santa Fe. "Governor Cargo clearly wanted to quell this thing," CdeBaca said. Cargo had appointed Vigil to serve as State Police chief and repeatedly had expressed confidence in Vigil's leadership abilities, CdeBaca said.

Martin Vigil was a commanding presence as New Mexico State Police chief from 1969-1982. Photo courtesy New Mexico State Police.

Friday, May 8th, orders changed for national guardsmen as well as for state and Albuquerque city police. "The occupation of the University of New Mexico Student Union Building by dissident students came to an abrupt end under National Guard bayonets and state and city police batons Friday afternoon," *Journal* State Editor Bill Hume reported. He said guardsmen had bayonets affixed to their M1 and M14 rifles. State and city police were armed with riot sticks and were helmeted, as were the guardsmen, Hume reported.

CdeBaca recalled how the State Police were prepared for a potentially serious confrontation. "I know that I never saw so much ammunition being disbursed out of the property and supply (unit) at State Police headquarters as I saw for that particular civil disobedience," he said. "We saw all this stuff leaving headquarters. I thought we were being prepared for a real rebellion."

About 40 state policemen from as far away as Chama and Clovis were called to the UNM campus, the *Journal* reported.

"I recall that Chief Martin Vigil got upset over the inaction by the chief of the Albuquerque Police Department so Chief Vigil took the initiative to take over the university. The university police were not capable of dealing with such a situation," CdeBaca said.

Indeed, Vigil on the Saturday of the unrest disclosed that it was he who directed national guardsmen and police to move onto the campus late Friday. UNM regents and President Heady said they had not been told of the move ahead of time, the *Journal* reported. It said that Vigil had first asked Cargo to have the guard on standby and that the governor agreed. "That automatically leaves the decision to use them or not to use them or how to use them entirely up to me," the *Journal* reported Vigil to have said.

Arrests that day totaled 122. Eleven people, including four news reporters, were injured as guardsmen stepped in to move people out of the Student Union Building. Most of the injured suffered stab wounds, the *Journal reported.*

UNM regent President Arturo Ortega was among those who questioned whether activation of the National Guard was necessary. But Vigil defended his actions. "The law provides that in a case like this, as much force as necessary can be used … I would do the same thing tomorrow or next week under the same circumstances," he told the *Journal.* He also told the paper, "Whether (UNM President) Heady wanted the National Guard or didn't want the National Guard didn't make a damn bit of difference. It was all up to me." He said he would resign if the governor thought he acted unwisely or unlawfully.

CdeBaca said that even though the State Police had been well prepared, he didn't really expect a serious confrontation at the UNM campus. "I wasn't concerned about going there and being confronted with the exchange of gunfire or anything like that, even though the riot at Kent State University was fresh in our minds," he said. "Throughout your training, it's drilled into you to use as much constraint as possible and not overreact to a given situation. When you're facing protestors, it's never really directed against you as a person. It's directed against the establishment."

CdeBaca said he did not believe that people from outside the UNM campus community were responsible for inciting the unrest. But he said that he and others he knew in law enforcement were like-minded in believing that general conditions that developed around a growing counter culture well beyond the university cultivated volatile unrest. "This was really part of the beginning of the drugs that had not only saturated the hippie communes but saturated the colleges and universities, and with that came the other problems that we saw on campuses," he said.

"These students at the University of New Mexico had some issues and they wanted to make a statement. But this was a wrong way to make a statement."

Jack Daniels, the Democratic candidate for governor, blamed the unrest on "irresponsible hotheads" at UNM. Republican U.S. Senator Pete Domenici said the unrest resulted from "a massive breakdown of authority" on the campus. Both were quoted in the *Journal.*

At the time of the unrest, students offered conflicting views of the situation. "It's time the students who are in the majority get together and stand up and tell the demonstrators to leave us alone and let us go to classes," 18-year-old freshman Robert Rhem III told *Journal* reporter Chuck Anthony. Rehm suffered a slight concussion during the unrest.

Other students blasted police and national guardsmen, accusing them of overreacting and injecting unnecessary violence into the situation.

8

Authorities Were Told the Prison Would Blow

State government offices everywhere are packed with shelving because of the innumerable reports and other bureaucratic paperwork that is churned out daily. Far too many of the documents serve only to accumulate dust.

Buried in all that paper during the late 1970s were several reports from grand juries that were assigned to review and evaluate conditions at the Penitentiary of New Mexico about 10 miles south of Santa Fe. *The Santa Fe New Mexican* reported more than once that the reports were filled with harsh findings as well as recommendations that would have required legislatures and governors to approve large new appropriations to the state Corrections Department. So much of what was recommended fell on deaf ears, the paper would report later.

A grand jury report in April 1977 said kitchen facilities were dirty and completely inadequate; the prison hospital was described as deplorable; security, inadequate.[1] A grand jury reported in February 1978 that the penitentiary was designed in the mid 1950s to house 850 inmates but was consistently 50 percent over capacity. It also said there was about a 50-percent shortfall in the number of required uniformed staff members. "Most of the problem areas at the penitentiary are derived from these conditions of overcrowding and staff limitations," the jury's report said.[2]

In May of 1979, a grand jury repeated concerns about overcrowding and understaffing then asserted: "During the orientation of the Grand Jury Panel, we were informed that as Grand Jurors we were a powerful body doing a civic duty. If our civic duty is to be taken seriously, and a meaningful solution be accomplished, it is essential that these matters be looked upon immediately."[3]

Concerns were echoed again in a grand jury report dated January 18, 1980.[4]

Less than a month later the Penitentiary of New Mexico exploded. Richard CdeBaca, working then as a deputy chief with the State Police recorded it in this notation:

"On February 2, 1980, one of the country's worst penitentiary riots ever took place at the main facility south of Santa Fe. During the infamous riot, 33 inmates were killed by other inmates and several guards were severely injured. Being in charge of the Criminal Investigations Bureau, it became my responsibility to oversee the investigation of all the crimes committed during the riot.

"Inmates had to be interviewed, fingerprinted, and photographed before they were transported to other penal institutions in the United States. A special task force was established under the district attorney's office to handle the prosecutions. Later, arrangements had to be made to bring the inmates back to face criminal charges.

"During the 36 hours of uprising, the prisoners had control of most of the penitentiary. They committed barbaric acts, murdering, torturing, pilfering and sodomizing both inmates and guards. It was history's worst prison riot in terms of loss of life and property. The death and destruction was a condemnation of man's inhumanity to man and it shocked everyone."

CdeBaca said later of the grand jury reports in years prior to the riot, "I'm not sure of the number of grand juries that were impaneled to investigate, if you will, conditions at the Penitentiary of New Mexico. Those grand jury findings that were made public stated clearly and unequivocally that crowded conditions at the penitentiary were a serious problem. But I don't recall that anything ever came out of those recommendations from grand juries. They were buried."

Well, they might not have been buried but they were placed upon government shelves without generating the kind of urgency that jurors considered necessary. Two governors and five legislatures had spent more than $20 million in renovations during the 10 years prior to the riot, *The New Mexican* reported. It said a multi-million-dollar renovation was under way at the time of the riot.

But work was far less than what was required, according to dire reports telling of impending disaster coming out of the prison.

The New Mexican reported that Clyde Malley, after resigning as warden in March 1978, predicted that the prison would "burst at the seams until the inmates burn it down to get attention."

Marc Orner, the prison's director of psychological services told the State Police in November 1979 that a riot was coming and that hostages were to be taken. He repeated the warning to the State Police in January 1980.[5]

In December 1979, reform-minded inmate Dwight Duran wrote to Governor Bruce King and said "terrible consequences" were coming soon because of the state's refusal to make necessary prison improvements. Paroled just before the riot, Duran told King "the prison's going to blow."[6]

Larry Flood, who had just come on as the prison's director of intelligence, told ranking prison administrators and the State Police on January 31st that the mood of the prison was "quite ugly."[7]

Author Roger Morris wrote that the prison at the time was being "ruled by a craven, unstable coalition between a few of the dominant felons of maximum security and an administration that could govern no other way."[8]

Writing immediately after the riot, Morris described prison conditions in terms even more graphic than those submitted by grand juries. Rats and roaches infested the prison by the mid 1970s, he wrote. He added that poor ventilation made the facility "stifling" in summers; inadequate heating left cell blocks "sickly chill" in winter; drinking and waste water systems were "cross-connected, spewing sewage into sinks;" food practices were "primitive and unsanitary;" gang rape was common.[9]

Morris wrote that inmates recalled a Thanksgiving Day meal when they were served spoiled turkey that one convict described as "smelling, green, rotten."[10]

On the enforcement side of the law, State Police officers are largely responsible for the flow of inmates entering New Mexico's prisons but CdeBaca said he is not aware of any meetings—formal or informal—within State Police headquarters where concerns were expressed about overcrowding and inadequate staffing at the Penitentiary of New Mexico. He said he was not aware of any occasion where the State Police chief or any other ranking officer might have met with prison administrators to offer a coordinated approach to the state Legislature in pursuit of funding necessary to make substantial improvements at the prison.

"I'm not aware of anything like that," CdeBaca said. "I am thinking that perhaps that responsibility was left to the warden. I am sure that the warden year after year requested more money, like the New Mexico State Police does, requesting more money for more officers."

"I don't recall any discussions at staff meetings about these grand jury conclusions. I honestly don't," he said. "It's the whole criminal justice system that contributed to this explosiveness. The police, the courts, the prosecutors. It's not one single entity."

Also to be considered, CdeBaca said, was the prevailing attitude not just among state legislators but the general public–the legislators' constituents–toward prison inmates and conditions they found themselves in after being convicted of crimes.

"The general attitude within police ranks, in the Legislature and in the public was that convicts deserved to be in prison," he said. "They weren't there because they were nice guys. The general attitude probably was why should convicts be treated better than the rest of us? They already have the opportunity to get a free education there paid for by the taxpayers, good health care. What do they think, that they deserve a country club atmosphere? That's my interpretation of what probably most of the people in New Mexico were thinking before the riot."

"All departments of state government showed up at the Legislature year after year, requesting, pleading for money to meet needs of the citizens. There just wasn't enough for everybody to get everything that they wanted. Sometimes it wasn't even close."

Anger and rivalries among some inmates ignited the bloody 1980 prison riot, CdeBaca said. In his view, little if any of the anger could be traced to how New Mexicans thought about the convicts. "I don't think they became rebellious because of any police attitude toward them, or the public's attitude toward them," he said. "To me, that was not a contributing factor that escalated into the riot.

"All of this had to be an attitude that fomented within the walls of that institution. It developed into a rage. The prison administration had been using so-called snitches. Word got around law enforcement circles about that and surely there had to be resentment inside the prison, certainly among the real-hardened criminals."

"Felix Rodriguez was an important figure at the prison leading up to the riot," CdeBaca said. "He went to work as a young guard around 1955, just before I started with the State Police. He eventually became warden and factionalism became the word for his administration. Felix Rodriguez was respected by a lot of the inmates. I knew him well and he wasn't one to side automatically with the guards. He would listen to all sides. But he was also the one who developed a far-reaching snitch system among inmates. In time, they had all the so-called snitches locked up in the protection unit. Resentment built up among the inmate population and, of course, they knew where the snitches were housed and that they would get special favors from the prison administration.

"When the riot took place, one of the first priorities of the rioters was to get the snitches, in particular a kid from one of the communities up north who was known as the king of the snitches. He was the second inmate they killed, only because they had trouble getting to him. Eventually they used a blow torch that they got from the plumbing department down in the basement to remove the hinges from this kid's cell door then they went at him with all the make-shift weapons that they had accumulated: pipes, bars, furniture legs, you name it. They beat him unconscious then revived him. They cut out his eyelids and pulled his eyeballs out of their sockets and left them dangling on his cheeks. They severed his penis and stuck it in his bleeding mouth then they torched his whole body. Even after they had killed him, they hung him from one of the baskets in the gym and his body continued to be brutalized."

The rage spread quickly once the terrible uprising began to unfold. CdeBaca was in Los Angeles en route back home to Santa Fe from a Hawaii vacation when he learned of the riot, which was in its second day. "I picked up a copy of the *LA Times* that was at the airport," he said. "The paper had a story about the riot on the front page along with a picture of the penitentiary with smoke coming out of it. I immediately called Captain Bob Carroll, who was in charge of the criminal investigation work under me."

CdeBaca's load as deputy chief overseeing criminal investigations was about to mushroom. He made these notations about what he learned upon his return to Santa Fe:

"At about 2 a.m. Saturday, correctional officers discovered a group of prisoners drinking something they had concocted. The prisoners managed to overpower the guards. Once the prisoners took over the control center, which was enclosed with glass that wasn't supposed to break, the bloody revolt began.

"The hard core and most dangerous prisoners from Cell Block 3 were released. With prisoners controlling everything, the prison population was at their mercy. The rampaging began, prisoners using blowtorches, cutting cell bars, setting mattresses on fire and leaving prisoners to burn in their own cells. They tied ropes around the so-called snitches and flung them down two or three tiers.

"The infirmary was raided and they consumed everything they could get their hands on. They got into a state of hysteria. On one inmate, they burned the word "snitch" across his bare chest with the blowtorch while he screamed. Another inmate had a cell bar hammered into his head from ear to ear. A black inmate was decapitated and his head was placed on his lap and carried out to the yard. Approximately 100 prisoners were responsible for all the havoc."

The inmates who were thrown down multiple tiers had ropes tied around their necks, CdeBaca said.

The glass that encased the control center only recently had been found to be of inferior quality to one that had been tested successfully earlier. The installed glass was to have been replaced. Inmates broke it with embarrassing ease. State Police officers were informed at 2:30 a.m. Saturday, February 2nd, soon after the glass was shattered, that control of the prison had been assumed by the convicts, *The New Mexican* reported.

CdeBaca's records told more about the destruction.

"Files had been ransacked and burned, the gymnasium was set on fire, plumbing was broken and water was pouring into the hallways and cells. Walls, windows, furniture, drinking fountains, toilets, washbasins and anything that got in the prisoners' path was smashed. The physical damage was unbelievable, but more horrifying was the human torturing. The stench of burning flesh permeated the air and human blood covered walls and floors. Debris and bodies were floating in ankle-deep water in the hallways.

"The sadistic mindset prevailed and seemed to take over. Some inmates had their skin peeled off from their bones with the blowtorches. Other inmates were castrated and some sodomized. A few cells were used as torture chambers, setting mattresses on fire and leaving inmates to burn. A guard who was hated by some prisoners was sodomized with a cell bar.

"When the prisoners broke into the pharmacy, they combined valium and aspirin, cold tablets and any other medicine they could find. Everything was put into a pot and cooked and injected into some inmates. With the exception of the prison's Catholic chapel, not much else was left untouched."

The New Mexican on February 3rd quoted one inmate who spoke of the rampaging convicts. "They just cleared out all the snitches, wiped all of them out," he said.

After 36 hours that included negotiations with inmates over their demands, the control of the prison was regained by State Police officers, national guardsmen, Santa Fe County sheriff's deputies and Santa Fe city police officers. Dead inmates totaled 33. Twelve guards had been taken hostage. Attacked in multiple ways, none of the guards was killed.

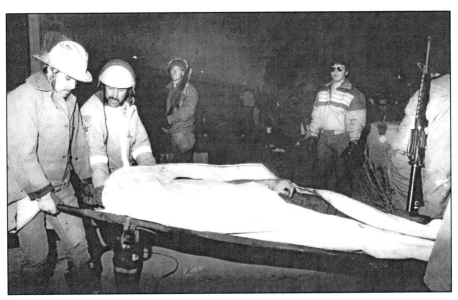

Thirty-three inmates were killed by other convicts during the February 1980 riot at the Penitentiary of New Mexico. Photo courtesy *The New Mexican*.

"Once the wild prisoners were totally exhausted from the rioting, the serious negotiations began," CdeBaca said. "Inmates wanted something done about overcrowding, prison food, recreational facilities, visiting conditions, and so on ... The penitentiary was finally secured and the task of tending to the injured sped along. Those with the most-severe injuries were transported to hospitals by ambulance and by helicopter, creating a chaotic situation at the hospital in Santa Fe."

CdeBaca did not get inside the prison until February 4th. "Most of what there was to see was vast destruction," he said. "Water, almost ankle deep in the hallways, blood smeared on walls, the glass in the communication center shattered, bars cut with torches, walls of steel-enforced cement busted, offices ransacked, burned hair, burned mattresses, the stench of death. No doubt, on a scale of one to 10, it was a 10 and 10 doesn't say enough. I had never gotten this close to the slaughtering of human beings."

"The prison was a disaster. It took days for anthropologists to sift through the mess in an attempt to find human remains to be able to identify the victims ... It's hard to conceive that so much destruction had taken place with the limited weapons that had been improvised, such as cell bars. It's not like they had a bull-dozer in there but it looked like they did. It was like nothing could stop them."

CdeBaca said it is remarkable that no guards were killed. "No deaths, but there are some that still to this day struggle to get through, one being a first cousin of mine," he said. "When the inmates captured the first correctional officers, they stripped them down. The inmates then tied the guards down, beat them and sodomized them: gang rape. My 24-year-old cousin was on foot patrol outside the prison when he heard over his two-way radio that a bunch of inmates were on the loose. He ran inside through the front entrance and saw a multitude of inmates standing outside the control center banging on the glass with all kinds of makeshift weapons that they had obtained. He and another guard who was inside the control center fled outside, where they remained for the rest of the riot. My cousin, who had been on the job for just a few months, was not physically injured but what he witnessed had a traumatic effect on him."

CdeBaca said it felt as if all energy had been sucked out of the wrecked facility once inmates finally surrendered control. "There was no attempt by in-mates to escape or do great bodily harm to the officers who came in," he said. "I think the whole inmate population was physically and emotionally exhausted. Their spirits had been shattered. Some of the pictures taken at the time showed inmates displaying the traumatic experience that they went through. Their eyes were fixed, glazed."

It's unlikely that authorities could have taken control of the prison sooner, CdeBaca said. "That's a question that will remain forever in everybody's mind," he said, "especially among those who don't realize the enormity of this riot. It may not have been possible to take it back sooner, not when inmates were in a frenzy and out of their minds. I don't think that any officer could have reasoned with these inmates in the condition that they were in."

Overseeing investigations of crimes committed during the riot and working with prosecutors was not the nightmare that might have been expected, CdeBaca said. He made this notation in his records:

"Of the 33 deaths, approximately 130 indictments were handed down. Ten prisoners pleaded guilty to murder charges, and several turned state's evidence, which helped with the prosecutions. It took three years to prosecute all of them. District Attorney Eloy Martinez and his special prosecutors, Joe Shattuck, Dick Baker and others did a remarkable job."

CdeBaca said that police investigators, even though images of the brutality were still fresh in their minds, did not turn to heavy-handed approaches in their work. "Actually, there was a lot of compassion shown toward the inmates. They were all informed of their rights; they were all treated with respect. I was not aware of any reports of inmates being subjected to abuse or intimidation."

A somewhat different account was provided by Santa Fe lawyer Mark Donatelli. "Many of the inmates who ended up being alleged eyewitnesses claimed to have been coerced," he said for this book.

Donatelli worked as the district public defender in the 1st Judicial District at the time of the riot. He later became director of the Prison Riot Defense Office, which was created by the Legislature to deal with cases growing out of the uprising.

He stressed that he was not present when inmates were interviewed or interrogated by prison officials or the State Police. But he said that several of the prisoners who survived the brutality inflicted on Cell Block 4, the protective custody unit, told him that they were taken to a facility in Las Cruces following the riot. Most of the prisoners taken to Las Cruces reportedly told interrogators that they didn't see anything, according to Donatelli.

He said multiple inmates speaking to him later said "the interrogators became impatient." Inmates reportedly were told that there were two buses waiting outside. One was for inmates who were willing to tell what they saw. The other was for those who remained silent. According to what inmates told Donatelli, interrogators said the first bus would take cooperative inmates to protective custody in a facility out of state. The second bus would take inmates back to the prison in Santa Fe where they had reason to fear for their safety.

Donatelli said some inmates told him that it was a prison administrator who made the threat; others said it was the State Police.

CdeBaca said, "I have no way to confirm or deny what Mr. Donatelli told you. This is the first time that I ever heard of anything like that. No complaints about such a situation came into my office."

CdeBaca said inmates involved in the riot were prosecuted whenever cases could be made against them. "There were many inmates, though, who were not prosecuted for lack of evidence," he said.

David King, serving at the time as secretary of the Department of Finance and Administration under his uncle, Governor Bruce King, told the Legislature just days after the riot that it would cost no less than $80 million to repair the battered Penitentiary of New Mexico and build new facilities to accommodate the growth of the inmate population.

"It took an all-out prison riot to make a statement to bring about much-needed changes," CdeBaca said.

9

A Murdered Priest and Other Unsolved Cases

Some time in 1981, a soft-spoken priest enamored by the history of New Mexico's capital city where he was assigned, sat down for dinner with his popular archbishop and several members of the Catholic parish served by the beautiful St. Francis Cathedral of Santa Fe.

"My wife's brother-in-law was the maintenance man at the cathedral so he made friends with all the priests there," said Richard CdeBaca, who worked at the time as deputy chief of the Criminal Investigations Bureau of the New Mexico State Police.

"My wife's sister and brother-in-law invited my wife and me to have dinner at their house with Father Reynaldo Rivera and Archbishop Robert Sanchez. It was a very pleasant evening that I'll always remember."

Less than a year later, on Aug. 7, 1982, Rivera was found dead on a muddy field about 12 miles south of Santa Fe. CdeBaca was called upon to apprehend the killer of the 57-year-old priest. He made this entry in his records:

"On August 3, 1982, during the evening hours, a telephone call was received at St. Francis Cathedral asking for a priest to administer the last sacraments to a person, whom according to the caller, was dying. The caller explained to the priest who took the call that they would meet the priest who was dispatched at the rest area south of Santa Fe located at La Bajada Hill. The caller did not ask for Father Reynaldo Rivera by name, and he identified himself only as 'Carmello.' Father Rivera volunteered to go and left on his own. Father Rivera did not return to the cathedral that night."

CdeBaca said he became directly involved in the case immediately. Two investigators from his Criminal Investigations Bureau were assigned to the case.

"Father Rivera's body was found close to the Waldo exit in an open field. A local man who found his body was returning from Albuquerque and he got off on the Waldo exit to urinate and he saw the human body and reported it. He was questioned extensively and was dismissed as a suspect."

Luis Perea of La Cienega is the man who found the shot and beaten body. "Luis Perea and I grew up together. He and a friend were returning from Albuquerque and they got off at the Waldo exit because Mother Nature called," CdeBaca said.

The priest who took the call at the rectory of the cathedral also was among the first to be interviewed by police. "He recalled that the man who identified himself as 'Carmello' said he wanted a priest to come deliver last rights to his grandfather. He said he would be driving a blue pickup and that he would meet the priest at the rest area. But that priest did not respond to the request. He told investigators that Father Rivera said he would respond to the call. The caller did not ask for a priest by name.

"Investigators surmised the caller was in his late 20s or early 30s. But they were told there was nothing else distinguishable about the voice, no accent, nothing."

It didn't take long for police to be stumped.

"We never could determine where Father Rivera met 'Carmello' and where he was ambushed. He must have been killed in one location and then dumped at another location. 'Carmello' could not have called from the rest area; there was no public telephone there. When 'Carmello' called, he said his grandfather had suffered a heart attack and wanted a priest to come to his Waldo residence to administer the last sacraments. No one lived in Waldo at the time."

"Father Rivera was wearing glasses and had taken his last sacrament satchel with him, neither of which was on his body when he was found. I used 32 recruits who were being trained to become State Police officers and several investigators to search the entire rest area and the surrounding area."

The recruits called to help search the area were pulled directly out of the State Law Enforcement Academy. "We searched up and down on both sides of that exit clear down to Bonanza Creek, about a quarter mile in all but we never found any evidence whatsoever," CdeBaca said.

Nor was a close examination of Father Rivera's car helpful. "The car was brought in after they examined the scene to State Police headquarters in Santa Fe," CdeBaca said. "It was examined by the crime lab technicians and they did not come up with any evidence—not finger prints, not hair, not anything that they could take to the lab for forensic evaluation. That was a detriment to the investigation."

An examination of the body offered no clues.

"Myself and one investigator went to the Office of the Medical Investigator in Albuquerque to view the body. We were told that Father Rivera had been struck with a blunt object over the head and stomach. He had been shot once in the chest and the trajectory of the bullet led us to believe he was in a kneeling position, as if to be begging not to be killed or, maybe, making a final prayer. He had scratch marks on his face from ear to ear, indicating he had been grabbed from behind with a rope or a wire."

Investigators started writing theories on a board at State Police headquarters. Among them: Rivera was killed at the rest area, then thrown into the killer's pickup and taken to the area near the Waldo exit. "There was no blood at the site where the body was found, and there was no blood in Father Rivera's car when it was found later at a rest area east of Grants," CdeBaca said.

Another theory suggested that the killer did not have a pickup or any vehicle when he made the call. Perhaps he needed transportation and figured that summoning a priest would get him what he wanted. "A blue pickup was never found. We asked ourselves, if the caller did have a pickup, why would he have fled in Father Rivera's car?"

Under yet another theory, the killer would, indeed, have been in a blue pickup that was mentioned during the phone call that night. An accomplice, or maybe more than one accomplice, would have been used to help get both vehicles—the pickup and Rivera's car—away from the scene.

"We could never determine whether more than one person was involved, though we theorized it had to be more than one. The motive for the murder was a mystery. We didn't rule out robbery but priests are not known for carrying much money."

"We questioned the priests assigned to St. Francis Cathedral and they offered very little, other than Father Rivera had volunteered to take the call. Father Rivera served on the Santa Fe Fiesta Council and was well known. I personally knew Father Rivera and believed he was well-respected in the community."

Rivera's ties to the Santa Fe Fiesta Council led police temporarily to a Santa Fe man who also had an immediate association with the city's annual fiesta. "The investigators came up with a person of interest," CdeBaca said. "He wrote a scathing letter to Father Rivera. He was upset that his daughter had not been named queen of the Santa Fe Fiesta. I directed investigators to bring this individual in and question him even though we knew that if it had been him, he would have asked for Father Rivera by name. The caller, remember, did not ask for anyone by name. That's the most baffling thing about this crime … We stopped looking at this Santa Fe man as a person of interest."

The staggering and much-publicized cases about priests abusing young boys nationwide still had not surfaced but CdeBaca said police considered the possibility that Rivera's killer felt that he had reason to strike out against a priest—any priest—because of something that occurred in the past. "That's one of the reasons that I asked investigators to talk to the priests at the cathedral," he said.

State Police also looked at the possibility of a roaming killer targeting priests wherever opportunities existed.

"This was the second killing of a priest in the Southwest. On Dec. 22, 1981, the Reverend Patrick Ryan from Denver City, Texas, was found murdered in a motel in Odella, Texas. Our investigators followed up on that murder and discovered there was no link between the two."

"Meanwhile in Las Cruces, an adult and a teenager, suspects in the killing of an Arizona clergyman, were questioned about Father Rivera's murder but, again, there were no similarities between the two."

Police did not rule out the possibility that the killer recklessly used his real name when he called the Santa Fe cathedral to request help.

"Investigators located a man by the name of Carmello in Phoenix, Arizona, and I sent them there to question him. He was polygraphed with his permission. The investigators dismissed him as a suspect."

"Hundreds of man hours were spent investigating Father Rivera's murder. Even with the help of a psychic and several thousand dollars offered for information, the crime remained unsolved. To this day, it still bothers me that those responsible have not come forward to confess."

Even before Rivera, CdeBaca had lost a friend to a high-profile, unsolved murder.

"On January 3, 1968, we received word that my good friend, Rio Arriba County Deputy Sheriff Eulogio Salazar, age 54, and father of four, had been murdered. His body had been discovered on a country road about 1.5 miles west of Tierra Amarilla. On his way home from work, he had stopped to open the gate to his property when apparently he was ambushed."

Salazar was the Rio Arriba County deputy who was to have testified in an impending trial that he had been shot in the face by land grant activist Reies Lopez Tijerina during the June 5, 1967, assault on the courthouse in Tierra Amarilla.

"Deputy Salazar was well respected in the community. He was expected to be a key witness at Reies Lopez Tijerina's trial, and that could be the only motive for killing him.

"Governor David Cargo termed the death of Eulogio Salazar as 'nothing more or less than a brutal murder.' He indirectly linked the murder with possible activities of Reies Lopez Tijerina's land grant alliance. He stated, 'It's terrorism and I won't have it.' State Police Chief Joe Black stressed the *Alianza* was a key target in the investigations. We immediately focused attention on *Alianza* land grant militants who were charged with the June 5th courthouse raid."

CdeBaca described Salazar as an unlikely target for murder had it not been for events of the courthouse raid. "I regarded Eulogio as an individual that would not be controversial, an individual that was compassionate, a man involved in his work at the courthouse and at his *ranchito*, CdeBaca said. "He was of the philosophy of live and let live. He did not raise any waves even with his badge and his authority. He was not one to rile anybody, abuse anybody's rights."

CdeBaca wrote this of Salazar's ambush and abduction:

"Mrs. Salazar said that the last time she had seen her husband was about 8 p.m. on the night that he was killed. That's when he drove up the driveway approaching the gate. Mrs. Salazar went into a bedroom and when she returned, she saw the car backing out of the driveway.

"A white cowboy hat which Deputy Salazar was accustomed to wearing and a piece of a broken pistol grip and blood were found on the ground. It was speculated that the assailants had been dropped off and were left hiding in the bushes waiting for Deputy Salazar. Mrs. Salazar did not see another car when she saw her husband's car going in reverse.

"The gate he got out to open was approximately 300 feet from the house. When he got out of his car, he must have been struck with a pistol on the head then thrown in the back seat of his car.

"In the next few minutes when his car was driven through Tierra Amarilla and west of El Vado road, Deputy Salazar was brutally beaten. Blood stained the inside of his car, soaking the seats, headliner and windows. The overhead lamp in the car was broken. He must have put up a good fight.

"West of Tierra Amarilla, his assassins stopped and threw his body into the front seat and stuffed it down onto the floorboard. The car was then pushed over a 40-foot embankment as if to make it appear that he had lost control of the car.

"Mrs. Salazar did not report him missing until after 8 a.m. the following day, when she called Deputy Daniel Rivera at his home. It is not clear why she did not report him missing earlier.

"Deputy Salazar's car was found about 11 a.m. on January 4th by a passing rancher."

The ferocity of the murder ignited passions, CdeBaca said. "Why did they have to abuse him so much? Why not just put a bullet in his head and get it over with? They prolonged this man's death by beatings that he took. The evidence inside the car proves that they abused him mercilessly. The question is, why would an individual or individuals display this kind of hatred and rage to get rid of this man? For what purpose?"

In his records, CdeBaca said he was not aware that Salazar ever spoke of having been threatened since the courthouse raid.

"Governor Cargo expressed dissatisfaction with the fact that no police protection had been given to Deputy Salazar. During my visits with Deputy Salazar, he never mentioned having received any threats and never said anything about fearing for his life. Whoever the assassins were, they should have been smart to know that Deputy Salazar had testified under oath when he gave his deposition on what happened at the courthouse in June. It made no sense to kill him. In that deposition, Deputy Salazar had identified Reies Lopez Tijerina as the man who shot him during the raid.

"Reies Lopez Tijerina made the statement that 'he was terribly shocked and sorry' over the news of Deputy Salazar's murder. Tijerina said that he was sure that nobody in his land grant alliance 'could have committed such a crude and savage crime against poor Mr. Salazar.' Tijerina added that the crime might possibly be attributed to what he called 'old traditional organized hatred between Democrats and Republicans in Rio Arriba County.' He further stated that he had nothing to worry about from Deputy Salazar, 'for I can prove that I was not in Tierra Amarilla at the time of the courthouse raid on June 5th.'"

CdeBaca said the apparent lack of threats on Salazar's life "was probably one of the reasons it was difficult to solve that crime." CdeBaca gives no credence to Tijerina's assertion that he was not at the courthouse when Salazar was shot during the June 5th raid.

"I am confident that it was Reies Lopez Tijerina who shot Deputy Salazar during the raid because Eulogio Salazar told me that it was him, and I have no reason to question his word," CdeBaca said.

He is nearly as confident, though, that Tijerina did not kill Salazar. "You would think that Reies Lopez Tijerina would be smarter than that because his attorneys could very well have challenged Deputy Salazar in court as to the veracity of his statements that he gave in his deposition," CdeBaca said. "Their chances to free themselves of the accusation that Tijerina shot Deputy Salazar during the raid would have been better if they had waited and discredited him on the witness stand."

Doubting that Tijerina himself was the killer, CdeBaca allowed that someone associated with Tijerina committed the crime, with or without Tijerina's knowledge.

CdeBaca dismissed Tijerina's repeated assertions that police, and well-placed public officials were behind Salazar's murder, which they purportedly hoped to use to quash him and his troublesome land grant movement. "I think it's farfetched to think that anything like that occurred," he said. "The theory that politicians and others got together to frame Reies Lopez Tijerina, I just don't see any importance to that. It's just something that's easy for him to say. The theory certainly was never discussed within law enforcement in my presence."

None of which, in CdeBaca's opinion, is to say that police couldn't have done a better job while investigating Salazar's murder. "The investigation focused on Reies Lopez Tijerina almost from the start," he said.

CdeBaca said that was largely due to comments made by District Attorney Alfonso Sanchez and State Police Chief Joe Black, both of whom openly suggested that Tijerina was the prime suspect. " If the word comes out from the chief of police or the district attorney that it was Reies Lopez Tijerina who is suspected of this crime, then who do you think the State Police investigators are going to look at? Investigators had this tunnel vision. They overlooked other individuals, whether they were followers or supporters of Reies Lopez Tijerina or they were activists from Tierra Amarilla or activists from Colorado who at times had been at Tijerina's side."

CdeBaca said five or six State Police investigators worked on the case for several months "until it reached a dead end." Years later, an investigation directed by then-Attorney General Toney Anaya also ended without indictments. Neither Anaya nor his investigators publicly named suspects.

More than 40 years cold, the case and much of what surrounds it still stirs emotions. "Reies Lopez Tijerina said State Police ran like scared coyotes during the courthouse raid but did he not do the same thing: run like a scared coyote after the shenanigans at the Tierra Amarilla courthouse in June of 1967? Most of his followers and sympathizers were picked up that night but he fled ... I'm not one of this man's admirers, not by a long shot. I just don't think it was Tijerina who killed Deputy Eulogio Salazar."

CdeBaca said he thinks Tijerina lacks the savagery that characterized Salazar's murder. He recalled in his records the thoughts of citizen who observed from a distance.

"An Albuquerque woman by the name of Mrs. Quincy Adams set up a fund for Mrs. Eulogio Salazar. Mrs. Adams started the fund with a $50 contribution. She was quoted as saying, 'The fact that we can have tyranny in our state, the fact that an underpaid policeman had to give his life to wake us up—that's pretty bad.'"

"Pretty bad" is a good description of what CdeBaca came upon one hot summer day while still at his first post of duty as a State Police officer.

"On July 18, 1958, a man from Tularosa called the State Police office and told the dispatcher that he needed to talk to an officer. I was south of Tularosa when I got the call. I met with the man at the city hall in Tularosa. He explained that he and his family were out hunting for arrowheads at the bottom of Round Mountain, west of Tularosa and that his 10-year-old daughter had stumbled onto decomposed human hands.

"I requested that he escort me to where these human hands were. When we got to the location on the old Mescalero road, I saw two human hands full of maggots, a quantity of skin and a portion of what may have been the victim's brain encased in a cardboard box. From what I could determine, the box had apparently been thrown out the window from a passing car. When the box landed on the slanted shoulder of the road, it flipped over and the human hands fell out.

"A search in an attempt to find other parts of the dismembered victim failed to turn up anything else. I took pictures and collected all the human specimens and took them to Tularosa to place them in dry ice and seal them in a box. On advice from my sergeant, I shipped the human parts to the FBI.

"I put out an APB for reports of a missing person. Representatives from the El Paso Sheriff's Office came to Alamogordo to talk to me in an attempt to tie the human finds with an earlier discovery of a butchered man they were investigating. They had discovered parts of a human body floating in a suitcase in the Rio Grande in El Paso. Only the victim's legs were in the suitcase. Later, a human torso was also discovered floating in the river. The head and arms were never found. Despite many hours of investigative work by multiple law enforcement agencies, the crime near Tularosa was never solved."

Multiple unsolved murders in Northern New Mexico during the 1970s drew considerable statewide publicity and, in the end, action by the State Police and the district attorney in Santa Fe. More about that brief controversial period in State Police history will be reported in Chapter 13. Among inquiries of the period was this one by the *Rio Grande Sun* of Española: "Are investigations of homicides and other violent crimes in Rio Arriba County bungled by incompetents or deliberately covered up?"

The weekly newspaper aimed much of its criticism at the State Police.

10

Standing Guard Against Legalized Gambling

Gambling in one form or another probably has existed since long before the first deck of cards was shuffled somewhere on a wobbly table. In this country, some states long have blocked gambling's spread as approved activity. But during the late 1970s legalized gambling started seeing serious cracks in New Mexico's door of prohibition.

It occurred during the second of three non-consecutive terms served as governor by Democrat Bruce King. State policeman Richard CdeBaca was around for it all. Aware of King's opposition to gambling, CdeBaca took steps that he concluded would have the governor's support. He made this entry in his records:

"While serving as Deputy State Police chief in charge of the Criminal Investigations Bureau in 1979, one of our criminal investigators stationed in Raton informed me that slot machines were being used for gambling, which was illegal. These slot machines were being used at the Country Club, the Elks Club and the Eagles Club.

"I authorized the investigator to obtain search warrants. Once the search warrants had been prepared, a team of State Police officers served the warrants and confiscated the slot machines. I gave orders to have the slot machines transported to headquarters.

"The district judge who authorized the search warrants issued an order that the slot machines be destroyed and a video tape be made of the destruction. These slot machines were of vintage quality and were worth a lot of money. A total of 12 machines were destroyed. Over $1,300 in coins was recovered from these slot machines. I delivered the money to the district judge in Raton and showed him the video of the destruction. A report was submitted to the district attorney on the illegal gambling and he declined to prosecute."

Gambling in those days was mostly in private clubs or offices, CdeBaca said. "You never heard of an arrest for petty misdemeanor of gambling," he said. "It carried a fine of $25 upon conviction. If it came to your attention, you took action. But no police chief that I ever worked under ever made gambling a priority."

He said he was not aware of any slot machines being used anywhere in New Mexico prior to the call he took from the officer in Raton. "If they existed before that incident, it had to have been in a very clandestine manner. Word didn't get out," he said.

CdeBaca referred strictly to his time with the State Police, beginning in 1956. Clandestine gambling drew much publicity less than a decade earlier when a Doña Ana County grand jury in 1949 issued multiple indictments for gambling that included machines. Indictments also were issued for gambling club payoffs to officials.[1]

"What we found in Raton was not a private card game. It was commercial gambling. What was confiscated by the agent and uniformed officers in Raton were vintage machines, so-called one-armed bandits. That's what they were, the slot machines with the lever. They were nickel, dime and quarter variety.

"I realized it was not a very popular move to take action when you're dealing with these private clubs—the Elks, the Eagles. I always informed Chief of Police Martin Vigil about what I was doing. He had no objections as to what action I was going to take. I never got any feedback from any member of those clubs. Chief Vigil didn't mention that he got phone calls or letters from Raton so I'm assuming he did not get any."

A few years went by before the State Police came upon a similar situation but on a grander scale or, at least, on a bigger stage. It was 1992 and CdeBaca was working at the time as the secretary for the Department of Public Safety in King's third administration. By then, according to the Associated Press, Sandia Pueblo and the Mescalero Apache Tribe already had begun video gaming, and others were maneuvering to do the same. CdeBaca wrote in his records:

"A gambling situation similar to the one in Raton was discovered in Albuquerque, but instead of using 'one-armed bandits' for gambling, they were using electronic video poker machines, including the Fraternal Order of Police. I ordered the confiscation of all the illegal gambling devices. The Bernalillo County District Attorney, Bob Schwartz, told me he would not prosecute and suggested that I ask the attorney general, Tom Udall. When I met with Tom Udall, he told me he would think about it. When I didn't hear from him, I called and was referred to Manuel Tijerina, his assistant, and that was the end of that."

CdeBaca said two weeks went by without him hearing back from Udall. "I went from Bob Schwartz, to Tom Udall to Manuel Tijerina. I was bounced around like a ping-pong ball," CdeBaca said. "I never got an affirmative or positive answer from Tijeriina regarding prosecutions. I saw I was just getting the run-around."

The cold response came after the State Police had made considerable efforts to bust the illegal activity. "We had infiltrated one of the clubs. One of our agents from the Special Investigations Division was hired in the club and he witnessed payoffs from these machines. It was printed paper that would be taken to a cashier and cashed out."

It was more than just a few elected officials that were less than impressed. The Albuquerque Tribune ran an editorial cartoon depicting police loading video poker machines onto the back of a truck while a citizen standing alongside a crime scene tape asks: "So, how goes the search for (murder suspect) Danny Martinez?" In the background, a police officer, with gun drawn on a poker machine, demands: "Freeze sucker!"

People, when caught breaking the law, often will ask police if they don't have better things to do, CdeBaca said. "You stop someone for speeding and often they'll ask you, 'Why aren't you chasing real criminals.' What they seemingly don't recognize is that we're simply doing what we were hired to do."

Even though he was hired to catch law-breakers, CdeBaca was not entirely surprised by the refusal of prosecutors to act against Albuquerque club owners who had been busted with gaming machines.

"I knew that this was a hot potato for any district attorney or the attorney general to handle," CdeBaca said. "They're elected officials and I'm sure they evaluated the political consequences of this type of prosecutions. Your private clubs kind of represent the higher social level of the community. It's not like you're confiscating one of these slot machines from some corner rinky-dinky bar. Prosecutors look at these individuals as probably being some of their stronger supporters come election time so why would you want to disenfranchise those individuals by filing criminal charges on those that are using the machines and punish them with what amounts to a $25 fine?"

CdeBaca said King did not ask him to leave gambling cases alone. But he did get stern direction from other quarters.

> "The clubs hired an attorney to represent them. A district judge in Bernalillo wrote a letter threatening me with contempt of court if I didn't release the video poker machines to its owners. I had no other recourse but to comply with the judge's letter. The video poker machines were returned and in the process, one of the video poker machines was accidentally dropped and destroyed, and we paid for it. Sometimes the justice system is a 'crapshoot.'"

While that issue went in circles, the situation involving proposed gaming compacts between the state and Indian communities intensified. The Mescalero Apaches and Sandia Pueblo sued King in 1992, looking to force the state to enter into compacts, the Associated Press reported. King seemingly felt a need to show more than intransigence, CdeBaca said.

King sent CdeBaca and Jerry Manzagol, director of Regulation and Licensing, to visit with Mescalero President Wendell Chino. "He was very congenial. He never raised his voice. But President Chino was determined that there was going to be gambling on the Mescalero reservation with or without the governor signing a compact," CdeBaca said. "He talked about economics on the reservation and he was personally convinced that this would be an economic stimulus for his people."

CdeBaca said he and Manzagol reported to King after the meeting. "I told the governor that I considered myself to be not just the secretary of the Department of Public Safety but one of his advisers on these issues. I told him, 'If you sign these gambling compacts, you're going to open the door wide open to Indian casinos. I'm sure that's not the kind of legacy that you want to leave behind.'

"My assumption was that the gambling interests from Nevada would come and establish themselves in New Mexico because most of these tribes were so poor that they had to have financial backing, and where was it going to come from if not from the gambling interests in Nevada?"

CdeBaca's assignments on gambling did not end there. King directed him to meet with Pojoaque Pueblo Governor Jacob Viarrial. "I respected Governor Viarrial but he was a different character than Mr. Chino," CdeBaca said. "Governor Viarrial was very outspoken about this issue and no one was going to tell him how to run his business. He wrote me a letter, and one sentence that I do remember in that letter was: 'Isn't it about time that you start walking in the proverbial moccasins?'

"I think in so many words, he was telling me that I needed to change my mind because he wasn't going to change his."

In its summary of Indian gambling developments, the Associated Press told how King lost his re-election bid for governor in 1994 to Republican Gary Johnson, who signed gaming compacts in 1995.

Both Chino and Viarrial ran aggressive gambling operations without signing compacts that others had negotiated with the state. The two men accused the state of claiming for itself too much of the profits, news reports of the time said.

Years after CdeBaca met with Viarrial to discuss the gambling issue, the two men came upon one another again. "My wife and I were gambling at the Cities of Gold Casino in Pojoaque. Governor Viarrial recognized me. He came over and took out a $20 bill and handed it to my sister-in-law, Cecilia, then he just walked away. Later, I saw him give money to another woman.

"The man had heart. He was a compassionate man and he fought for what he thought was right for his people. He died of an apparent heart attack while in Mexico in 2004."

II

Alcohol, DUI and Drugs Galore

Alcohol abuse and then, increasingly, access to illegal drugs have been societal concerns that have occupied law enforcement and the courts day and night for generations. While in law enforcement, Richard CdeBaca fought alcohol and drug abuse as a patrolman on state highways, then as deputy chief and chief of the New Mexico State Police. He later addressed the problems as the state's drug czar and cabinet secretary of the Department of Public Safety.

"Drunks have been killing innocent people since drivers were licensed to drive," he said.

His entries include these two from his early years as a patrolman:

"It was about 6 p.m. on a Christmas Eve when I investigated a fatal accident north of Alamogordo. A 1954 Chevrolet failed to stop at the stop sign at the junction of highway 83 and U.S. 54-70. It broad-sided another car. The driver of the Chevrolet, a resident of Alamogordo, was an acquaintance of mine. He had been drinking and was thrown out of the car. I found him lying on the roadway critically injured.

"I radioed for an ambulance and a wrecker. I sat the man up because he was choking from his own blood from severe internal injuries. He was bleeding from his nose and mouth. He was taken to the hospital by ambulance. The driver and passenger of the other car were not seriously injured but I made them go to the hospital.

"By the time I had finished investigating the accident and went to the hospital, the driver of the Chevy had been declared dead. It was very difficult notifying his family the day before Christmas."

"I was on my way home one night at about 11 when an officer with the Tularosa Police Department called for help. The officer had arrested a drunk driver and his two passengers and had taken them to city hall to be booked. When they arrived at city hall, the three men refused to be booked.

"When I arrived, I told them that if they didn't go inside, they would be charged with resisting arrest. Suddenly two of them threw punches at me and while I was defending myself, the jailer came out to help me and a motorist who was driving by also came to help. In no time, we had all three offenders in jail.

"The Tularosa officer had locked himself in his police car and I told him not to call me again if he ever needed help. I complained to Chief of Police Julian Martinez. Either the officer was terminated or he resigned because I never saw him again."

CdeBaca said drunken drivers have always been "the nemesis for law enforcement ... As long as there have been cars and law enforcement, there has been the enforcement of DWI laws. But for a long time, there was public apathy toward the problem."

CdeBaca made this observation in his records midway through his career:

"I do not believe people are aware of how many individuals are driving under the influence of illegal drugs and alcohol, which combined makes for a lethal weapon."

If not fully aware of the number of substance-impaired motorists, New Mexicans have long known of this problem alongside which they drive on just about every roadway. *The Santa Fe New Mexican* reported this account in a 1935 edition:

"Six months in the penitentiary for a drunken automobile driver who ran down a car and injured several people; and he will spend six months there unless turned loose by 'a politically minded governor or a weak-kneed parole board,' quoth the vigorous and outspoken District Judge Mike Otero, who is occasionally available when not disqualified by his eminent district attorney or some of the beneficiaries of the rotten Hannett-Vogel law firm, to strike a blow for law and order. The carnage of the automobile is bad enough when drivers are sober; and the drunken driver is a menace which must be exterminated."

Despite such vitriolic writing in the capital city's leading newspaper, drunk driving laws have not always received the attention they deserve in the Legislature, said CdeBaca, who lobbied lawmakers for years on other issues. "The attitude toward DUI has changed considerably since the 1950s when I began patrolling as a state policeman," he said. "Sure, there were pictures of fatal accidents and stories about drunk drivers and innocent people getting killed. But there wasn't a public outcry then. The message today is loud and clear: The public wants something done. It probably has become issue number-one with the public. "

CdeBaca said much of what fuels today's growing intolerance of drunk driving continues to be the highly publicized tragedy of Christmas Eve 1992 when Gordon House of Gallup killed an Albuquerque mother and her three daughters while driving drunk and in the wrong direction on Interstate-40.

What he considered to have been an inattentive public did not keep CdeBaca from aggressively pursuing DUI offenders and other violators of laws written to curb alcohol and drug abuse. Here are some of his numerous notations:

"On May 7, 1976, I was traveling south on I-25 and when I approached mile marker 271, traffic was slowing down due to construction. I was the last car in line when a man driving a Nissan car at a high rate of speed swerved to the left to avoid rear-ending my car. He lost control of his car and plowed into a 25 MPH sign. The car then rolled over and landed on its wheels in the middle of the median.

"The windows in the car broke and personal belongings were scattered all over. The engine of the car had stopped running but the driver managed to get it started and began to move forward in a northerly direction even though he had been traveling south. By this time I had gotten out of my car and yelled at him to stop, which he did.

"The door to the driver's side was jammed from the accident and I ordered him to get out on the passenger's side. When he moved himself from the driver's seat, I saw a lit marijuana cigarette on the floorboard. The man's eyes were glassy-looking and he appeared to be 'stoned.' He asked me why I had stopped him. Obviously he didn't realize he had rolled his car. The man was transporting D.A.R.E. literature to Albuquerque. Quite an advocate for the anti-drug program—smoking pot. A uniformed officer arrived at the scene and arrested the man."

"One morning, a man reported finding a dead Mescalero Apache woman next to a cattle guard at Three Rivers, a small community north of Tularosa. Officer Sam Chavez was called to investigate the mysterious death. Officer Chavez discovered that two other women had been with the victim the night before and that all three had been drinking.

"The owner of the Three Rivers Mercantile Store knew the women. Officer Chavez radioed me to help him locate the two Indian women so that an inquest into the cause of death could be held at the scene before removing the body. I asked Julian Martinez, the chief of police in Tularosa, to assist me in finding the two women. By some stroke of luck, he found them at Moller's Lounge in Tularosa. I took them into custody and placed them in the back seat of my car and proceeded to take them to Three Rivers.

"Both women were under the influence of alcohol. I explained to them that their companion had been found dead and I was taking them to the inquest. On the way, one of them tapped me on the shoulder and said, 'Say, good looking, why don't you pull off the road and make love to us.' I told her that I had important business to take care of. One of the women made positive identification of the victim who had passed out and froze to death. I left the women with Officer Chavez and told him I'm not about to take them back to Tularosa."

"Sometimes, enforcement can be quite comical but what I encountered one night while on patrol deserves an Academy Award. I came up behind a car whose driver was driving in all directions but straight. The car was occupied by two women. I followed the car for a short distance until I was convinced that the woman behind the wheel had no business driving in that condition.

"I turned on the emergency equipment to stop the car, and while I had the spot light on the car, the two women proceeded to change positions in the car. I didn't think it was possible, but they accomplished it while the car was moving. When the car finally stopped, I walked up to the passenger side of the car and asked the woman who had been the first driver to show me her driver's license, but she denied driving. I opened the door and arrested her for drunk driving and put her in the back seat of my car. I then ordered the second driver to step out of the car. I made her submit to a sobriety test, which she failed miserably. I also arrested her for drunk driving and took them to jail.

"After booking them, I told the jailer to allow them to make a phone call. One of the ladies asked me if their names would appear in the newspaper and I told her I had no control over what the newspaper published. The next morning they were arraigned before Justice of the Peace Howard Beacham. They pleaded guilty to DUI and were fined $100 plus $5 court costs."

"One night of March 21, 1959, I had left Tularosa and I was on my way to the office to catch up on reports when I came across a car parked at an angle on the shoulder with the left rear on the highway. I stopped to find out if the driver needed assistance. The driver was passed out behind the wheel. After struggling to get him out, I managed to put him in my car.

"I radioed the dispatcher to call a wrecker to pick up the car. The driver was incarcerated. At his trial before Justice of the Peace Howard Beacham on charges of DUI, his attorney entered a plea of not guilty. His attorney argued that his client was not driving and should not be found guilty. I testified that the defendant was passed out behind the wheel, the engine to the car was running and there was no one else in the car and the car was obstructing traffic.

"The attorney told the judge that if his client was guilty of anything, it would be for illegal parking. Judge Beacham found him guilty of DUI. His attorney appealed the case to District Court. Judge Allan Walker heard the case and he affirmed the judgment of the lower court."

"One afternoon in November, I was patrolling U.S.-83 west of Cloudcroft when I caught up with a slow-moving car crowding the center line one too many times. I stopped the car and ordered the driver to step out. He was having trouble balancing himself. I told him he was under arrest for drunk driving and handcuffed him.

"When I asked him how much he had to drink, he gave me the standard answer every drunk gives, 'I only had two drinks.' I searched his car and found a fifth of Jim Beam under the front seat with almost half of its contents gone. I opened the bottle and poured out the whiskey on the shoulder of the road. The driver said, 'Jesus Christ, I just bought that expensive whiskey.'

"I replied, 'You aren't going to need it where you're going.' The next morning at his arraignment before Justice of the Peace Howard Beacham, he pleaded guilty to DUI and was fined $100 and $5 court costs."

"During the 1958 Christmas holidays, Governor Ed Mechem assigned the National Guard to assist us with roadblocks. I have no idea if Chief A.P. Winston had requested the help of the guard. On the evening of December 24, 1958, we set up a roadblock north of Alamogordo on U.S. 54-70 and we were being assisted by national guardsmen. We were checking drivers when we heard the screeching of brakes. A drunk driver had run over the reflectors on the highway and we took off running. One of the guards took it for granted that the car would stop and he got hit and suffered minor injuries.

"A guardsman in Gallup helping with a roadblock was not so fortunate. He was run over by a drunk driver and killed. That is the last time any governor called out the National Guard to assist with traffic checks."

"In January, 1960, the dispatcher received a telephone call from a woman who claimed she had been thrown out of a car on State Road 83. She gave the dispatcher the description of a two-tone white/blue 1955 Chevrolet. Later on that night, I observed a car answering the same description headed south on U.S.-54 toward El Paso. I caught up with the car and noticed it was weaving all over the highway.

"When I stopped the car, I detected the driver was in no condition to be driving. I arrested him and took him to the office to unravel the bizarre events. The driver admitted he had picked up the woman who had filed the complaint earlier in the evening at a bar in High Rolls. He said they got into an argument and he pushed her out of the car, but he said the car was not moving.

"The woman was picked up by a passing motorist. The following day she filed assault charges on the drunk driver. He appeared before Justice of the Peace Howard Beacham and pleaded guilty to assault and was fined $50. He also pleaded guilty to DUI and was fined $100 and $5 court costs. Judge Beacham also suspended the man's driver's license for one year."

"I had investigated many accidents with injuries, but the one that occurred on the night of December 15, 1958, deserves mention because of the circumstances.

"The driver of a 1956 Buick lost control while traveling west of High Rolls on State Road 83 and finally left the road, plunging head on into Dry Canyon. The last 50 feet of the canyon wall are perpendicular but lucky for the driver that he was thrown out of the car before it landed at the bottom.

"The car was a total loss and the driver was taken to Gerald Champion Memorial Hospital, suffering from lacerations, contusions and abrasions. He had been drinking before the accident and I cited him to court on a reckless driving charge. Very few drivers that plunged to the bottom of the canyon in that location lived to talk about it. To this day, the remains of the car lie at the bottom."

"On the morning of November 20, 1966, I answered the telephone at the Santa Rosa office and the caller reported that there was a car submerged in the El Rito Creek on Highway 91. Within five minutes, I arrived at the scene, then Sheriff Bobby Serrano showed up. Several people were standing on the bridge looking at the car in the river. There was no way of telling if anyone was trapped inside the car. It was totally submerged and its top was barely visible.

"I instructed the officers who had arrived to clear the traffic and disperse the people while I went home and changed into my swimming trunks. On my way home, I radioed the dispatcher and told him to send a wrecker to the scene. When I returned, I dove into the water and received the shock of my life. I didn't expect the water to be that cold. To my surprise, there was no one inside the car. By some stroke of luck I managed to tie the wrecker cable to the rear bumper. The wrecker operator pulled the 1957 Chevrolet out of the river.

"While I went home to get into my uniform, the driver of the car and his companion showed up at the city police office. Chief of Police Willie

Ronquillo radioed me to report to his office. The 18-year-old driver admitted that he and his friend had been drinking the night before. He said he lost control of the car, hit the bridge and plunged into the river.

"The driver said he got out through the right front door and the passenger got out through the rear broken window. Both walked home without reporting it. I told them they were lucky they didn't drown. I filed reckless driving charges on the driver, and he was fined $100 and was jailed pending payment of the fine. His passenger was not charged with any crime."

"One weekend in Gallup I was assigned to drive the patty wagon. As I was driving through the city, I heard the dispatcher reporting a disturbance at the Aztec Bar. I radioed the dispatcher and told her I was approaching the bar and I would check it out and asked that she send me some backup. I entered the bar with my baton ready to protect myself if I had to. A city officer responded to the call also.

"Inside the bar, a drunk woman armed with a broken bottle was threatening a drunk man who had apparently been fighting with her. We took the broken bottle from her and arrested both of them and put them in the patty wagon.

"I called the dispatcher and told her that I had two 10-15s (prisoners) and was on my way to the jail. In order to get to the jail, I had to circle the block and it must have taken me five or six minutes to get there. When I arrived, I opened the rear doors and saw the man on top of the woman. I ordered them to get out and I heard the man tell me in slurred speech, 'Officer, take us around the block one more time, please.'"

"While patrolling U.S.-66 west of Gallup late one night, I saw a set of headlights from a car that was upside down. The Navajo police car had gone off the road and landed on its top. The Navajo police officer was passed out in the car. With the assistance of the truck driver, we managed to pull the uniformed policeman out of the car. I took him to McKinley County jail.

"When I searched him, I found a piece of peyote in his possession. The next day, he was arraigned before Judge Edward Romero on a DUI charge. He pleaded guilty and was fined $100. He also was terminated from his job."

"Officer Leroy Urioste and I stopped an 18-wheeler on U.S.-66 east of Santa Rosa and arrested the 38-year-old driver for possession of dangerous drugs. He had in his possession 29 Benzedrine (Bennies) and amphetamine sulfite pills. The driver was taken before Justice of the Peace Manuel Ulibarri where he posted a $200 bond and was released.

"These drugs are not considered narcotics but are widely abused by truck drivers to keep them awake."

"My district commander in Las Cruces, Captain Archie White, sent me on a special assignment to Silver City. The sheriff from Grant County had requested help with curbing Sunday liquor sales in the county. I reported to the sheriff in late October 1958 about the time that hunters are getting their beer. The sheriff loaned me an old pickup and assigned a deputy in civilian clothes to show me the bars in the county that were suspected of selling liquor on Sundays.

"The first Sunday, I managed to purchase beer from a bar in Hurley. The following Sunday, I had no luck buying liquor from any of the bars, even those in remote areas. I was convinced that word got out that a state policeman was working undercover trying to buy liquor on Sundays."

"I reported to Captain White that I believed my assignment had been compromised and I could no longer be effective. He agreed with my assessment and I returned to Alamogordo. Months later I heard that the deputy who was assigned to help me had announced as a candidate for sheriff. Get the picture?"

"One day, the wife of one of my officers came to see me to tell me that her husband was drinking and seeing another woman, whose husband was in the military service. I told her I had not detected any of that but I would be more observant. I called the officers one evening to set up a roadblock on U.S. 66 east of Santa Rosa. When the accused officer arrived, I could smell alcohol on him. When I pulled him to the side and confronted him, he admitted having a drink before dinner and said he didn't expect to be called out. I sent him home. I believed he had had more than one drink.

"The following day, I called him into my office and warned him that I would not tolerate drinking and I didn't want him to jeopardize his career. He requested a transfer and shortly thereafter he was transferred to Taos.

Later he resigned or was forced to leave, and he was hired by the Taos County Sheriff's Department.

"One night while off duty and driving under the influence, he lost control of the car, rolled it and was fatally injured."

CdeBaca said he is among those who are pleased to have seen the Legislature set a lower legal limit for blood-alcohol content of drivers and stiffen penalties that include larger fines, more jail time and impoundment of vehicles. It all should help, he said, but the problem won't go away. "Every time there is a multiple fatal accident caused by a drunk driver, we hear the public outrage that we need more stringent laws," he said.

Public pressure has led government officials to redouble efforts at getting drunk drivers off New Mexico roads. Photo by Clyde Mueller, *The New Mexican.*

"But alcoholism, being an addiction, is not going to stop with the bigger fines, harsher jail sentences and confiscation of cars. The alcoholic has to stop drinking and not get behind the wheel of a car, period. Ignition inter-locks, electronic ankle bracelets, designated drivers, suggested DWI license plates, pink hats and all the other absurd stuff have not worked effectively."

At least some of that might be open to debate. *The Santa Fe New Mexican* reported in October 2009 that in December 2008, a total of 8,891 people were driving with interlock devices. Information compiled by Dick Roth and reported by Anne Constable showed that 6,186 such devices were installed in 2008 alone. Records showed that there had been a 31-percent decrease in the number of alcohol-related crashes from 2002-2008, some of the credit for the drop was assigned to interlock devices, wrote Constable.

A week later, the newspaper reported that New Mexico had dropped substantially in national rankings that measure alcohol-related deaths on roadways.

As attempts are made to address alcoholism, CdeBaca said, more people need to stop automatically associating men with drunk driving. He said women often are the impaired drivers in serious automobile crashes and that mothers with children in their cars account for many of the DUI tickets issued by police.

Tickets and arrests alone, he said, have proven to be little deterrence in some cases. "We read about individuals who have been arrested numerous times, some as many as 20 or more, and they are still driving."

Indeed, Rachel O'Connor, state DWI czar in 2009, told news reporters that one New Mexico man had been cited 26 times for DWI, another man 23 times. The information came out after a Mora man was arrested for his 22 DWI.

"My uncle, Jimmy CdeBaca, was hit by a five-time loser—a man with five DWIs—who T-boned his pickup and killed him in Albuquerque," CdeBaca said.

Political favors too frequently can get in the way of effective DWI lawmaking and enforcement in the courts, CdeBaca said. "Just about everybody has friends or relatives who get into trouble because of alcohol. But that should have been considered when these public officials were campaigning for office. Surely you have to know when you seek an office that you're going to face some very, very tough decisions."

Sometimes in the not-so-distant past, he said, political influences were deeply ingrained in the arena of public service and could have a corrupting effect. He referred specifically to a time in 1959 when state liquor inspectors were sent out to sell fund-raising tickets for the dominant political party and spent much of their time peddling the tickets to those who they were supposed to regulate.

"Nothing much was mentioned when, under the administration of State Liquor Director Kern Aldridge, liquor inspectors were conducting a campaign, collecting political donations from liquor dispensers. The Democratic dinner tickets were being sold for $25 each," CdeBaca said.

And, of course, there was the much-publicized 1963 incident in Santa Fe's La Fonda Hotel when Frank "Pancho" Padilla, president of the New Mexico Liquor Dealers Association, boasted loudly that he "owned" the Legislature because of his strategic support of lawmakers. (More on this will appear in Chapter 15.)

Being well connected hasn't always proved useful when it comes to alcohol and trouble. One fatal accident involving alcohol sticks to CdeBaca's mind more than so many others.

"On December 22, 1972, I was called out of a department Christmas party at the Holiday Inn in Santa Fe. Bob Patton, one of my communications equipment operators told me that Jeffrey Balling, another one of my operators had just been killed in a car accident and that there were other people killed who had not yet been identified.

"A few minutes later, I was called out again by the registration clerk at the hotel to tell me that I had a telephone call. When I answered the telephone, another of my operators at headquarters told me that Sharon Fox, a 21-year-old secretary who worked for Captain Alexander and myself, was also killed while riding with Jeffrey Balling. The operator also told me that the driver of another car involved in the accident had also been killed but had not been identified. He said that all the victims had been taken to the hospital morgue.

"I went back into the party and got Bob Patton and Stan Williams, another of my operators to go with me to the hospital. On the way to the hospital, Stan Williams said he felt real bad about the accident because he had been drinking after work with Jeffrey Balling and Sharon Fox. When we arrived at the hospital morgue, all the bodies were covered.

"A city police officer asked me if I would step into the morgue and help identify the third victim. He said the woman had no identification on her but that the car she was driving was registered to a Richard Stanley Williams. When the officer uncovered the body, I had to take a second look. It was Stan Williams' wife.

"Stan Williams and Bob Patton were waiting for me outside in the hallway. I gave Stan the bad news and he broke down and blamed himself for the cause of it all. He had called his wife, Alice, from the party to come join him.

"The city officer explained that Jeffrey Balling was driving south on

Cerrillos Road at a high rate of speed when he lost control of his car and it crossed the divider and sideswiped a car then bounced straight into the path of the car driven by Alice Williams, hitting it head on. The 20-year-old driver of the car that was sideswiped was hospitalized with back injuries.

"We returned to the Christmas party where only a handful of employees were left. My wife and I took Stan Williams to pick up his two sons, Ronnie and Mark, from the babysitter and took them home with us where they spent the night. The following morning, we went to express our condolences to Jeffrey Ballings' wife and to Sharon Fox's parents.

"The funerals took place after Christmas. Back at work, the mood was somber.

"Stan Williams sued Jeffrey Ballings' insurance company. Stan had to get a loan, which I co-signed, to pay for his wife's funeral expenses. We established a fund at headquarters to help defray expenses."

As noted in a previous chapter, CdeBaca and others in law enforcement began seeing increased availability and use of illegal drugs in the 1960s. In 1975, State Police Chief Martin Vigil placed CdeBaca in charge of the State Police Criminal Investigations Bureau, which oversaw several divisions, including Narcotics. He promptly began to clean house.

"Changes in the Narcotics Division were necessary. The commander, assistant commander and other supervisors were transferred out of the Narcotics Division. Tighter controls on the inventory of confiscated drugs and the accountability of money used in the purchase of drugs were implemented. In one drug deal alone, an agent had to show $300,000 in cash as good faith to negotiate a large amount of marijuana. It was an effective way to make purchases of illegal drugs.

"The risk of the agent's safety and the loss of the state money was always of great concern. Confiscated vehicles and aircraft used in the transportation of illicit drugs were sold at the annual State Police auction every July."

"Confiscated drugs kept coming in almost on a daily basis, larger amounts being confiscated by uniformed officers on the highways. A garage at headquarters that was converted into a drug storage room was designated as the evidence room. Large sums of money confiscated were safely stored in an undisclosed vault. A huge parking lot was used to store confiscated vehicles. On one occasion, one of the confiscated cars was stolen from the State Police property."

CdeBaca said he was always aware of the danger faced by his officers.

"One night in Las Vegas, two narcotics enforcement agents, Jerry Noedel and Louie Gallegos, were in pursuit of a suspected drug trafficker. After stopping the car, the agents approached the driver who pointed a .22 rifle at them in a threatening manner. He refused to put the gun down and the agents shot him to death.

"Sergeant Harold Byford and I traveled to Las Vegas to lend moral support to the agents and gain firsthand knowledge of the shooting. We met with the family of the victim and they accused the agents of being murderers and said they should be arrested and jailed. The victim's mother told us that her son was killed in cold blood, that he was a good boy and would never harm anyone.

"When we told her that her son was armed with a rifle and had pointed it at the officers and was suspected of selling marijuana, she didn't believe it. In order to try to assuage their feelings, I told them that I would ask the attorney general for an independent investigation.

"Mr. Benny Flores, the district attorney in Las Vegas, impaneled a grand jury to look into the circumstances of the shooting. After all the testimony was heard, both agents were exonerated. The consensus of the jury was that the agents acted in self-defense.

"The State Police Department was eventually sued and the state Risk Management Division settled the civil suit for an undisclosed amount."

"During an intensive recruiting campaign to attract uniformed officers to become narcotics agents, only two officers applied. The additional $100 per month incentive pay and the type of work did not seem to entice any of them. The difference in pay was an issue among some uniformed officers, but these officers who are in the minority get in a 'comfort zone' and complain about anything."

Complaints soon started reaching CdeBaca's desk from other quarters.

"The destruction of confiscated drugs could only be done by a court order from a district judge, and as time went on, there were tons of marijuana to be disposed of. We used to take the drugs to the Duke City Lumber mill north of Española to dispose of them in the incinerator. The state Environmental Improvement Division made us stop doing it, claiming we were polluting the entire Española Valley. Then we moved to a more-remote area to a mill near Cimarron and we were ordered to stop that, too.

"We had no choice but to ask the Legislature for money to build our own incinerator behind the Narcotics Division offices. This one was built in compliance with environmental regulations."

If dealing with complaints was part of the job, CdeBaca's records suggest that most of the time he spent overseeing the Narcotics Division was devoted to tracking down marijuana and hard drugs. Conditions unfolding within the state appeared to demand it.

"After lengthy undercover investigations, regular early morning raids were conducted in cities across the state. My participation in some of these early morning raids was to lend moral support to the agents and uniformed officers. State, county and city officers participated in these raids. No matter how much of a combined effort was used to combat the illegal drug trade, the drug dealers seemed more determined. There was never enough manpower and city mayors and school officials kept asking for help with the drug problem in their areas."

"With the availability of federal grants, we established regional task forces involving federal, state, county and city law enforcement resources. No matter how much effort was put into drug interdiction, the illicit drug trade flourished, contraband kept being smuggled in and transported across state lines."

"In 1980, for the first time in the history of the division, we recruited two female officers from the uniformed bureau and assigned them to the Narcotics Division. These undercover agents proved to be very successful. Despite the danger involved, they did their jobs very well."

"On November 5, 1979, 28 suspected narcotics violators were arrested in a sweeping raid early in the morning in San Juan County. A total of 11 law enforcement agencies were involved with 100 officers from different jurisdictions. The arrested included many persons well known to police who had been suspected in crimes ranging from murder to burglary.

"Most arrests were on charges of pushing hard narcotics, particularly 'meth' and LSD. There were also numerous arrests on distribution of cocaine charges. District Attorney Paul Onuska described the raid as a 'quality raid.'"

Smuggling of drugs across borders pressed CdeBaca to rely increasingly on specially trained officers within his unit.

"The Narcotics Air Detail was responsible for tracking aircraft used to smuggle drugs across the border.

"In 1977, narcotics agents recovered a single-engine aircraft in a remote area a few miles west of Springer. The pilot had removed several hundred pounds of marijuana and stashed it so that it could be picked up later by a ground crew. He drained the fuel tank and poured the fuel all over the aircraft. In doing so, he accidentally got gas on himself and when he set fire to the airplane, he became engulfed in flames. His charred body was found a few feet away from what was left of the aircraft."

"In 1978, a twin engine aircraft landed on a dirt road near El Vado Dam and unloaded untold amounts of marijuana. The aircraft was then set on fire and left to burn. The smugglers were never apprehended. The Narcotics Air Detail salvaged the two engines, which were auctioned off by the department. Drug smugglers could afford to destroy aircrafts because of the lucrative drug profits."

"After months of surveillance in 1978, the Narcotics Air Detail tracked a private airplane suspected of smuggling marijuana. The small aircraft landed in Santa Rosa where narcotics agents were waiting. Two suspects were arrested for unlawful possession of marijuana with intent to distribute. The airplane was loaded with a large amount of marijuana. One of the suspects arrested was the brother of state Senator Manny Aragon of Albuquerque."

CdeBaca increasingly found cooperation with other agencies to be productive.

"Late in 1979, we signed an agreement with the Drug Enforcement Administration and the Albuquerque Police Department to sponsor a Diversion Investigation Unit to share information on drug interdiction. Prior to Phillip Jordan's appointment as regional DEA special agent in charge, DEA and State Police Narcotics agents had not worked well together. It was a matter of who was going to take credit for what."

There was one agency, though, that continued to frustrate CdeBaca.

"In September of 1982, Captain R.D. Thompson, Narcotics Division commander, informed me that narcotics agents had discovered 50 acres of marijuana which was ready to be cultivated in the small farming community of Arch, located in Roosevelt County.

"I traveled to Arch and met with narcotics enforcement supervisors and agents who had secured the field and were waiting for a decision to be made on what to do. The marijuana plants were camouflaged by milo plants. However, most of the marijuana plants had outgrown the small milo plants. Many of the marijuana plants had grown seven and eight feet tall.

"There was one area of this field on the north side which had been stripped by poachers. Still, this would be the largest marijuana harvest for us, and it presented an enormous problem on how to dispose of it.

"Before doing anything with the illegal crop, I consulted with the state Environmental Improvement Division to determine if they would give us permission to burn it once it was cut. But the division would not issue a permit for such purposes. We had no place to store 50 acres of weed, which would amount to several tons.

"After consulting with the district attorney, we agreed to have it mowed, but not before we would photograph it. I hired two local farmers to bring their tractors and cut the plants, disc them into mulch and plow them under.

"The owner of the land disavowed any knowledge of the illegal contraband. He leased the property and did not live there. A year later, the seed that was plowed germinated and the number of plants multiplied in numbers. We had the young plants eradicated."

Turns out people at the Environmental Improvement Division weren't the only ones concerned about how the marijuana was to be destroyed. The Associated Press reported that area farmers protested when they learned that the herbicide, Hellfire, was sprayed on the crop and that the plants were to be burned. Farmers worried that fumes would get into their homes.

A year after the record marijuana crop seizure, State Police busted the largest cocaine ring that they had ever encountered.

"On September 1, 1981, undercover narcotics agents busted the largest cocaine ring after seizing 23 pounds of the drug worth an estimated $2.3 million in street value at the time. Six residents of Albuquerque's Northeast Heights were arrested in connection with the three-month undercover operation.

"The cocaine that was smuggled came from Columbia and moved through Florida on its way to Albuquerque. It was packaged in kilo bricks, the customary way of shipping drugs. Sergeant A.J. Riccio of the Narcotics Air Detail coordinated the operation."

As pleased as State Police were with that operation, just a few months would pass before they would make a much-larger bust.

"On June 16, 1982, State police officer Phillip Baiers conducted a careful and exhaustive search in the Santa Rosa area and finally located several duffle bags loaded with 213 pounds of cocaine. It was the largest recovery of cocaine in the history of drug enforcement in the state.

"The duffle bags loaded with cocaine had apparently been tossed out of an airplane. What prompted Officer Baiers to look for the cocaine was his knowledge of an ongoing investigation. The investigation had been a cooperative effort among the State Police, DEA, U.S. Customs Air Support, Arizona Department of Public Safety, U.S. Attorney's Office in Phoenix, U.S. Attorney Bill Lutz in Albuquerque and District Attorney Benny Flores in Las Vegas, New Mexico.

"We were informed earlier by the Arizona Department of Public Safety that an airplane was suspected of smuggling the cocaine from Mexico into the U.S. An airplane suspected of carrying the cocaine flew into the Santa Rosa airstrip on June 7th. The two pilots were questioned and released. Later, officer Baiers arrested three men for criminal trespassing on a ranch south of Santa Rosa. Three people from Mexico were arrested; two of them gave addresses in Florida."

CdeBaca's work with the Narcotics Division and other elements of the Criminal Investigations Bureau would further his rise to the top of the State Police chain of command. Although he was successful in climbing the career ladder, he did not always have confidence in how the department went about its personnel promotions.

12

Promotions in the Ranks

Richard CdeBaca's parents in La Cienega south of Santa Fe thought that their education-hungry son with a commanding presence would make an outstanding public school teacher and sought to guide him in that direction. Recently back from military service in the Korean War, the strapping young man was directed not toward a career in education but into the State Police by a ranking aide to the governor.

Once in uniform, CdeBaca excelled in his assignments, winning numerous recognitions from his superiors and repeated praise in the news media. Dedication to his charge and loyalty to those who gave him orders drove his success. "I grew up with good work ethics, taught to me at home by my father," he said. "I was disciplined with the Christian Brothers throughout high school, disciplined in the military and then disciplined more while going through basic training with the New Mexico State Police. It all molded me into an individual who was self-motivated. I did my job the best that I could and I minded my own business."

Well, CdeBaca minded his own business to a point. The ambitious young man, after nearly a decade with the State Police, began to question privately at least some of what transpired around him within the department. He made this entry in his records:

"By 1965, I was beginning to wonder if the department was ever going to offer competitive examinations for promotion. It seemed that a handful of promotions were made through the sole discretion of the chief or through the State Police Board political influence."

CdeBaca had first-hand knowledge accumulated during his posting in Southern New Mexico on which to base his doubts.

"Early one fall in Alamogordo, my sergeant, A.B. Munsey, ordered me to get up early the following morning and pick up one of the members of the State Police Board, then drive to Albuquerque and pick up the chairman of the board. The next day, the commissioner and I arrived at the commission chairman's house at 9 a.m. From there to Santa Fe, both of them sat in the back seat of my car. In no time, the conversation turned into police matters.

"By the time we got to the State Police headquarters for the 10 a.m. board meeting, a lot of wheeling and dealing had taken place. The chairman told the commissioner at his side that he wanted to promote Sergeant Munsey to lieutenant.

"Later, on our way back to Albuquerque, the commission chairman commented on how smooth the meeting had gone and what they had accomplished. Before the chairman got out of the car, he told me, 'What was discussed in this car stays in this car.'

"On our way back to Alamogordo, I asked the commissioner riding with me how the police chief had reacted to the promotion of Munsey and the commissioner answered, 'We had the votes.'"

CdeBaca recalls that he was driving his patrol car that day, a 1958 Chevrolet. He said he was in full police uniform; the two men who rode with him were in suits and ties. "What happened in the back seat of my car that day was a done deal. I was basically told to keep my mouth shut about it, and I did. I learned later that Sergeant Munsey had hired a relative of the commission chairman to work as a dispatcher in Alamogordo."

"Up to this time in my career, I was too naïve to understand internal affairs in the department, and I was too busy to care. But it bothered me to know that one police officer had been promoted in the back seat of my police car without competing for the promotion. Not only did Munsey get promoted to lieutenant, but he also got transferred to Portales, his home town."

CdeBaca made multiple entries in his records about Munsey, beginning with one that told of Munsey's arrival in Alamogordo.

"Sergeant Floyd Miles was transferred and replaced by Sergeant A.B. Munsey. We had been used to having an easy-going supervisor and we would miss him. Before Sergeant Munsey arrived in Alamogordo, we had heard rumors that he was in the horse breeding business. The rumors were confirmed when he moved his stud horse, Jack Straw, and other horses to the small village of La Luz.

"Jack Straw was a proven quarter horse stud and race horse owners were always bringing their brood mares to be bred to Jack Straw. There would be days when I would be on patrol on U.S. 70, north of Alamogordo and horse owners would stop and ask me for directions to Sergeant Munsey's stables."

CdeBaca said Munsey tolerated little dissention among officers around him. "Officer Rudy Gonzalez got in cross-wise with Sergeant Munsey and he had Gonzalez transferred from Alamogordo to Chama," CdeBaca said. "Another rookie officer who wasn't afraid to question the system, John Tixier, was also transferred out of Alamogordo.

"It was like J. Edgar Hoover in the old days at the FBI, transferring people if they bucked the system. I'm sure it happened in other districts, too, not just Alamogordo."

A welcomed crack in the old system finally came as CdeBaca began his tenth year on the force. Testing would be relied upon to select the next crop of sergeants.

"In September of 1965 an announcement was made that those officers eligible for promotion to sergeant would undergo testing. By law, any officer with five years or more became eligible for promotion to sergeant."

CdeBaca said the five-year law had meant little and was further minimized when what he called "an arbitrary rule" came down from the chief's office, saying officers needed to complete nine years of service before becoming eligible for promotion to sergeant.

"I had completed nine years and this would be my first opportunity to compete. There were 80-some officers that were eligible and word got out that only 10 would be promoted.

"I obtained books from the library on police examinations to prepare myself. During the process, we were given written tests, problem solving and oral interviews. A few days later, Chief Bradford met with the State Police Board and after the meeting, the names of those officers who were promoted were made public. Fortunately, I was one of those few promoted and the only Hispanic from those who were promoted.

"One week later I was told to report to Chief Bradford. When I did, he told me I was being transferred to Santa Rosa. I would be in charge of the officers stationed in Santa Rosa, Ft. Sumner and Vaughn, and I would answer to Captain Frank Lucero, the district commander in Las Vegas.

"My first official action was to visit the captain in Las Vegas to get my orders as to what he expected of me. While in Las Vegas, I visited with the district attorney, Donaldo 'Tiny' Martinez. He thanked me for visiting him and wished me well. His mother and my father were related."

As district attorney, Martinez arguably warranted a visit from the newly assigned sergeant to the area. But even while welcoming a crack in the internal politics of the State Police Department CdeBaca, with his visit of Martinez, a man of mounting influence, seems to have recognized an even-more entrenched political system, the one that drove so much of the public's business in Las Vegas.

Visible changes in the ranks of the State Police, actually, had begun even before the sudden change in the manner used to promote sergeants. Some were long overdue. "At the time of my commission, the New Mexico State Police was a predominantly Anglo-Saxon organization," said CdeBaca, whose father was Hispanic, his mother an Anglo from the Midwest. "Hispanics were the minority and there were no Native Americans, no African-Americans and no women. I do not recall that there were any priorities to recruit these minorities.

"When I was transferred to Santa Fe in 1963 and assigned to desk duties in the Records Office, Chief K.K. Miller called me into his office and told me that a committee in the Legislature had asked for a roster of Hispanic officers. Chief Miller directed me to compile the names of Hispanic officers and to include those who were Hispanic but had Anglo surnames. Apparently there was an awareness among legislators that not enough minorities were being hired and they were making an issue out of it by challenging the chief."

Other changes continued to unfold.

"In 1972, a group of five officers began a movement to unionize the department. A vote was taken among patrolmen and sergeants but the majority opposed it and that was the end of the union movement. However, in 1973 a New Mexico State Police Association was established, which has served its purpose well."

"In October of 1976, two women broke the all-male officer ranks for the first time in the history of the New Mexico State Police. We knew it was just a matter of time. This was nothing new for law enforcement. Other law enforcement departments had been hiring women.

"Immediately, questions were being asked, 'Are they going to be asking for back-up every time they arrest someone?' 'What will the department do when they get pregnant? Are they going to have to be taken off patrol?'

"Dorcas Bailey, one of the first women to be hired by the State Police put things in perspective when she said, 'It will probably take a while for the novelty of having women on the force to wear off.' However, officer Bailey did not stay with the department very long. No one in the department performed an exit interview in order to learn something from her experience."

"More changes came about when the minimum height of 5'10" was eliminated and the minimum age was dropped from 23 to 21 and later to 18. The Federal Labor Standards Act brought about significant work changes as well. It did away with 12- and 14-hour days. Now the department had to pay overtime for any time worked over 40 hours, double time for holidays."

CdeBaca said efforts were being made not only to increase the professionalism of the department but to ensure that it had a broader, more diverse pool from which to fill its ranks. Some of the changes were long overdue, said CdeBaca. "There hadn't been much change to the status quo and when change came, it wasn't always real clean. Early in the 1960's, the state attorney general issued an opinion that sought to deal with nepotism, saying that a State Police officer could not be related to a member of the State Police Board. But there was nothing to prohibit State Police officers from being related to each other. It meant that father and son, uncles and nephews, brothers and cousins could serve in the State Police."

It was 1976 when the first women were enlisted in the New Mexico State Police. Thirty years later, Sergeant Jennie Pierce employed her skills at Cochiti Lake as part of the State Police dive team. Photo by Karl Stolleis, *The New Mexican.*

CdeBaca was called upon to help police departments outside New Mexico address mounting concerns and complaints of minorities.

"When the Federal Office of Equal Opportunity caught up with police departments that had discriminated in promoting minority officers, it forced chiefs across the country to evaluate their method of promotions. Some came up with a creative idea and established assessment centers and staffing them with non-biased ranking officers from other departments to perform the oral evaluations for promotion.

"The Louisville Police Department requested that a Hispanic officer be assigned to be a part of their assessment center and Chief Martin Vigil assigned me. Those of us assigned spent four days interviewing officers eligible for promotion. The Louisville Police Department had problems promoting blacks. After we were done with our oral interviews, we recommended two black officers for promotion."

"I was assigned to participate in another assessment center in Denver, Colorado. The Denver Police Department was having its own problems promoting minorities. Some chiefs of police welcomed this method of evaluating officers but other chiefs preferred promoting their own officers without outside assistance. The assessment center only made recommendations based on a consensus. It didn't mean that the chief had to take the assessment center's recommendations. But it did put some pressure on the chiefs."

CdeBaca said he personally had never experienced discrimination based on ethnicity even though other officers around him claimed that they had. CdeBaca acknowledged that Martin Vigil, a Hispanic who became chief in 1969, mentored him and seemingly decided to groom him for advancement in the department.

13

Challenges to the Department's Integrity

When challenges to the integrity of the New Mexico State Police arise, perhaps no case is mentioned more often than the decades-old murder mystery involving Ovida "Cricket" Coogler. Coogler was a reckless, petite 18-year-old Las Cruces waitress. Her 1949 brutal demise, the apparent conspiracy to conceal the killer or killers and a reckless zeal to pin the death on an innocent man have been linked to ranking government officials of the time, including State Police Chief Hubert Beasley.

More recently, the man with the longest tenure as State Police chief ran into his own firestorm of controversy late in the 1970's. Martin Vigil faced multiple accusations, including attempts to link him to his own wife's death.

Richard CdeBaca was mentored by Vigil. His records include notations on both Vigil and Beasley. First, Beasely:

> "One of the worse cases of civil rights violations and the most notorious one that took place in the department was in the 1949 murder of Ovida 'Cricket' Coogler investigation. This case involved a cover-up by law enforcement, exposed illegal gambling and prostitution operations in Southern New Mexico. It tainted the reputations of some state politicians who used to frequent Doña Ana County gambling houses.
>
> "In this case, State Police Chief Hubert Beasley and others were convicted of torturing a black suspect by the name of Wesley Eugene Byrd to obtain a confession from him. Mr. Byrd suffered a terrible injustice and was later freed. However, Chief Beasley and the other officials were sentenced to serve time in a federal prison. The Coogler murder was never solved."

Beasely, a 48-year-old Tennessee native who had settled in Tucumcari, was convicted by a federal jury in Santa Fe of civil rights violations after jurors heard sworn testimony that he and Doña Ana County Sheriff A.L. Happy Apodaca applied two padlocks around a 28-year-old mechanic's penis and part of his testicles while trying to get a confession.[1] Apodaca, 37, was convicted on the same charge of violating Wesley Byrd's civil rights plus one that alleged conspiracy to violate those rights. One of Apodaca's deputies also was convicted of conspiracy.[2]

Byrd was described as "a slender, good-looking, volatile man who was not shy with women."[3] He married a Santa Fe County woman who said he was the biggest liar she had ever known.[4]

When the Coogler case broke, Governor Thomas Mabry sent in Beasley to direct the state's investigation and called him the best police chief ever to serve New Mexico.[5] It was Mabry who accepted Beasley's resignation following his conviction.[6]

For Vigil, biting criticism during the 1970s started with investigative reports by the weekly *Rio Grande Sun* in Española, Vigil's hometown. Vigil joined the State Police in 1946, three years before Beasley's career-ending controversy. Republican Governor David Cargo, who was popular in much of Northern New Mexico, appointed Vigil chief in December 1969.

Criticism directed at Vigil a decade into his tenure as chief began with questions about how he chose and supervised those around him. CdeBaca was serving as a major under Vigil at the time. The *Sun*, in a series of articles, suggested that the State Police under Vigil were no match for the growing number of drug dealers and killers who remained unidentified and on the loose.

Lesser accusations soon were aimed directly at Vigil and members of his family.

"In 1978, the *Rio Grande Sun* newspaper in Española began publishing a series of articles critical of law enforcement. The first article written by Ms. Sally Denton asked the question, 'Are investigations of homicides and other violent crimes in Rio Arriba County bungled by incompetents or deliberately covered up?' Other stories alleged law enforcement agencies were aware of heroin trafficking but did nothing about it. The State Police were the target of most of Ms. Denton's allegations. The *Sun* reported that Chief Martin Vigil had covered up the arrests of his two sons in separate incidents, one north of Santa Fe and the other in Portales.

"The *Sun* articles produced citizen outcry for an investigation into seven unsolved murders in the area alleged to be tied with drug trafficking. A citizen's group from Rio Arriba County made an appointment with Governor Jerry Apodaca, demanding an investigation. One case that generated a lot of publicity was the Laura Dupree murder. There were rumors that a State Police officer in Española had had a relationship with Ms. Dupree.

"Chief Vigil assigned me to meet with Governor Apodaca and assure him that we would name a special investigative team which would be supervised by Captain T.J. Chavez. Most of these murders were old and had been investigated by different jurisdictions—the county sheriff's department, city police and Indian police—and had not cooperated exchanging information. Captain Chavez was allowed to pick his own investigators. He requested Sergeant Jim Sedillo, Agents Willie Garcia, Gilbert Silva and Leo Martinez. I hired Cecilia Baca from Chamita as their personal secretary.

"The special team was furnished with an office in Española. Not many days after the investigation was under way, Ms. Sally Denton began calling me and criticizing me for lack of support to the team. I don't know where she was getting her information from. Captain Chavez didn't complain to me about lack of support.

"After several months of investigative work, the special team did not come up with sufficient evidence to indict anyone. Finally, Captain Chavez and I agreed to disband the special team. Captain Chavez was instructed to brief Governor Apodaca. To this day, it remains a mystery who killed all these women."

In time, the *Sun* wasn't the only publication stirring concern about the unsolved cases. An article with an Española dateline that was distributed by the New York Times News Service reported: "The state attorney general believes that Rio Arriba County has a serious drug smuggling problem, both in marijuana and heroin. The head of the State Police believes it, the district attorney believes it, the local newspaper believes it. But no one believes much of anything is being done about it."

The article told of a grand jury having been impaneled and then disbanded without being able to issue indictments. "The grand jury concluded that the biggest problem the police have is a shortage of manpower," the article reported.

Vigil had been wounded by the controversy, which attracted statewide publicity. Some ranking members of the State Police apparently sensed an opportunity to oust their chief and shake up the agency. "Several ranking officers were positioning themselves to become chief even though there had been no indication that Chief Martin Vigil was going anywhere," CdeBaca said. "While talking with one of these officers, he told me he'd like to see Chief Vigil run over by a dump truck."

CdeBaca made this entry in his records:

"A handful of dissident officers, mostly supervisors, were conspiring to have Chief Martin Vigil removed from office. It began with a sergeant delivering a copy of the arrest of one of Chief Vigil's sons to Albuquerque Senator Eddie Barboa at his office at the Legislature. Also, a report was circulating among senators, claiming that Chief Vigil had bungled a drug smuggling operation by not cooperating with the Maricopa County Sheriff's office in Arizona, which was not true."

The tenacious Española weekly soon re-entered the picture and accusations grew nastier.

"The *Rio Grande Sun* published reports that Chief Vigil had covered up the arrest of his two sons for possession of marijuana and that he had destroyed the arrest report. He was also accused of using the State Police aircraft to fly to Portales to get one of his sons out of jail. The most disturbing accusation was that he was responsible for his wife's death.

"The district attorney, Eloy Martinez, impaneled a grand jury to look into allegations contained in the *Rio Grande Sun*. Sergeant Al Miller, Sergeant Tommy Holder and one of Chief Vigil's sons were called to testify as was Captain T.J. Chavez and others. As custodian of the records in the Criminal Investigations Bureau, I was the last one called to testify.

"I produced the original arrest report of Chief Vigil's son."

CdeBaca said that he had taken it upon himself to put the arrest report of Chief Vigil's son away for safe-keeping. "Too many things were disappearing from within headquarters during this period when information that appeared in the papers was being fed to reporters by insiders," he said. "I told the grand jury: 'Let's set the record straight. There have been a lot of allegations about Chief Vigil.' I reached into my attaché case and showed them the original arrest report. I knew that copies had already been made and distributed to the news media. I made the decision to confiscate the original report and lock it up and it had been in my possession ever since.

"I told the grand jury that when Chief Vigil was advised of his son's arrest he told the arresting officers, 'Do what you have to do.' I took that to mean: Do your job and don't be intimidated by my position. I don't think charges were ever filed against anyone in that case," CdeBaca said.

He also testified about allegations made against the chief regarding the drug smuggling case, which originated with the Maricopa Sheriff's Office. There was no truth to reports that Chief Vigil had refused to offer assistance, he said.

> "When it was all over, one juror recommended to the district attorney that two officers who testified be charged with perjury for lying. The juror did not specify their names in my presence. The chief was cleared of any wrongdoing and the grand jury report was sealed, meaning it would never be made public.
> "Chief Vigil sued the *Rio Grande Sun*."

Vigil sued even though there was truth to at least some of what had been reported. The chief, for example, did take a State Police plane to Portales to help one of his sons following an arrest.

Vigil's wife, Theresa, died in January 1976 of an apparent overdose of prescription drugs, according to news reports. CdeBaca said he had had a conversation with Mrs. Vigil just days earlier in which she said, "You won't see me after the first of the year." It was at a little Christmas party at Martin Vigil's house. I didn't know what she meant by it at the time. I didn't mention anything about it to the chief and have lived with it the rest of my life."

Vigil eventually dropped his libel suit against the *Sun*. It was dropped "in exchange for the offending newspaper simply running a story about (Vigil's) retirement," wrote author Roger Morris.[7] Robert Trapp, founding editor and publisher of the *Sun,* said for this book that he was never worried about being able to defend his paper's position against allegations made in Vigil's lawsuit.

Vigil died in April 1993.

Prior to the public and private storm that swirled around Vigil, the chief had appointed CdeBaca to begin a unit within the State Police intended to ferret out corruption and other misconduct within the department. CdeBaca had just completed an extraordinarily successful administration of the agency's Communications Division (More on this in Chapter 14).

"In June of 1973, Chief Martin Vigil took me out of the Communications Division and assigned me to establish the Office of Internal Affairs. The Office of Internal Affairs would become the investigative arm of the department. Previously, complaints against officers would be handled at the district level and each commander had his own standards of reprimanding officers, and there was no real uniformity.

"Sometimes officers are falsely accused and it becomes the responsibility of the department to exonerate them. My orders were to report directly to the chief and on any investigation I made and whatever conclusions and recommendations I made, he had the final authority to make a decision.

"Chief Vigil promoted Sergeant C.E. Tow to lieutenant and assigned him to assist me. These investigations were time consuming because we had to travel great distances to interview officers and witnesses. In most investigations, officers were cleared of any wrongdoing."

Some officers were left wishing that they had been exonerated. Here are some of CdeBaca's entries from the period:

"Chief Vigil assigned myself and Major M.S. Chavez, the northern zone commander, to investigate a complaint against the district commander in Gallup, including some of the officers under his command. The complaint alleged that they were defrauding Ford Motor Company by installing AM/FM radios in their police cars and charging the installation to the vehicle warranty, claiming they were mechanical repairs. The local car dealer went along with it.

"In those days, State Police cars were not equipped with factory radios. Some officers used to carry portable radios even though it was against department rules.

"The allegations against these officers in Gallup proved to be true. Chief Vigil reprimanded the captain and transferred him. The officers under his command who were guilty of the same thing also received letters of reprimand.

"We recommended to the chief that future police cars be equipped with factory radios. It made no sense not to have them. From that day, all police cars were ordered with factory radios."

"Complaints of all different types kept coming in to the chief's office. Two officers were accused of selling Indian jewelry out of the trunks of their police cars. One officer was accused of selling Hatch green chili. A captain was accused of accepting a hindquarter of beef from a rancher north of Española and transporting it to his home in the trunk of his police car. One officer during an inspection was transporting piñon for sale in the trunk of his police car. All of the above incidents proved to be true.

"Frivolous lawsuits were filed against officers, alleging excessive force during arrests. The majority of these lawsuits were dismissed."

Bribing of State Police officers was not nearly as common as some in the public might have suspected, CdeBaca said. He said the only offer he got while on patrol came along busy Route 66 when a Chicago man offered him $50 to escape a traffic ticket.

"I would not have taken a bribe of any amount," CdeBaca said. "The New Mexico State Police is a paramilitary organization and is held to higher standards. Anything less than that is not acceptable to the public, who places its trust in law enforcement. Very few officers would risk their job by accepting some small bribe."

Perhaps. Yet CdeBaca's own notations show how officers might go out of their way to create conditions where small amounts of money can buy favors.

"Among all the duties I was assigned to, I was still classifying fingerprints and teaching classes. One day a clerk in the bureau brought to my attention a series of missing traffic tickets. Copies of all the tickets are required to be submitted to headquarters for filing. This discrepancy was brought to the attention of the chief. An investigation revealed that two officers from the Santa Fe District were writing tickets for DUI and then dismissing them. There were allegations that the officers were accepting money. The officers hired attorney Fred Stanley to defend them before the State Police Board. Both received 30-day suspensions without pay and were transferred."

There are plenty of temptations, CdeBaca acknowledged, for the few officers who are willing to stray and risk their careers. "What has lured officers to money is the profits in drugs and there have been cases documented that State Police officers got themselves into trouble because they were tempted to make quick money with the sale of drugs," he said.

He made this notation about such a case that came after he had assumed duties outside the Internal Affairs Office:

"In 1980, a narcotics agent was arrested by agents of the federal Drug Enforcement Administration on charges of possession with intent to distribute marijuana. When the agent appeared for sentencing before federal Judge Edwin Mechem, the judge told the agent that he was giving him the maximum sentence allowed by law to set an example and to discourage other police officers from doing the same thing.

"Our legal advisor and I debriefed the agent and he admitted being lured by the money from the sale of drugs. He said, 'The temptation was always there and inventory controls were very lax.' The agent was a well-liked policeman and I heard other officers say that he was 'set up.'"

Sex, like quick money from drugs, must always be considered among temptations capable of derailing police careers, CdeBaca said.

"One case that merits attention is that of a sergeant who had complaints against him for stopping women and propositioning them. On one occasion, he admitted having consensual sex with a woman in the back seat of his police car. The victim complained that he had forced her to have sex, which in fact was not true. She recanted her story when I interviewed her.

"Chief Vigil wanted to demote and transfer the sergeant but the State Police Board spoke in his defense and he was only transferred. One day while attempting to light the pilot to the furnace located in the basement, there was an explosion and he suffered severe burns to his hands and face. He was retired on a medical condition."

"Another officer who graduated with me from the basic training was caught by a Bernalillo County deputy with a 13-year-old boy in the police car in a remote area. This officer had been reported for this same kind of behavior on a previous occasion. The officer, who had been with the department for 17 years and attained the rank of sergeant, resigned.

"One day I was in Carrizozo on an investigation and I ran into him at a local restaurant. He told me he was living out of a dump truck. Years later, he died partially paralyzed in a nursing home where he was committed after stumbling and hitting the back of his head on a coffee table."

And, of course, there are cases of police misconduct—whether true or contrived—that end up costing the taxpayers, CdeBaca said. Here's one of his notations about a case that wove through a dispute over jurisdiction, a dispute that the arresting officer seemingly was ill-prepared to handle:

"This complaint involved the governor of Pojoaque Pueblo, who filed a lawsuit alleging that his rights were violated when an officer arrested him for drunk driving inside the reservation and then jailed him in the Santa Fe City Jail. While being transported to Santa Fe, Governor Jacob Viarrial told the officer that he should be taken before the tribal court but the officer ignored him.

"The department decided not to defend the lawsuit in court and the state Risk Management Division settled the case for $40,000.

"Many other civil lawsuits have resulted in similar settlements."

Taxpayers often are required to bear other costs associated with alleged police misconduct, as seen in this notation by CdeBaca:

"The most misunderstood policy is when an officer is accused of wrong-doing and the officer is placed on paid administrative leave. Some officers have gone on to second jobs while being paid by the department. This may last weeks and months.

"One officer attended St.. Mary's University in San Antonio, Texas, while on paid administrative leave.

"The general public has never accepted this. In private industry, which I have experience in, an employee accused of wrongdoing is terminated, and not placed on paid leave."

Public records of the state Legislative Finance Committee from May and June of 2005 show that some State Police officers had drawn pay for six to 24 months while on leave for legal reasons. Steps were being taken to correct conditions that department administrators asserted required them to provide such payments.

CdeBaca was still directing the Internal Affairs Office when Chief Vigil promoted him to major.

14

Building an Academy and State-of-the-Art Communications

Even under the old standards of basic police communication, law enforcement in New Mexico often fell on the laps of people who were ill prepared to get from Point A to Point B. Consider this entry in the records of Richard CdeBaca:

> "In the 1950s, there were not many police departments in New Mexico with police standards. Some police officers were hired because of whom they knew at city hall, and Alamogordo was no exception. One night, I was visiting with the radio dispatcher when a man came in asking for one of the city officers by name. The officer was about 70 years of age. J.D. McDaniels, the dispatcher, radioed the officer and the call went like this: 'Alamogordo to Alamo 2.' The elderly officer answered, 'This is Alamo 2.' 'Headquarters to Alamo 2, if you are not 10-6 (busy), 10-19 (report to the office); 10-12 (visitor) 10-23 (standing by); 10-4 (acknowledge).'
>
> "Complete silence for a moment from the officer, then we heard him reply, "Speak to me in English."

Then there was the night that the same poorly trained officer was riding with another policeman while in pursuit of a speeding car.

> "I was in the office and I took off to try to help them stop the car. A few minutes after the chase began, it was called off. I found out that Alamogordo City Police officer Frank Ochoa was driving the patrol car and ordered his 70-year-old companion to roll down the window of their unit and try to shoot the tires out of the speeding car.
>
> "The elderly officer stuck his revolver out the window and began to fire.

His first shot put a hole through the spotlight mounted on the right side of the police car. The second round put a hole in the police car's right front fender. Officer Ochoa gave up the chase and drove to State Police headquarters to examine the damage. I don't know if the elderly officer had ever fired his gun before."

Situations like that, said CdeBaca, made it clear to some of the state's highest-ranking police officers that substantial improvements needed to be made in the training of personnel as well as in the equipment on which they relied upon to communicate and otherwise carry out their responsibilities. "At the smaller police departments, if people had pull with the chief or the mayor they might be hired as officers on the spot without any training whatsoever," he said.

Major changes began unfolding after the surprise election of Republican David Cargo as governor in 1966.

"When David F. Cargo was elected, Chief John Bradford retired and Governor Cargo appointed Captain Joe Black to replace him. Chief Black called me and fellow sergeant, Don Moberly, to his office and told us he was assigning us to the Legislature. Chief Black explained to us that one of his top priorities was to get the Legislature to appropriate money to build a State Police Training Academy, and he wanted us to convince the legislators.

"This was a mighty tall order, having to coordinate planning with Senator Edmundo Delgado, the sponsor of the bill and Philippe Register, the architect for the project.

"The State Police had been leasing the facilities at the Glorieta Baptist Assembly and it just made good sense to have our own training facility. Besides, training at the Baptist Assembly could only be done on a seasonal basis, since the Assembly was occupied through the summer months. Chief Black told us in no uncertain terms that he wanted the academy built in Santa Fe and nowhere else.

"One major move in our favor is that Santa Fe City Mayor Pat Hollis cooperated with us and offered 35 acres south of Santa Fe to build the academy and promised to provide water and sewer services to the site.

"It took time to convince our legislators of the necessity of such a training facility and how it would upgrade the quality of law enforcement in New Mexico,"

CdeBaca said. "The state to that point did not provide training facilities. I graduated from training in the barracks at the old Army Bruns hospital in Santa Fe. You could see daylight through the walls of those dormitories, if you want to call them that.

"The state then turned to leasing facilities at the Glorieta Baptist center. Training had to be arranged around the center's schedule. Joe Black took over as chief, recognizing that the state was always paying someone for the use of their facilities to train police officers."

Capitol and hometown politics quickly came into play as CdeBaca, Moberly and Black worked on lawmakers.

"When the bill to create the State Police Academy was introduced by Senator Delgado, it was assigned to the Senate Finance Committee. It didn't take much time to discover who was our main opposition to the bill. Senator Penrod Toles, representing Chaves County, was adamantly opposed to building the academy in Santa Fe. His argument was that the abandoned Walker Air Force Base in Roswell was the ideal place for such a facility.

"Despite his efforts to kill the bill, it received a 'do-pass' vote in the committee. A few days later, the bill went before the full Senate, where it passed by a unanimous vote. The bill was then referred to the House Appropriations and Finance Committee.

"We realized the vote was going to be very close in the committee, and we contacted every member of the panel. The chairman, Representative John Mershon, would not make a commitment.

"When the bill came up for a hearing before the committee, Chief Black, Senator Delgado, the architect Phil Register, Sergeant Moberly and I testified on its behalf. The bill was killed in committee by one vote and it was Representative Mershon's vote that prevented it from passing.

"Chief Black was very disappointed and so were we, but I mentioned to the chief that we did not have the necessary time to do the planning."

Only a few months passed before Black called upon the two sergeants whom he had assigned to the Legislature to prepare to renew their battle for an academy. This time there would be a major change in strategy, one that was not immediately embraced by Black.

"In November of 1967, Chief Black assigned myself and Sergeant Moberly to pursue again the work of establishing the Law Enforcement Academy. We took a more-aggressive approach to garner support for the proposed academy. This time we had two months to prepare feasibility studies to be submitted to key members of the Legislature.

"Sergeant Don Moberly and I were very busy with our plans for the police training academy as 1968 began. Sergeant Moberly and I visited with everyone else in law enforcement we could talk to about the proposed academy. In discussing the plans with one representative, we learned that the reason some were opposed to it was because they wanted an academy that would include all law enforcement agencies and not just the State Police, which was ignorance on their part. The academy that we wanted would have trained more than State Police officers. But apparently we had not done our homework in clearing that misunderstanding the previous year.

"We recommended to Chief Black that the name should be changed from State Police Academy to New Mexico Law Enforcement Academy and explained to him why. Reluctantly, he agreed to change the name, if it meant passage of the bill.

"Senator Delgado drafted a new bill designating it as the New Mexico Law Enforcement Academy, creating an independent board which would set policy for the operation of the academy."

One hurdle had been crossed but another yet remained. Crossing this one would require more than a simple name change. It would require addressing well-founded concerns of a hard-hit community hundreds of miles away and those of the region's legislators.

"We made arrangements to meet with Senator Toles, the Mayor of Roswell and area representatives. On January 7, we flew Senator Delgado to Roswell. After we met with the local delegation, we were given a tour of Walker Air Force Base, which had been closed by President Lyndon B. Johnson. We were shown the buildings there that could be used for training.

"The abandoned structures would need some remodeling but they were in good condition. What would not be feasible is that the entire training staff would have to be moved from Santa Fe, and we would never own the facilities.

"With Santa Fe being the seat of state government, it would be very difficult to do state business from Roswell. We were also shown military houses that were vacant and could be occupied for practically no cost. The mayor and other officials were doing their best to lure new industry to Roswell to revitalize the local economy."

Back at the Legislature, the law enforcement academy bill faced familiar foes but attracted open support from key quarters.

"Senator Delgado's bill establishing the Law Enforcement Academy was referred to the Senate Finance Committee, as it had been the previous year. The construction of the academy would be paid out of severance taxes in the amount of $2.5 million. Governor David Cargo came out publicly endorsing the academy and said he would sign the bill if it got to his desk.

"Senator Toles spoke against the bill, but it got a 'do pass' recommendation in committee. When the bill came up for debate before the whole Senate, Sergeant Moberly and I were in the gallery listening to Senator Toles trying to kill the bill. Senator Toles accused me of submitting a biased report on the Walker Air Force Base facilities. Over his objections, the bill passed by a good majority."

CdeBaca said Toles was not working against law enforcement; he was working to help his constituents battle back against depressed times. "Senator Toles was not opposed to having a training academy. What he was opposed to was the location that we proposed, arguing that facilities already existed in Roswell. It was a sound argument on his part because Roswell was hurting after the Air Force base had been closed."

With the Senate won, CdeBaca and others turned their attention again to the House of Representatives.

"The bill was assigned to the House Appropriations and Finance Committee, where it had failed to pass the previous session. Chief Black was apprehensive about the bill being killed in the House Appropriations and Finance Committee and he told us, 'I hope you have done your homework.'

"Senator Delgado and Chief Black knew that if this bill passed, it would be a feather in their hats, but they also knew that Representative John Mershon was a force to be reckoned with. He ruled the committee with an iron fist.

"As soon as the bill was scheduled for a hearing, Sergeant Moberly and I wasted no time calling every sheriff and police chief we had talked to on our visits throughout the state. We asked them to please call and telegram every member on the committee and we furnished them with the names and telephone numbers. We constantly checked with the mail clerk to monitor the incoming telegrams. The committee members were inundated with telegrams and telephone calls. We contacted every committee member and asked them for their support.

"The day of the hearing, the bill generated a lot of discussion. We got called to testify. When the final vote was called for by Chairman Mershon, the bill got a 'do pass' recommendation, and we were all ecstatic, even though it was not the final step. The House of Representatives would have to vote on it.

"We had Representative Bruce King, who was speaker of the House, carry the bill on the floor. At the time the vote was being taken, Representative Bill Shrecengost got up and told the representatives that Sergeant CdeBaca and Sergeant Moberly were up in the gallery listening and that if they didn't vote for this bill, they would be getting tickets. The bill passed by a majority vote. We already had assurances from Governor Cargo that he would sign the bill, which he ultimately did.

"During the legislative session, the Senate passed a memorial (No. 44) complimenting me for my friendly and helpful attitude and for serving with distinction at all times, especially during various emergencies. It referred to me as one of the finest members of the New Mexico State Police force, and that I symbolized the great dedication to the public welfare. This was a great honor for me.

"With the New Mexico Law Enforcement Academy approved, Chief Black would now leave a legacy, something he had wanted from the day he was appointed chief. On April 10, Chief Black called me and Sergeant Moberly to his office, congratulated us on a job well done and promoted us to lieutenant. I was named assistant director of the Criminal Investigations Bureau."

If Black considered the academy his legacy, CdeBaca also was moved by the success of their two-year effort. "It was my pride and joy," he said. "If I was to be asked what was my major contribution to the department, the one thing that I am most proud of, without hesitation I would say it was having worked under Chief Joe Black and having been selected to lobby for the funding to create the New Mexico Law Enforcement Training Academy.

"Chief Joe Black retired in 1969 and Captain Martin Vigil was appointed to replace him. Chief Black did not get to see the completion of the Law Enforcement Training Academy, but he had participated in the ground-breaking ceremonies."

CdeBaca said the training academy soon made an impact. "A retired police officer, Bill Norris, who served 21 years in the Los Alamos Police Department and retired from the Santa Fe Police Department related that at one time, the local police looked up to the State Police and that this was the general perception of the public," he said. "The required training at the law enforcement academy and the certification of all law enforcement officers that comes with it has leveled the playing field. Sheriff departments continue to grow, and they are putting their footprints into every aspect of law enforcement while at one time years ago they were primarily involved in the civil process."

"Political hirings in police departments have been sharply reduced or eliminated in most places. Exhaustive background checks are made of all applicants, which eliminate many of them. Because of the method of selection and the extensive training, law enforcement has become more professional."

It was more than the training academy that grew out of the effort spearheaded by Black. "Funding for a State Police crime lab was part of the package that was approved by the Legislature, which definitely improved the quality of crime-solving," CdeBaca said. "It took the State Police almost 40 years before it entered the realm of police science ... Previously, we relied upon the FBI crime lab for forensic science examination. It translated into long waits for results to come back.

"With the inception of our own crime lab, came the expediency of solving more cases. It helped with successful prosecution because of the expertise that came out of our lab's results. It was definitely a big boost not only to the New Mexico State Police but to other law enforcement agencies."

While still working as a sergeant, CdeBaca had been named director of the State Police communications office. Black relied upon him while in that office to secure needed advances that would complement the new training academy.

"Prior to Colonel Black's retirement as chief, he had assigned me to attend the National Crime Information Center training sponsored by the FBI in Washington, D.C. This was the most advanced tool in law enforcement in having an automated system to track fugitives and stolen vehicles. I got to meet J. Edgar Hoover, FBI director, when he welcomed us to the FBI training program.

"The NCIC terminal was installed in the criminal bureau. Access to NCIC came via Teletype messages addressed to the radio room at headquarters then the dispatcher would have to telephone the NCIC operator and wait for a response. This was a cumbersome way for an officer to get a return on a driver or a vehicle license number but it was a vast improvement over the old method of officers having to make telephone calls."

"In August 1970, Colonel Vigil promoted me to captain. I was elected president of the New Mexico Public Safety Association and later was elected president for the Mountain West Region. I traveled extensively, attending seminars and conferences and in so doing, I got exposed to the different communications systems in the different states.

"As communications director for the New Mexico State Police, it was my responsibility to oversee the telephone, radio and Teletype communications. A new state-of-the-art telephone system had been installed before we moved to the new State Police headquarters in south Santa Fe. In addition, the low-band radio frequency of 39.9 that had been used forever was upgraded to a high-band frequency. This eliminated radio transmissions from other police departments, including interference from as far away as Maine. We used to hear officers in Maine telling their dispatcher to repeat the call because they were getting interference from them 'New Mexico cowboys.'

"Upgrading the Teletype network became the next priority. The Model 28 Teletype machines had served the department well but they were becoming obsolete and finding parts for them was a problem.

"I contacted the Mountain Bell regional director in Albuquerque and asked him if he could spare one of their data specialists to assist me in modernizing the State Police Teletype system. After I explained what I wanted to accomplish, he could see monetary gains for Mountain Bell. He called an employee by the name of Jon Evans and told him he was going to be assigned to a project to work with the State Police on a part-time basis. This was the same Jon Evans I had given a ticket for drag racing when I was stationed in Alamogordo. I asked him if he remembered me and he said, 'What a coincidence.'

"Over time, Jon Evans and I became good friends. We traveled to other states to get acquainted with their communications network. In Phoenix, Arizona, Western Systems introduced us to the latest line of Teletype hardware. In Dallas, Texas, Texas Instruments demonstrated the state-of-the-art computer switchers. Many months went into planning and designing a unique communications network for law enforcement in New Mexico."

Laying of that groundwork produced results.

"On June 21, 1972, the New Mexico State Police took a giant leap forward in the handling and exchange of police information. With the installation of a computer switcher and Model 37 ASR Teletypewriters, messages could be transmitted automatically, thereby eliminating manual transfers. The department and other law enforcement agencies were able to add speed and flexibility in the exchange of information.

"Remote terminals now had direct access to the Law Enforcement Teletype System, the National Law Enforcement Teletype System and the National Crime Information Center. We traveled hundreds of miles training 275 communications equipment operators throughout the state. The installation of this communications system was made possible through a Law Enforcement Administration grant in the amount of $36,000.

"The National Teletype Publication gave the department recognition for pioneering a new system in teletype communications."

It was a big jump. "We now had a system for sharing information across the country," CdeBaca said. "Before all this, let's say that someone at a remote terminal in Las Cruces wanted to send a teletype to Cleveland, Ohio. Maybe, the remote terminal operator in Las Cruces would send a teletype message to State Police headquarters in Santa Fe. The teletype operator in Santa Fe had to take the tape that was received from Las Cruces and transfer that tape to the National Law Enforcement Teletype System.

"Many times, they had these tapes, which resembled ribbons, just hanging there, waiting for availability for the national system to pick up on behalf of our far-off community that sent it in.

"As our State Police communications director, I appeared before the national Law Enforcement Teletype Board and proposed that we get rid of this cumbersome method of transmitting information from one state to another. I told them of our new Teletype switcher at headquarters in Santa Fe that had the capability to do an electronic transfer bypassing headquarters and going directly, say, from Las Cruces, New Mexico, to Cleveland, Ohio."

CdeBaca said he encountered skepticism. "The national board was concerned that there would be too much garbage that could not be monitored because information was bypassing the main terminal. They feared it would clutter everything in the exchange of information."

CdeBaca said he persuaded the national board to let him run a pilot program. "I had to train all the radio dispatchers that handled the Teletype that if we were going to be successful with this proposal, I would have to rely on them to be able to discipline the system. It was so successful that within about three months, the National Law Enforcement Teletype Board lifted the restriction, thereby opening direct communication from state to state.

"Since we pioneered this new system of sharing information, the national board gave formal recognition to the New Mexico State Police."

15

Working among the Politicians, Celebrities

Unaware that he eventually would be assigned to lobby legislators in the state Capitol, Richard CdeBaca in 1964 was posted at the old statehouse, now part of the Bataan Memorial Building, to provide security. Chief John Bradford, newly appointed by Governor Jack Campbell to head the State Police, gave CdeBaca his orders.

This woman, who did not give her name, reportedly told Richard CdeBaca that she would not leave the state Capitol until he agreed to pose with her for a picture.

The variety of incidents that he came upon rivaled what he had encountered as a patrolman on the highways. He wrote in his records:

"On March 13, 1965, I was paged to report to the Senate chambers reference an emergency. I found Senator Vincent Vesely lying on the floor, apparently the victim of a heart attack. I administered first aid until the ambulance arrived. He was still conscious when he was picked up by the ambulance but died in the emergency room shortly after his arrival.

"Senator Vesely was from Silver City. After his funeral, I received a very nice letter from Mrs. Vesely thanking me for helping her husband."

The new Capitol, the Roundhouse, opened in 1966 and promptly began generating drama of its own.

"One day, Sergeant A.P. Wickard and I were in the House gallery when two young men got by the assistant sergeant-at-arms who was standing at the door to the House chambers and started shouting at the legislators. The sergeant-at-arms locked the door to prevent anyone else from entering. I obtained a rope from the media room next to the gallery and lowered myself to the House floor. The speaker ordered us to escort the two demonstrators out of the building and keep them from returning. Sergeant Wickard could not believe seeing me rappel down into the House chamber. To this day, Wickard still talks about it."

"On another occasion while the House of Representatives was in session, I was standing in the gallery when a local artist and activist by the name of Tommy Macaione stood up in the gallery and at the top of his voice said, 'Mr. Speaker, I arise on a point of personal privilege.'

"Everyone in the house chambers looked up to see who would be so daring as to interfere with the session. The House speaker, seeing me standing in the gallery, banged his gavel and said, 'Officer CdeBaca, please escort the gentleman out of the gallery.'

"I told Mr. Macaione, 'You heard the speaker. Let's get out of here.' He replied, 'I know my rights,' and I answered, "So do I,' and grabbed him by the arm and escorted him out. The man's clothing was covered with dog hair and I got it all over my uniform. Mr. Macaione owned at least a dozen dogs."

Liquor, whether as a topic of debate or a beverage to be consumed, seemingly never had trouble generating drama. CdeBaca alluded to one piece of legislation while recalling an incident that occurred at La Fonda Hotel just down the street from the Capitol years earlier. Frank "Pancho" Padilla, president of the New Mexico Liquor Dealers Association, was in the thick of it.

"There was plenty of debate one legislative session over a bill that called for making it legal to sell liquor in the state on Sundays. The liquor lobby was strong. A Mr. Frank 'Pancho' Padilla, who was director of the retail liquor association, told Senator Fabián Chávez at a local bar in 1963 that he 'owned the Legislature.' The news media got word of it and the legislators didn't take his remarks too kindly and barred him from the Legislature.

"Mr. Padilla also made the same remark to me. He was outspoken and the legislators knew him well."

CdeBaca said Padilla also boasted to him about the influence that his association's contributions to lawmakers had secured him. "He told me that he owned the Legislature. I was in uniform and stationed in a hallway outside the House of Representatives. He was a powerful lobbyist and he knew how to get the legislators' attention."

Reports of bribes from the liquor industry were common but CdeBaca said he never saw money change hands while working among lawmakers. "I was never in a position to see that happen. What I did see now and then came when a senator or representative would ask me to give them a ride back to their hotel when I was assigned to security," he said.

"One evening, Representative Louis Romero from McKinley County asked me to give him a ride to La Posada, where he was staying. Inside his room, he showed me a case of hard liquor, which he said had been given to him by the liquor lobby."

It was a vote on a liquor bill in the state Senate that one year ignited rage in a lieutenant governor. He had just cast a tie-breaking vote on the measure and was called on the carpet by the governor.

"One morning before the Senate convened, I got paged to report to Lieutenant Governor E. Lee Francis's office. He was livid and told me that he wanted to get a restraining order on Governor Cargo. When I asked him why he wanted to do that, he told me in a straight face, 'Because the son-of-a-bitch threatened me and I don't appreciate it.'

"I didn't know what to say so I told him, 'I'm sure whatever Governor Cargo said, he didn't mean it,' and the lieutenant governor replied, 'The hell he didn't.' He added, 'I demand full State Police security around the clock.'

"I found out later that Governor Cargo had called the lieutenant governor to his office over a tie vote that the lieutenant governor broke and went against Governor Cargo's interests.

"I had sensed after the raid on the Tierra Amarilla courthouse that Governor Cargo had not been happy with the lieutenant governor over his activation of the National Guard, and they didn't get along that well.

"I informed Chief Black of my conversation with the lieutenant governor and Chief Black had a good laugh. He told me he would call the lieutenant governor and address his concerns. The lieutenant governor was a man who liked to be catered to. He complained that he should have the same security as the governor."

CdeBaca said he suspected that Black took it upon himself to calm Francis down. He said he doubted that Black found it necessary to inform Cargo of the situation.

Indeed, that apparently is what occurred. Cargo recalled visiting with Francis following his tie-breaking vote but the governor had not been aware of Francis' angry demands made later of CdeBaca. "I never heard about that incident," he said, "but I know that Lee Francis did not get along well with the State Police.

"I got after Lee when he cast the tie-breaking vote on a bill to change the old pricing system on liquor. I talked to him about the measure before he went down to the Senate chamber. When the vote came up, it was a tie and Lee voted against the bill to break the tie. He told me later, 'That's the most popular thing I ever did. I was getting congratulations from 'Pancho' Padilla and liquor dealers and on and on.'

"I said, 'Listen, Mr. Lieutenant Governor, tomorrow you're going to get words that aren't quite along that line and they're going to come from the *Albuquerque Journal* and *The Santa Fe New Mexican*.

"Lee could be a little temperamental but generally speaking, I got along pretty well with him."

Francis died in 2001.

If liquor legislation had a way of attracting heat, so too did bills addressing public employees and their compensation.

"During the 1968 legislative session, a hotly contested public employees bargaining bill was being debated. Senator William Sego, a Republican from Albuquerque, sparked a major parliamentary fight when he successfully asked to reconsider the public employees bargaining bill.

"That night Senator Sego's sister-in-law's car was burned. According to Senator Sego, she was baby sitting for his wife who was attending a movie with a friend. When Senator Sego's wife got home, she got a telephone call from an anonymous person who told her, 'More of this can happen if you don't vote the right way.'

"Senator Sego said he had 'no idea' who burned the vehicle but stated, 'Evidently it was someone who is unhappy about my vote on the recall of the bill.'

"That same night, Republican Senator Junio Lopez from San Miguel County, was driving his car in Santa Fe when he was run off the road by two unidentified men in a pickup. Senator Lopez had also voted with Senator Sego to kill the public employees bill.

"We increased our security in the Legislature and provided security for both Senator Sego and Senator Lopez in addition to their families. There were no other overt acts of criminal behavior."

Serious business like that faced by Sego and Lopez in 1968 was broken up one day that same year after the State Police acquired its first drug-sniffing dog.

"Officer Dean Stuyvesant was the dog's master. The dog's name was Thor. One day in February, we introduced Thor to the House of Representatives. We wanted to demonstrate how effective Thor was in sniffing marijuana. I had known Representative Paris "Pete" Derizotis from my tour in Gallup, and we planted a baggie of marijuana in a drawer in his desk without his knowledge. The House was in session when he turned Thor loose among the lawmakers at their desks. He eventually ended up at Representative Derizotis' desk, where he located the marijuana and opened the desk drawer with his front paw.

"Representative Derizotis was speechless. Everyone had a good laugh, including many of the spectators in the gallery. Representative Derizotis was a good sport about it and never made an issue about it.

"Thor went on to be very successful at sniffing out drugs, helping make cases not only for the New Mexico State Police but also for other law enforcement agencies.

"A handful of spectators cleared the House gallery as soon as they saw how effective Thor was at sniffing out marijuana."

Controversy it could appear was never far away. State officials often arrived at their posts more than familiar with controversy, sometimes having faced it in elections that won them their seats.

"On Election Day in November 1968, I was assigned to the Tierra Amarilla County courthouse. According to Chief Joe Black, the Rio Arriba County clerk had requested that a State Police officer be present during the voting to prevent trouble.

"Fabián Chávez was running against Governor David Cargo and it was predicted that the vote was too close to call.

"I recall an elderly man who could not read needed assistance to vote and the presiding judge allowed another man to help with the ballot in the voting booth. When it came to the vote for governor, the man assisting told the voter, '*Vota por Chávez*,' trying to influence the voter. The man voting replied, '*Yo no voto por Chávez. Yo quiero votar por Cargo*,' and the man assisting insisted, '*No, no. Vota por Chávez*.'

"At this time, the presiding judge called me to take the man out of the booth. I told him, 'It's against the law to try to influence a person to vote in the voting booth or in the voting line,' and I escorted him out.

"After the polls closed, District Judge James Scarborough ordered all voting boxes in Rio Arriba County impounded. After the election, I heard that deceased people in Rio Arriba County were still registered to vote and some were still voting.

"Fabían Chávez lost the election to Governor Cargo by the narrowest of margins."

Cargo was a heck of a campaigner but he also was more than adept at positioning himself in roles outside of politics.

"One Saturday morning, Chief Black assigned me to take Governor Cargo to the old western town located at the Eaves Ranch. The governor had a bit part in the movie, Gatling Gun, in which he played the part of a confederate officer. After bungling his first line, he managed to get it done on the retake. On the way back to Santa Fe, Governor Cargo asked actress Rita Moreno to ride back with us."

CdeBaca said Cargo and Moreno conversed easily until the actress was dropped off at her Santa Fe hotel. Cargo was returned to the Governor's Mansion.

Cargo's razor-thin re-election victory accompanied the election of Republican Richard Nixon as U.S. president. Nixon handily defeated Vice President Hubert Humphrey in New Mexico. Cargo's defeated opponent, Fabián Chávez, asserted that if Humphrey had done even slightly better in the Land of Enchantment, it would have meant more votes for other Democrats on the ticket and likely would have denied Cargo a second term as governor.

Humphrey left a few memories for New Mexicans while stumping in New Mexico for the Democratic ticket in 1964.

"When Hubert Horacio Humphrey was campaigning in Santa Fe, several of us were assigned to security. Mr. Humphrey asked that we take our picture with him."

CdeBaca's duties in and around the Capitol during the 1960s wound up being wide ranging. Early on, they included driving two of the state's ranking elected officials around New Mexico, across country and even beyond an international border. Some of what he was asked to do went beyond what would be permitted today.

Democrat Hubert H. Humphrey found plenty of police protection in New Mexico while campaigning in the state in 1964. Pictured (back row) are State Police officer Richard CdeBaca, State Police Sergeant T.J. Chavez, Humphrey, State Police Captain A.P. Winston, and Santa Fe City Police Chief A.B. Martinez. Pictured (front row) are State Police officer Freddie Martinez, State Police Deputy Chief Joseph Black, State Police Lieutenant A.J. Smith, and State Police Lieutenant Monroe Alexander.

"I had only recently been assigned to security at the Legislature in 1964 when Chief John Bradford assigned me to other duties that included helping with security at the Governor's Mansion and chauffeuring Governor Jack Campbell and Secretary of State Alberta Miller. Some of my weekends were occupied taking the governor or the secretary of state to special functions. Officer Red Pack was the designated governor's security but it took both of us to keep up with all the functions Governor Campbell attended.

"In August of 1964, Secretary of State Miller asked if I would chauffer her and her daughter and another staff member to New York City to attend the World's Fair. That turned out to be an experience of a lifetime.

"When I was working security at the Mansion, Mrs. Ruth Campbell, the governor's wife, would ask me to take Mac, their pet bulldog, to get bathed and groomed or to take her to run errands. I enjoyed being in her company. She was not demanding. On some weekends, I would have to drive to Roswell to pick up their son, Michael, who attended New Mexico Military Institute and then take him back on Sunday afternoon. One evening, Mrs. Campbell asked me to take their two daughters, Kathy and Patty, to the drive-in in Albuquerque to see Alfred Hitchcock's suspense movie, 'The Birds,' which I also enjoyed.

"Alberta Miller liked to combine weekend business trips with visits to the horse tracks in Raton and Sunland Park. On one occasion, she asked me to take her across the border into Mexico to bet on the dogs. Her favorite time of the year was going to the State Fair to bet on the horses."

CdeBaca found himself in more-stoic company on his trips with Governor Campbell. "He almost never talked to me," said CdeBaca.

"One evening I was assigned to take Governor Campbell to Albuquerque to attend a social function at the Four Hills Country Club. On the way there Governor Campbell told me that he had instructed his secretary to reserve him a room at the Western Skies Motel on east Central so that he could change into casual clothes after his speaking engagement.

"There was hardly any conversation exchanged between us on any of our trips. On the way there, I mentioned that I was taking a Dale Carnegie class on 'How to win Friends and Influence People,' to which the governor replied, 'Maybe I should do the same thing.'

"After he was done at the country club, I took Governor Campbell to the Western Skies, where he changed clothes and went to socialize. About 1 a.m., he showed up feeling no pain. I had gone to sleep on top of the covers and I quickly put my boots on. On top of everything, Governor Campbell was exhausted and he wanted to get to the Mansion ASAP.

"When we got out of the city limits, he told me to stop the limousine and get the pillow out of the trunk for him. He fell asleep in the back seat right away. When we arrived at the Mansion, I woke him up and he told me to get his suitcase and take it inside. I told him that we had left the suitcase behind and he said, 'Go get it.'

"I radioed the dispatcher and told him to have an officer from Albuquerque go to the Western Skies and pick up the Governor's suitcase and meet me between Albuquerque and Santa Fe. That morning, I rang the doorbell at the Mansion at 6:30 a.m. and waited for the governor to open the door. He never said a word."

Relations between the two men were a little warmer sometime later when CdeBaca approached Campbell for a favor.

"On one of Governor Campbell's speaking engagements in Roswell, I told him of officer Alfred Leyba's unfortunate accident in Las Cruces. In brief detail, I described how officer Leyba had been in pursuit of a stolen car on the night of November 4, 1963, when his car struck a horse and the impact caused a carbine to dislodge from the back of the car and strike him in the back of the head, causing blunt trauma and leaving him in a coma for several months.

"I asked the governor if he would take time from his busy schedule to visit officer Leyba, which he did. When I took the governor, officer Leyba was in no condition to communicate but I believe he was able to register who the governor was. He seemed to be excited.

"Governor Campbell was elected to office when he lived in Roswell. I am sure that officer Leyba was familiar with the governor. Anyway, I thought the governor showed a lot of compassion by taking time to see officer Leyba."

CdeBaca's account of driving Governor Campbell back home after a night of drinking in Albuquerque brings to mind the countless public officials who over the years lacked chauffeurs but still had to get home after consuming alcohol. CdeBaca's records tell of one such incident near Alamogordo.

"While returning to headquarters late one night in 1958, I met a car with its bright lights on and though I tried to get the driver to dim the lights, the driver did not do so. I turned around and stopped the late-model white Cadillac. The driver was one of our area's state district judges, and he was accompanied by his wife.

"I explained to him why I had stopped him and asked him for his driver's license. At first, he was very cooperative. But when I asked him if he had been drinking, he became highly indignant. He told me they were returning from the country club and he had only had two drinks and asked me why I questioned him when he wasn't drunk driving. I returned his driver's license and told him to please dim the lights at oncoming cars, and I told him he could be on his way.

"About one hour later, the dispatcher radioed me to report to headquarters, saying that the judge who I had stopped wanted to see me. When I arrived at the office, the judge and his wife were sitting in Sergeant Floyd Miles' office.

"I asked the judge, 'Do you mind telling me what this is all about?' He replied, 'I don't appreciate you stopping me and embarrassing me, and remove your weapon while I'm talking to you.' I answered, 'My weapon is part of my uniform and I am not going to remove it. I am not going to threaten you with it.' The judge then warned me that he could have my job. I told him, 'My job is a profession, just like yours.'

"I didn't know where this meeting was headed, but I was surprised to hear the judge's wife tell her husband, 'Why don't we go home and you can talk to his supervisor tomorrow.'

"The following morning, I informed Sergeant Miles about my encounter with the judge. Sergeant Miles never heard a word from the judge."

(Sergeant Miles was the son of former Democratic Governor John Miles.)

CdeBaca said he did not ticket the judge for the infraction that prompted the traffic stop. "I don't think I ever issued a ticket to a driver for failure to dim the lights," he said. "It had nothing to do with who the driver was in this case. Not one supervisor ever told me not to ticket someone because of their positions, because of their status."

CdeBaca's aggressiveness while on patrol more than occasionally produced indignation.

"On July 10, 1959, I stopped a limo for speeding on U.S. 54-70 between Alamogordo and Tularosa. I expected to meet some celebrity. Little did I know that the passenger was the notorious governor from Louisiana, Earl K. Long. I had heard much about the Long family political dynasty in that state.

"Governor Long was being chauffeured by a Louisiana state trooper. I told the trooper why I had stopped him, and before I could say another word, the governor called me a 'Mexican bandit.' And he said that I had no business stopping him, that he was immune from arrest.

"I told him that in New Mexico, the laws applied to everyone. Rather than subject myself to more humiliation from the governor, which I felt I didn't deserve, I told the trooper to go on and drive safely. Later on that day at the Ruidoso Downs, the governor got into a confrontation with Lincoln County Sheriff 'Sally' Vega."

Sometimes, traffic stops led to pleasant surprises.

"One afternoon, officer Joe Cotton and I were checking vehicles at a roadblock west of Gallup when a black limousine stopped. Inside was the legendary 'Fats' Domino. He got out and shook hands with us."

Because of his multiple and varied assignments through the 1960s, CdeBaca brushed up against some of the period's biggest stars.

"On the first week of September, Chief Black assigned me as liaison to the State Fair Commission for the duration of the State Fair. I reported to Mr. Finlay MacGillivray, director of the State Fair. Sometimes, he would assign me to pick up celebrities at the airport and take them to the Western Skies Motel on east Central.

"The State Fair commissioners kept me busy taking them to meetings and social events. They had box seats assigned to them at Tingley Coliseum, and Mr. Leo Smith, whom I had made friends with at Tierra Amarilla, was a member of the commission, and he invited me to sit with them. I enjoyed watching the celebrities perform and also the professional rodeo.

"In the three consecutive years I was assigned to the State Fair Commission, I met Tennessee Ernie Ford, Eddie Arnold, Johnny Rodriguez, Glen Campbell, Jimmy Dean, Ray Price, Marty Robbins, Johnny Cash and June Carter. The day I picked up Johnny Cash and June Carter, he introduced himself with that signature voice of his, 'Hello, I'm Johnny Cash.' Before the show, I had my picture taken with him and June Carter and he autographed an album for me, which I still own.

"Marty Robbins did not wish to be around a lot of people. After he checked into his room, I took him for a ride up to the top of Sandia Crest, which he enjoyed. When I was taking Eddie Arnold back to the Western Skies after his performance, he complained about the dusty manure inside the coliseum and said it bothered him while he was singing. I told him that I didn't think anybody had noticed."

Richard CdeBaca provided security to multiple performers, like Glen Campbell, at the New Mexico State Fair during the 1960s.

Something that couldn't escape attention came several years after CdeBaca had stopped chauffeuring state officials and Western celebrities. CdeBaca was one of many State Police officers who didn't like what they saw unfolding in the state Capitol.

"In 1978 under the administration of Governor Jerry Apodaca, state agencies were reorganized into cabinet departments. On April 1, 1978, the State Police became a division within the Criminal Justice Department.

"Governor Apodaca appointed Dr. Charles Becknell, an African American, to be the director. Dr. Becknell had excellent credentials but what didn't fare well with the State Police were some of his appointments. Dr. Becknell hired John Ramming, an attorney to be the liaison between his office and the State Police. John Ramming was an ex-con but so was another man who was hired and placed in the records bureau, of all places to have an ex-con working."

CdeBaca said State Police officers feared losing their autonomy through the reorganization. "Prior to Governor Apodaca, no governor had taken it upon himself to make any major changes within the New Mexico State Police. The chief of police always answered to the State Police Board, which answered to the governor.

"But Governor Apodaca convinced the Legislature to establish a Department of Criminal Justice. Under the umbrella of criminal justice, came the State Police, the Corrections Department and others. Suddenly, the chief of police answered to the director of the Criminal Justice Department. And, actually, what demoralized so many at the time was not so much that the State Police lost autonomy but that it suddenly had to answer to civilian authority.

Governors David Cargo, Jerry Apodaca and Bruce King all left imprints on the New Mexico State Police during Richard CdeBaca's long tenure in and around the agency.

"It also was troublesome that the liaison between the new Criminal Justice secretary and the State Police was an ex-con. By that time, I was deputy chief in charge of the Criminal Investigations Bureau. John Ramming on a daily basis was wanting to get briefed on activities taking place within the narcotics division, the criminal division, the intelligence division. To be honest, many times I had to withhold information from Mr. John Ramming because of the confidential nature of the investigations that were ongoing.

CdeBaca wrote in his records:

"The governor's intention of streamlining state government was a good idea but it created more bureaucracy in the State Police. We resented the reorganization, but in all fairness to the governor, we remained a dedicated and professional agency. Being in charge of the Criminal Investigations Bureau, I spent a large portion of my time answering to John Ramming, sometimes in matters that seemed mundane. He was always telling me, 'I have to keep the boss informed.'"

CdeBaca said that Apodca's reorganization was "never fully accepted" by State Police. "The State Police is a very proud organization. Over the years, there's been this attitude that we are an elite, professional organization; don't mess with our department. But as deputy chief, I realized that I had to set an example and not criticize the new way that we had been structured."

He also knew that help might be on the way.

"When Bruce King was campaigning again for governor at the end of Governor Apodaca's term, he was asked by a reporter, 'Did you hear many complaints from individual officers as to re-organization?' Bruce King's reply was, 'Frankly, I never did see a State Police officer that agreed that it should have been under re-organization the way it was.' When Bruce King got elected, he convinced the Legislature to pass a bill making the State Police an autonomous department again."

CdeBaca said State Police generally thought Apodaca had a short fuse. "Still," said CdeBaca, "Chief Martin Vigil respected him for one reason: Governor Apodaca didn't interfere with personnel matters in the New Mexico State Police."

Bruce King, said CdeBaca, was "the real gladiator" of State Police. King was responsible for getting the department much of what it needed going back to his days in the House of Representatives when he was instrumental in securing funding for the new law enforcement academy and crime lab, according to CdeBaca.

David Cargo was "very supportive" of Chief Martin Vigil as well as the department that he ran, CdeBaca said. Cargo, he said, also kept from injecting himself into personnel matters.

There was no interference from Jack Campbell as governor, CdeBaca said.

John Simms is remembered by CdeBaca for something he told State Police recruits while CdeBaca was in training in 1956. "He said if you stop someone that is going to tell you that he has influence with me or my office, you can give him my telephone number and don't let that distract you or intimidate you from doing your job."

CdeBaca recalled Governor Edwin Mechem for the time that he directed the National Guard to help State Police in roadblocks. "The guardsmen weren't trained for such duty," said CdeBaca. "One got hit by a car and killed in Gallup. At another roadblock that I was manning with two other officers, a guardsman got clipped by a car and was hurt, fortunately not very seriously.

"No governor since then called out the National Guard to help State Police at roadblocks."

But if that was a faux pas for Mechem, the Republican who was elected governor four times drew credit from CdeBaca on another front. "Back in the 1950s, clan and cronyism was pervasive at most levels of government," CdeBaca said. "When I was employed at the Motor Vehicle Office after my discharge from the Navy, a $5 monthly fee was deducted from our paycheck and the money went to the political party in office. Governor Mechem did away with the system that allowed for such 'spoils.'"

Mechem, formerly with the FBI, was among governors most respected by State Police officers, according to CdeBaca. "Along with Governor Mechem, I believe you would have to include Governor David Cargo and Governor Bruce King in that group that was well respected by the State Police," he said.

Toney Anaya's time as governor revives dark memories for CdeBaca (more in Chapter 17). "Toney Anaya interfered with personnel matters at the State Police like no other governor I ever knew. When he left office, he had a very, very low popular rating. This, in itself, says volumes about him," said CdeBaca.

16

Family Life

Looking upon his career with the State Police, Richard CdeBaca said police chiefs did not appear to be too preoccupied with concerns about their officers' family lives, particularly during his first decade on the force. Work became a life-style as opposed to a job, he said.

"I don't know that family matters got due consideration," he said.

For years, officers got one day off per week; 12-14-hour days were routine-ly expected, said CdeBaca. "You knew you were always going to have to answer calls," he said.

"One day off limited what you could do with your family, especially if it was on a Monday. If you booked someone into jail during the weekend, you knew you'd have to be in court come Monday ... I had four supervising officers in Alamogordo and not one of them changed my day off. I never had a weekend or a holiday off to be with my family during that period."

Sometimes officers simply had to enjoy their own company during off hours, and even that did not always work out. CdeBaca recorded this entry about life in Alamogordo.

"Late one night, all five officers from the district met at the State Police office. Officer Sam Chavez brought his accordion. He was an excellent musician. Officer Felix Work brought his guitar. Officer Allan Whitehouse brought his fiddle. Officer Jim Syling, his Jewish Harp and I had a harmonica. We all tuned up and started playing.

"We had it going when Sergeant A.B. Munsey came out of the family living quarters in his pajamas and asked us if we didn't have anything better to do and added that his family deserved peace and quiet. We all dispersed in a hurry, from then on, I guess, we could serenade the coyotes at night with our instruments."

Then there was the constant moving required of State Police officers. Beginning with their first training, said CdeBaca, officers were told they likely would get multiple postings around the state. "For those officers that are moved around, you learn to live from pay check to pay check," CdeBaca said. "It really forces you into a different lifestyle and environment because you cannot afford to buy a house everywhere they transfer you. So you do the next best thing and live in what you can afford. You may not like living that way but what other choice do you have? You go shopping for a trailer. A large number of officers have to resort to that type of living conditions. Some mobile home parks don't have the best accommodations."

Officers who made waves, might get more postings than others, sometimes to remote areas, CdeBaca said.

"One transfer that I was involved in had an officer move from Raton to Vaughn in the late 1970s. He sued Chief Martin Vigil and the department for discrimination, claiming that he had to live in deplorable housing after the transfer. Many of us had experienced the same situation and we never complained.

"A jury in Albuquerque consisting mostly of women awarded the officer a large sum of money. Needless to say, he was not the most-liked officer in the department, and he was very much aware of it. He lost the respect of his fellow officers. You have heard the old cliché: Don't bite the hand that feeds you.'

"I had recommended the transfer to Chief Vigil because the officer's activity was not meeting expectations in Raton."

No matter where the posting, danger could be hiding behind any corner. CdeBaca recalled one incident in Alamogordo that was sparked by a minor fender-bender. It was an incident where his service to the State Police—along with his life -- could easily have been cut short. "A 1957 Ford and a 1955 Chevrolet pickup were involved in a minor collision at the Starlite Drivein one night. The driver of the Ford jumped out of his vehicle and approached the driver of the pickup. The man in the truck asked his wife to give him his gun from the glove compartment.

"The man from the Ford jumped onto the truck's running board and with his knife slashed the face of the woman in the truck. He then took the gun away from her in the middle of the fight just as I arrived. I guess any one of us could have gotten killed that day but I was able to put a stop to it, confiscate the weapons and take the offender to jail."

Threats to life and limb seemingly could not be avoided, as evidenced years later when, ironically, a police chief sought to create more family time for his officers. An officer who CdeBaca was supervising narrowly escaped murder. CdeBaca made this notation in his records:

"Chief Martin Vigil had assigned his immediate staff to rotate weekend duties to handle department matters. Late one Saturday night while I was on call, officer Robert 'Big Foot' Martinez went to a bar in Peñasco and arrested two brothers for disorderly conduct. Officer Martinez was acquainted with the two brothers.

"While taking them to jail, one of the brothers pulled out a .357 magnum and pointed it at officer Martinez's head. He told officer Martinez they were going to kill him. They found a location they wanted and ordered the officer out of the police car. When he got out of the car, he ran for his safety and jumped down an arroyo. He was shot at but escaped without being hit.

"Officer Martinez had not reported in from an accident he had been dispatched to investigate. A search had already been initiated by the time he got to a telephone to call the district office. His police car was found destroyed by fire. The two brothers were arrested later and charged with kidnapping, assault with intent to commit a violent felony and destruction of state property."

A year after CdeBaca joined the State Police, he married a woman whom he had met while at his first posting. If she did not know initially what she was in for as a wife of a State Police officer, she promptly found out.

"On September 14, 1957, I married Frances Sanchez, whom I had met at the local bank in Alamogordo where she was employed. During the wedding, three relentless State Police officers confiscated my 1957 Chevrolet convertible, which was parked in front of the church. They had conveniently replaced it with a wheelbarrow decorated with ribbons and flowers. After the wedding ceremony was over, they placed my wife in the wheelbarrow and made me push her up the street all the way to the courthouse while they escorted us with the police cars' red lights and sirens going.

"Employees from the local businesses came out to see what all the commotion was about. Our parents took it all in and I am sure they talked about it for a long time. When my wife and I returned from a short honeymoon and moved into our house, I discovered cowbells attached to the bottom of our bed's box spring."

Little more than a year went by before the young married couple truly had to begin juggling the demands placed on a State Police officer with those of a family.

"I had received orders to report to Gallup from Alamogordo to be part of a 'wolf pack' operation against drunk drivers. At the time I got my orders for this special assignment, my wife was expecting our first child. My orders did not specify how long my assignment would last. As it turned out, we were released from our assignment just in time for me to see my wife give birth to a beautiful and healthy baby boy, who we named Richard Allen, born October 24, 1958."

Richard CdeBaca plays with son, Richard Allen, in 1959.

A year later, there was another son. This one, too, might well have come while CdeBaca was out of town at work.

"On December 4, 1959, I received orders to report to Santa Fe on another special assignment. The purpose of this assignment was to try to apprehend arsonists who were burning houses on the north side of Santa Fe. There had been a rash of house fires in the affluent section of the city

"When I received my orders, my wife was expecting our second child. I reported to Santa Fe and the supervisor in charge assigned us to patrol the neighborhood on the north side with instructions to stop every car that moved during the night hours between 11 p.m. and 5 a.m.

"On December 9th, I received word that my wife had been taken to the hospital. I went to Deputy Chief Joe Black and explained the situation. He gave me permission to return to Alamogordo. On December 10th, my wife gave birth to another healthy, beautiful baby boy who we named Ronald Wayne.

"My stay with them in Alamogordo did not last long. As soon as I took my wife out of the hospital, I had to return to Santa Fe. Two days later, I was dismissed from my assignment and returned home."

Stories about police officers and members of the opposite sex likely have circulated since the existence of uniforms. CdeBaca tells of an incident where his own police car played a role in a dalliance by a young officer whom he was coaching.

"I was serving as a coach officer for a newly commissioned officer assigned to Alamogordo. We spent many hours in my police car together. I liked the young officer from the beginning. Within a few days, I had him driving the car, chasing speeders, writing tickets, arresting drunk drivers and investigating accidents. My wife and his wife made friends right away.

"One Sunday after he had been under my supervision for almost four weeks, I told him I was going to recommend to Lieutenant Hoover Wimberly that he be assigned his own police car. That night, I told the officer to drop me off at my house, take my car home with him and have it washed first thing in the morning and then pick me up.

"At 1 a.m., the telephone woke me up. It was the officer's wife. She asked me how long I had been home, and I told her since about 9:30 p.m. Then she said that her husband was not home yet. I called the radio dispatcher and told him to call my unit number, which he did and got no answer. Then I asked the dispatcher if the missing officer had checked out of the car. He had not. I instructed the dispatcher to keep calling my unit and if he got an answer to let me know. I grew alarmed thinking of what might have happened to the officer between my house and his.

"Before I called his wife back, I called Lieutenant Wimberly and explained to him what was going on. I told him I would take my personal car to the office and meet there to start looking for the officer.

"Lieutenant Wimberly and I got into his police car and we kept radioing my unit without success. We alerted the city police officer on duty to look for my police car. When we passed the Red Rooster Restaurant, I saw my police car parked there. It was locked and there was no evidence of foul play. My shotgun was located where I always carried it. The restaurant was closed and my police car was the only one in the parking lot.

"I told Lieutenant Wimberly to take me home so I could pick up the extra set of keys to my police car. When we left my house, the dispatcher radioed Lieutenant Wimberly and said that the wife of the missing officer had just called and told him that her husband was home. Lieutenant Wimberly and I immediately went to the officer's residence.

"Lieutenant Wimberly asked the officer for a full explanation. The officer explained that he had gone to the restaurant after dropping me off and met a girl there and they went for a ride in her car up to High Rolls.

"Lieutenant Wimberly suspended the officer and asked for a full written report. Lieutenant Wimberly got a detailed report then terminated the officer, who was on probation. The officer told me on his way out, 'I am sorry that I let you down.' I told him 'So am I.'"

After four years in Alamogordo, CdeBaca was told to prepare for his first transfer.

"In June 1960, Lieutenant Hoover Wimberly called me into his office and told me that Captain Archie White, our district commander, wanted to talk to me about a transfer to Anthony. One never knew when the day would come that you get transferred. The next day, I reported to Captain White in Las Cruces. He told me that officer Bob Gilliland was being transferred from Anthony and he was going to transfer me to replace him.

"I told Captain White that under any other circumstances I would accept the transfer, but at that time, it would be a real hardship on us since my wife had been scheduled for lung surgery in El Paso. He explained that one advantage was that we would be closer to the hospital from Anthony. I replied that I didn't deny that but that my mother-in-law would not be available in Anthony to baby-sit our sons, who were just one and two years old. I asked him to delay the transfer until my wife recovered.

"He told me that he didn't want to leave Anthony vacant for that period of time. I realized then that he was determined to transfer me. I told him that if I got transfer orders right away, I would have to consider quitting my job. He advised me to think twice about it.

"When I returned to Alamogordo, I told Lieutenant Wimberly that my family was my first responsibility and that should be taken into consideration. I asked why the transfer couldn't be delayed. I don't know what conversation took place between Lieutenant Wimberly and Captain White, but the next day Lieutenant Wimberly called me and told me to disregard my transfer.

"I asked him if he had wanted me transferred and he replied that he did not. My wife had her surgery as scheduled, and when she recovered she returned to work at the bank."

CdeBaca eventually was transferred to Gallup in 1961 and he braced himself for how it might impact his family. "My wife was born and raised in Alamogordo," he said. "The move would be more difficult for her than for me. I would have a job in Gallup but she didn't plus she was leaving her family and friends." Life continued to take many turns.

"I reported to Captain E.A. Tafoya, the district commander in Gallup. He welcomed me to the district and told me to report to Sergeant Eddie Jaramillo to get my assignment from him. I was assigned to patrol U.S. 66, west of Gallup to the Arizona state line. My regular day off would be Monday, and it couldn't be a worse day off. If I arrested someone over the weekend, I would have to appear in court on Monday, which happened too often.

"I spent two weeks living in the dormitory at the State Police headquarters before I rented a duplex on Gladden Street. My wife and I listed our three-bedroom Dale Bellamah house for sale and moved to Gallup.

"My wife got employment at the Merchant's Bank, and we found excellent babysitters at a day care center run by nuns. I remember taking our sons to the babysitter the first morning, and it hurt me to hear Rick tell his younger brother, Ron, 'If you don't cry, I am not going to cry.' But before I dropped them off, they were both crying. After two or three days, they got over it.

"I had spent five years in a warm climate and now I had to get used to one of the coldest places in the state. I also had to get used to the amount of traffic on U.S. 66 compared to what I was accustomed to in Alamogordo."

"Little did we know what hardships my transfer to Gallup would bring. When we bought our house in Alamogordo in 1957, the local economy was booming and housing was very scarce. We were extremely lucky to buy a used house, which we could barely afford.

"When we left Alamogordo, the economy was terribly depressed. Houses were not selling. We finally decided to rent our home. Three months later, the tenants were gone and they left the house in a mess. We painted it and replaced the carpet in the living room. Now we had monthly payments on the house, the duplex in Gallup, the family car and the babysitter. My salary was $480 a month.

"One day, I received a call from our Realtor and he asked me if we would accept $300 for our equity. He told me that houses were being foreclosed. We accepted the $300. It was hard to swallow but we had no choice.

"Rather than continue paying rent, we bought a trailer in Albuquerque and had it moved to the Hawaiian Village Trailer Park west of Gallup. The name of the trailer park sounded attractive but it was nothing special."

"In August of 1961, one of my wife's sisters, Inez, moved in with us and enrolled at Gallup High School, where she graduated."

"My parents came to visit us in Gallup one Sunday and they reminded me that they had lived in Gallup in the 1930s. My father had worked in the coal mines. My oldest sister and her husband had also lived in Gallup for a couple of years when he worked for the gas company."

"On Sunday mornings, we attended church services on a regular basis. It gave us an opportunity to be together as a family, at least for a couple of hours. Being on duty, I was subject to call. Fortunately, I never was called out of church. One Sunday, before the services, the priest approached me and asked me to help with the collection. I felt awkward passing the collection in full State Police uniform but the parishioners didn't seem to mind. I don't know if the contributions were up for that service."

"On my regular day off, I enjoyed spending time with our sons. The manager of the Shalimar Motel allowed me to take our sons swimming in their swimming pool."

"Approaching Easter weekend, I asked for time off for the holiday and much to my surprise my request was approved. This would be the first time in six years I would be off on a holiday. We went to Alamogordo where our sons enjoyed an exciting Easter hunt with their cousins."

With an eye on advancing within the police department, CdeBaca enrolled in a La Salle Extension University law course. Three years went by before CdeBaca's final examination was mailed to Gallup District Attorney Ed DePauli, whom CdeBaca had designated as his official monitor.

"When the district attorney received the examination papers, he called me and offered one of his offices for me to take my exam in privacy. About two weeks later, I received a letter of congratulations from the university. About one week later, I received my bachelor-of-laws degree. I sent a copy to Chief K.K. Miller to place in my personnel file. There had been a handful of State Police officers who had enrolled at the same time I did, but none of them completed the course."

One cold winter night, CdeBaca got a scare that would change his career path.

"Late one night in February 1963, I was on patrol on U.S. 66 west of Gallup when I suffered a mild heart attack. Officer Joe Cotton took me to St. Mary's Hospital. Dr. Keney attended to me and kept me in the hospital until test results were completed. I was diagnosed with acute angina and Dr. Keney referred me to Dr. Richard Streeper in Santa Fe, a renowned heart specialist.

"Dr. Streeper recommended to Chief K.K. Miller that I be relieved of patrol duties and be assigned to administrative work until my condition improved. Chief Miller accepted the advice of the doctor and transferred me to Santa Fe.

"Our trailer was moved by the department to the Vagabond Trailer Park located on south Cerrillos Road in Santa Fe. My wife found employment at the First National Bank and we managed to get a good babysitter for our sons.

"I took a course through the Institute of Applied Science to learn how to classify fingerprints. Once I received my diploma, I was assigned to the Criminal Bureau to classify fingerprints and keep statistics on traffic accidents. All this time, I was under the care of Dr. Streeper.

"My police car was issued to another officer and during this time my day off was on Sunday, which was a blessing. Now I could spend quality time with my family."

Aware that he had too little of it, CdeBaca sought to create family time whenever he could. One day, he got help from a high-placed source.

"For one of the recruit class graduations, Governor Jack Campbell was invited to be the guest speaker, as was customary. My wife and I took our son, Rick, dressed in a State Police uniform. Governor Campbell saw him and shook hands with him. A photographer was on the spot and took a picture of him, which was published in *The Santa Fe New Mexican*."

The same son later had an experience worthy of public attention but for far different reasons.

"Rick wanted to work part time when he was a junior in high school, and we gave him permission with the understanding that he would have to keep up with his school work. He found employment at a 7-11 convenience store after school.

"Soon after he began working there, three punks came into the store one night as our son and a female clerk were getting ready to close. They demanded the money and placed a paper bag over the girl's head and locked her in the freezer. Brandishing a knife, they took the money from the cash register and forced our son into the freezer. In those days, the convenience stores did not have an unlocking device to open the freezer doors from the inside. Fortunately, the manager, Bill Hindi, arrived to count the receipts for the day and close the store. He got our son and the girl out of the freezer."

Two years had gone by since CdeBaca's heart attack. Nine years since his enlistment in the department, he was eligible to be considered for promotion to sergeant. He passed the required test and was one of 10 men who secured promotion.

"Following my promotion to sergeant and transfer to Santa Rosa in 1965, I was once again confronted with the problem of displacing my family, and this time it was going to be more difficult because our sons were already in school. I looked for a place to park our trailer, but I couldn't find any. This meant my family would stay behind in Santa Fe temporarily, and I would have to find an apartment for myself.

"I visited city hall to ask Mayor Sotero Sanchez if he could be of any assistance. The city clerk, Rita Sanchez, offered me a cramped one-bedroom with commode and shower but no kitchen, which I accepted for $50 per month. It was equipped with a small gas heater that I had to turn on and off manually. At times, I feared asphyxiation.

"After three months, I moved into a newly constructed unfurnished apartment, which I rented for $200 per month plus utilities. I bought a used table with chairs and a bed; no television. I began to do some cooking for myself. It was expensive to eat out every day.

"When I got promoted to sergeant, I received an increase of $50 per month. My total monthly salary was $580. I figured that if I didn't find a place to park our trailer, my family and I would go broke in a matter of a few months."

"One day, I came upon a pickup parked on the shoulder of the road with a flat tire near Puerto de Luna and I stopped to help. I introduced myself and asked Mr. Gallegos, the truck's driver, where he lived. He told me he owned a ranch nearby, bordering the Pecos River. When we were done, he asked me to join him and his wife for a cup of coffee, which I accepted.

"During coffee, I told Mr. Gallegos that his ranch reminded me of my father's ranch where I grew up. Mrs. Gallegos told me to bring my wife to visit and I thanked her but told her that my family was in Santa Fe and that I lived by myself because I couldn't find a place to park our trailer.

"After coffee, I thanked them for their hospitality and left. The next day, Mr. Gallegos stopped by the office and offered me a place to park our trailer. He told me, 'You can park it there if you don't mind investing in putting in a septic tank and hooking up the utilities.' I accepted his offer and made arrangements to park our trailer.

"On my next trip to Santa Fe, I made arrangements with the department to move our trailer and to move my family. My wife had to give up her job and we registered our sons in school. There were no jobs available for my wife so she stayed home on the ranch where we had been provided some space."

"While in Santa Rosa, I submitted a letter to Chief John Bradford recommending that officers work six straight days and get two consecutive days off. I mentioned that such a schedule would allow officers to be off on Friday and Saturday and the following week they would be off on Saturday and Sunday and so on. This would be a major departure from the one-day off per week. I never got a reply to my letter."

It must have seemed like the family had only settled in on the Guadalupe County ranch when an opportunity arose that they knew might require yet another move.

"In December 1966, Chief John Bradford announced that the department was going to create an auto theft unit and any officer that was interested to apply in writing. I applied for the position, knowing that if I was selected, I would be moving my family once more.

"Those of us that applied received written notice that we would have to appear before a panel for oral interviews. I got busy and prepared a proposal on how the auto theft unit should function and how it would enhance law enforcement in the state. Specifically, every officer should receive specialized training in the recovery of stolen vehicles. The State Police, the FBI and the National Auto Theft Bureau should provide the training.

"When I was ordered to report to Santa Fe for the oral interview, I was informed that a total of 16 officers had applied. When I showed up for my interview, the panel consisted of Chief John Bradford, Captain Hoover Wimberly, Captain Monroe Alexander and Fred Creech, the National Automobile Theft Bureau regional representative.

"I had worked for Captain Wimberly when he was a lieutenant in Alamogordo, and had also worked for Captain Alexander when he was a lieutenant in the Criminal Bureau, and now he was still in charge of the bureau and the auto theft unit would be under him. I felt very confident about my presentation, and when my interview was over, Chief Bradford complemented me for being prepared.

"About one week later, I received a letter from Chief Bradford notifying me that I had been selected and I was being transferred to Santa Fe after the Christmas holidays. During the holidays, I made arrangements for our trailer to be moved to Santa Fe, and we were lucky to get a space at the same trailer park we had lived in before. We enrolled our sons at Kearny Elementary School.

"Before we left Santa Rosa, I said my goodbyes to many people, especially to Nora Carpenter, owner of the Spanish Inn where I used to eat and to Mr. and Mrs. Gallegos for letting us park our trailer on their property. The *Santa Rosa News* published a nice story about my transfer, and I took the opportunity to thank the newspaper and the citizens for their cooperation.

"Once we moved to Santa Fe in January 1967, my wife returned to work at the bank and our sons started school. I returned to work in the Criminal Bureau and got busy setting up the auto theft unit. My day off was scheduled for Sunday, and that was a blessing because I could once again spend quality time with my family.

"Our sons were growing fast and soon after we returned to Santa Fe from my assignment in Santa Rosa, we contracted to have a house built on Placita Circle. When the time came to sell our trailer, we had a problem finding a buyer for it. Finally, a couple wrote us a check for $3,000 but the check bounced. In time, the trailer sold at a loss."

Frances CdeBaca's return to work was not without incident. She and her sons in 1967 were thrust into the center of trouble that authorities apparently feared might be connected to Richard CdeBaca's work while on assignment in Rio Arriba County following the raid on the Tierra Amarilla courthouse.

"A bizarre set of circumstances took place at First National Bank of Santa Fe where my wife worked while I was assigned to keep peace in Tierra Amarilla following the Rio Arriba County courthouse raid. A man from San Diego wearing a red scarf and a chain around his neck entered the bank waving a gun.

"The FBI took my wife and our two sons and placed them under protective custody. I was not notified at the time of what was going on. Later, I found out that my family had been taken to my wife's parents in Alamogordo.

"I never knew what connection, if any, this incident had with the raid at the courthouse nearly 100 miles from the Santa Fe bank."

Family life continued unfolding amid strains accumulated during nearly 25 years of marriage.

"I enrolled my sons in a firearms training class sponsored by the Game and Fish Department. After completion of the class, I bought both of my sons 410 shotguns. I took them to Cuervo, where a friend I knew from Santa Rosa let us hunt quail on his property."

Then, wham!

"In May of 1981, my wife and I divorced. Our two sons had already left home. My father passed away a few days after our divorce. I had visited with my father the morning before he suffered a massive heart attack. This was a very low point in my life. As Proverbs says, "A happy heart doeth good like medicine, but a broken spirit drieth the bones.""

17

Promoted to Chief, Out in Controversy, Then Returned Amid Praise

Few could dispute that as he worked his way through the New Mexico State Police, Richard CdeBaca had become a protégé of Martin Vigil, a long-time ranking officer who in time would become the organization's longest-serving as well as one of its most-controversial chiefs.

CdeBaca owed four of his six rank promotions to Vigil dating back to 1971. CdeBaca's ascension to chief came after Vigil seemingly maneuvered to ensure that the man whom he had mentored for years would not be denied the department's coveted top post amid political changes in the state Capitol.

Little did Vigil know that his actions would ignite a political firestorm that would sweep through the upper levels of the State Police and singe others high into the governor's office.

Arguably, Vigil began showing favor toward CdeBaca in the 1960s even while Vigil, himself, was working his way up. Cde Baca was a sergeant assigned to headquarters in Santa Fe at the time. Consider this entry from CdeBaca's records:

"During the month of July 1968, Chief Joe Black informed me that Captain Martin Vigil, district commander in Española, was going on a two-week vacation and he requested that I be assigned to Española to take charge of the district in his absence. I reported to Chief Vigil for briefing.

"After the captain left, I met with Sergeant Joe Tarazon, stationed in Chama, who had graduated with me from basic training, and Sergeant Tommy Cantu, stationed in Taos, who had worked under me when I was in Santa Rosa and he was in Vaughn. I explained to them that I was there on temporary assignment and I was not changing any of Captain Vigil's policies.

"During my short time there, I got exposed to a high crime rate, domestic violence and a high number of DUI arrests. Officers in the district were busier than officers in other districts and worked longer hours. When Chief Vigil returned, I briefed him on the activities of the officers and returned to my job at the criminal bureau."

CdeBaca said he had no reason early on to believe that Vigil had cast an eye toward him as someone who he might help climb the ranks. "I never had anything to do with Martin Vigil. I didn't get to know him until I was placed in charge of the State Police detail after the raid on the Rio Arriba courthouse. It happened to be in his district. While there, I was instructed to report to the chief but I also knew that Martin Vigil was the chain of command on certain things.

"Later, I can say that I was surprised when Chief Black called me and said that he had a special request from Captain Vigil to run his district while he was on vacation. He had Sergeant Tommy Cantu in Taos and Sergeant Joe Tarazon in Chama. It entered my mind: Why could they not serve as acting commanders in their own district?"

Vigil succeeded Black as chief in December 1969. In 1971, he promoted CdeBaca to captain and made him director of communications. Vigil elevated CdeBaca to major in 1973 and directed him to create and head the department's first Office of Internal Affairs. In 1975, Vigil placed CdeBaca in charge of the Criminal Investigations Bureau, a post that he continued to hold after 1978 when Vigil promoted him to deputy chief.

It was just before that promotion that CdeBaca concluded that Vigil had plans for him. "I became more cognizant of it on the day that Chief Vigil called me into his office and said he wanted to submit my name to the FBI so that I could attend the FBI academy in Washington, D.C. It was a three-month course. I was a major at the time but had not yet been promoted to deputy chief.

"I told Chief Vigil that I was honored, however, 'I'm only a few years away from retirement. Why not send some young sergeant who has many years ahead of him in the department and can contribute for many more years than I can?'

"He asked, 'Are you sure?' And I said, 'Yes, I am.' He went ahead and assigned a sergeant but I think that was probably the first time that I thought that maybe this man was thinking about me being his replacement. He never came right out and said anything like that to me. After all, he had deputies who he could promote. He had deputies Bill Bullock, Steve Lagomarsino, Sam Chavez. He also had other majors besides me who he could promote."

But if the crop of potential successors was rich, it began thinning itself out in time.

"While I was serving on weekend duty in September 1978, Deputy Chief Bill Bullock was killed in a truck accident. He was returning from Tucumcari with a load of watermelons when he lost control of the truck. He was killed when the truck rolled over."

"In November of that same year while I again was on weekend duty, Major C.A. 'Red' Pack died of a heart attack while hunting in the southwestern part of the state. He had served on the governor's security for years and years."

Other, less-fateful developments also depleted upper ranks. Sam Chavez retired. Others left, too, but under different circumstances.

"It was one of the most difficult times in Martin Vigil's career. There was a move by some officers to have him replaced as chief," CdeBaca said. "A lot of misinformation was being fed to the press and it was coming from inside the department. He did not say who was "feeding" the press.

But several men were angling to succeed Martin Vigil, CdeBaca said, and any of them, knowingly or not, might have had supporters within the department working on their behalf. "If Vigil was ousted, one of these men was going to be chief and the others would be assistant chiefs if they pulled together. It wasn't really a conspiracy. It was disgruntled men who were no longer loyal to Chief Vigil and they wanted changes," CdeBaca said.

Among those who CdeBaca said were positioning themselves to succeed Vigil were Lagomarsino, T.J. Chavez and Hoover Wimberly. "Lagomarsino denied doing anything to hurt Chief Vigil but the chief demoted him to captain and Lagomarsino retired," CdeBaca said. "Hoover Wimberley told me one day that he didn't like Chief Vigil and there came a time when he just stopped showing up for work. Chief Vigil sent me to talk with him and let him know that what he was doing was not acceptable. Wimberly told me that he still had a lot of comp time coming to him, and I told him that we didn't get comp time. I told him to express his position in writing and he retired, instead.

"Chief Vigil took T.J. Chavez out as director of the Narcotics Division and transferred him to Las Vegas."

Vigil's long tenure at the top of the State Police clearly had begun to wear on some of those around him. But CdeBaca said Vigil, always a firm leader, had not grown tired, abusive or arrogant. "I don't think any of those things were discussed openly," said CdeBaca. "He had made enemies. He had terminated, demoted, suspended, reprimanded and transferred. All of those things are going to catch up with you. You are going to make enemies—and he did. But he was still generally respected. He was still popular among officers of the department."

Vigil in 1979 told Tomas Martinez of the *Albuquerque Journal*, "As chief, it's impossible to please all 360 officers in the department, but I think the fact that I've been chief almost 10 years should indicate that I have done something right."

Still, warranted or not, Vigil during that same period would purge his own upper ranks of the State Police. That coupled with two deaths and two planned retirements left CdeBaca looking more and more like Vigil's heir apparent. But if that's what Vigil wanted, there was still the 1982 gubernatorial campaign to be considered.

The oft-bitter 1982 race for governor was between Democrat reformer Toney Anaya and conservative Republican John Irick. Relations between Anaya and outgoing Governor Bruce King, also a Democrat, were more than strained. Irick, if successful, would be the first Republican elected governor since 1968. Anaya promised change; Republicans would have insisted on change from Irick.

Polls consistently showed Anaya running strong. Behind the scenes, it was being said that Anaya faced pressure to replace Vigil and that much of the pressure was coming from an Anaya supporter who wanted the chief's post for himself.

Little of it could have escaped the politically astute Vigil, who by 1982 was in his 13th year as chief.

At a State Police Board meeting on October 29, 1982, Vigil surprisingly announced his retirement. Within minutes and on Vigil's recommendation, the board unanimously approved CdeBaca as the new chief. The five-member board served at the pleasure of the governor but CdeBaca acknowledged that he did not remember a time when the outgoing chief–not the governor–recommended his successor.

It was five days before the November 2nd general election.

"What's the hurry?" *The Santa Fe New Mexican* asked about Vigil's sudden retirement in an Election Day editorial. "Instead of having a clear shot at appointing a person of his liking as State Police chief, the new governor first must deal with CdeBaca's future in the department," the paper said.

The 60-year-old Vigil said little more than that the time was right. "I just decided a couple of months ago. I'm in good health ... I've been here 13 years. It's time that someone else takes over," he told David Steinberg of the *Albuquerque Journal.*

King told the United Press International that he tried to convince Vigil to remain on the job long enough for the new governor to appoint a successor. Vigil reportedly told King that he simply did not want to go through another transition."

CdeBaca said Vigil had told him about his plans two or three days prior to the meeting of the State Police Board. "We met for breakfast at the Village Inn in Santa Fe and he told me he was going to retire and that he was going to recommend me as his replacement. He didn't tell me that he had discussed it with the governor or with the State Police Board. If he had such a discussion, he would have told me."

Vigil once before had told CdeBaca he was on the verge of retirement. "It was 1979 or 1980. Martin Vigil understood the treachery that he was facing from top-level commanders," CdeBaca said. "It seemed everybody was after him, not only high-level commanders, but members of the Legislature as well as the news media, particularly the *Rio Grande Sun.*

"The chief had been invited to speak at a social gathering of some sort in Roswell. He asked me to go with him. On that trip, he told me that he was thinking about retiring and I advised him not to, 'not while this cloud hangs over you. It would be a mistake for you to do it at this time.' He did not resign. He weathered the storm."

Elected with the largest margin in a governor's race since 1964, Anaya believed he had a mandate for change as he prepared to take office.

CdeBaca, himself, was well-schooled in politics and braced for the weeks ahead, armed with information about maneuvering within Anaya's camp.

"By now, I had completed 26 years with the State Police. Having served in many different capacities with the department, I felt very confident being the head of the department. The New Mexico State Police Board who served under Governor Bruce King confirmed my appointment.

"I asked District Judge Michael Francke to administer the oath of office.

When he was with the attorney general's office, he and I served on a multi-state border task force working with our counterparts from Mexico to craft a compact for the retrieval of stolen motor vehicles. Judge Francke had warned me to 'watch my back,' that Lieutenant Freddie Garcia was 'tight' with Toney Anaya and that Lieutenant Garcia wanted to be chief. I thanked him for telling me. I began to lay the foundation for a very ambitious program as chief."

Garcia, while employed with the State Police, had been assigned to work as an investigator for Anaya when he was attorney general from 1975-1978. Francke later resigned his judgeship to accept Anaya's appointment as Corrections Department secretary. Anaya apparently was unaware of Francke's purported comments to CdeBaca about Garcia.

Having previously worked together to recover stolen vehicles, Richard CdeBaca in 1982 asked Michael Francke, by then a state district judge, to administer the oath of State Police chief.

CdeBaca, even while looking over his shoulder, went about his work as the new chief.

"I implemented an aggressive enforcement initiative against crime and established visible patrols in rural areas, where there was no visible law enforcement. In an editorial, the *Albuquerque Journal* complimented me on my agenda. I began communications with Indian tribes to cross deputize officers since State Police officers had no jurisdiction inside Indian reservations, and it was always a problem."

Drawing closer to the day that he would be sworn in as governor, Anaya prepared to make top-level appointments. CdeBaca grew increasingly uneasy.

"Soon after Toney Anaya set up his transition office, he began asking for resignations and resumes from incumbents in office. I visited with him and asked him if his request for resumes applied to me, and his reply was that he was going to review all positions. (Martin Vigil had served as chief for 13 years under four different governors and had never been asked for a resume.)

"Toney Anaya asked me if I had any strong feelings about any of the State Police Board members, and I took the opportunity to tell him that Commissioner Mahlon Love had been a very hard-working board member, and he said that Mahlon would be one of the first ones to be replaced. Eventually, he replaced all the State Police Board members, which was not unusual as most newly elected governors did the same thing. Mr. Tom Brown from Artesia was named chairman of the board."

"After Toney Anaya was sworn in as governor, he named a new State Police Board. The new board confirmed my appointment as chief."

Although CdeBaca said Vigil was never asked for a resume by incoming governors, Vigil told the *Albuquerque Journal* in 1979 that as a matter of courtesy, he offered his resignation to each new governor. CdeBaca did not tender such an offer to Anaya; his prompt confirmation as chief by Anaya's newly appointed State Police Board gave CdeBaca a temporary boost of encouragement. And he drew support from other quarters, too.

"On Friday, January 14, 1983, the Hobbs newspaper congratulated me and I quote from the editorial: 'First CdeBaca wants to make State Police patrol units more visible on the highways. Instead of stationing themselves behind billboard signs or in a cluster of trees, waiting for a speeding motorist.'

"A concerned citizen wrote a letter saying, 'I am happy to know that we finally found someone that considers crimes, such as rape, theft, shootings, etc., more important than issuing of traffic tickets.'"

CdeBaca said he tried to win Anaya's confidence. "I had a staff meeting of all the top State Police commanders in one of the classrooms of the law enforcement academy," he said. "I invited Governor Anaya and he came. While there, he made the statement that there were cliques in the department and that he was going to do something about it. He referred to cliques in the Corrections Department and other areas."

Richard CdeBaca during his first days as chief of the New Mexico State Police.

The *Albuquerque Journal* in 1979 raised the issue of purported cliques within the State Police. "There is dissention in the ranks," it reported in a special tabloid section that looked in-depth at State Police operations. The paper asked: "Is there indeed an intra-departmental split in which officers are identified as 'Vigil men,' 'dissidents' or 'fence-riders'? Are there ethnic overtones?"

"Not all sniping is directed at Vigil," the *Journal* reported. "Other officers have been known to bad-mouth practically anyone in the force. Rank hath no privileges here ... There are persistent and recurring reports of ethnic grapplings within the force."

Anaya, convinced that cliques were hurting the State Police, continued laying the groundwork for his new administration. CdeBaca said he began feeling pressure that he knew he would not be able to tolerate.

"Governor Anaya called me one day to discuss personnel changes in the State Police. He told me he wanted some changes at the top to accommodate officers of his choice. I explained that I needed the most-trusted and qualified officers on my staff.

"On an ensuing visit to the governor, he showed me a copy of the State Police organizational chart. He named those commanders at headquarters that he wanted replaced. I explained to him that these command officers were nearing retirement and it wouldn't be fair to displace them and their wives who were also employed in town."

Among ranking officers who Anaya wanted replaced, CdeBaca said, were Major R.D. Thompson, who was in charge of Internal Affairs; Captain Al Briggs, who was in charge of the Intelligence Division; and Captain Bob Carroll, who was in charge of the Criminal Division. And, said CdeBaca, Anaya was very specific about another move that he wanted.

"He told me that he wanted Lieutenant Freddie Garcia promoted to deputy chief. Freddie Garcia had worked as an investigator in the attorney general's office at the request of Toney Anaya when he was attorney general. To promote Freddie to deputy chief, I would be jumping him over the ranks of captain and major and this would surely cause morale problems in the department. Freddie Garcia had not served in a top managerial position and did not have a broad exposure to the department.

"I discussed the programs I had implemented and the direction I was taking the State Police and the governor had no problem with this. I always respected the office of the governor, having served under 10, but I never heard in all my years of service of any governor getting involved in promotions and demotions."

Anaya said he had not promised jobs to anyone during the campaign. He denied that he had ordered Garcia promoted but acknowledged that he discussed a deputy chief position with Garcia after the election. Unfolding events suggested otherwise, said CdeBaca.

"At my next meeting with Governor Anaya, which was at the Governor's Mansion, he asked me when the next State Police Board meeting was scheduled. He told me to promote Freddie to deputy chief. I did not promise him anything. By this time, I was beginning to resent the governor's intrusions into State Police personnel matters."

The next scheduled meeting of the State Police Board was February 8th. CdeBaca said that one more attempt would be made to get him to do as the governor wanted.

"The night before the board meeting, Tom Brown, the chairman of the State Police Board, asked me to meet him for dinner. He tried to convince me to recommend the promotions desired by the governor to the State Police Board. I told him that if I did, I would be known by every police officer as the governor's 'boot polisher.'

"When I asked Tom Brown if he agreed with me that such promotions would demoralize the officers, his reply was, 'They will get over it.' He underestimated the professionalism in the department. I told him I would lose all respect from the officers, that I had principles to uphold. I emphasized to the chairman that the governor was politicizing the department and circumventing my job as chief and that he might as well be the chief."

Brown, who had just turned 80 when approached to comment for this book, said he did not remember many specifics about the period surrounding

CdeBaca's resignation. He said he did not recall having dinner with CdeBaca the night before the meeting of the State Police Board on February 8, 1983.

CdeBaca later called it selective memory. "Politicians forget quickly for their convenience," he said.

CdeBaca recalled how he was disheartened as a young patrolman in Alamogordo when he heard the man who served then as State Police Board chairman speak in the back seat of CdeBaca's patrol car about a promotion to be made later that day without regard to formal procedures. Ironically, years later a different police board chairman purportedly was privately asking CdeBaca as chief to make a promotion that he considered to be even more egregious.

Even though Brown did not remember the February 7th dinner meeting, CdeBaca insisted that the meeting occurred, recalling the conversation in considerable detail. "I believe the meeting was at the Hilton Hotel in Santa Fe. It was just the two of us," CdeBaca said. "I told Tom Brown that I wasn't going to promote Freddie Garcia to deputy chief. I told him that my deputy chief had to be one of the most-trusted and loyal members of my staff. He told me to give it some thought. He said, 'I don't know what I'm going to tell the governor.'"

It turned out that all involved were heading toward what is commonly referred to around politics as a train wreck. The timing of Vigil's resignation as chief and the immediate appointment of CdeBaca as his successor cast a shadow on the outgoing administration of Bruce King. Anaya, as the governor-elect who had been denied the opportunity to cleanly appoint his own chief, likely had public opinion on his side at the start.

But Anaya badly played the cards that he was dealt. It got messy and the news media put some of it out for the public to see. But much of what occurred was not openly known or reported and appears here for the first time.

Public opinion on the issue before long began turning against Anaya. It hurt him very early in his administration and likely left its wound until the end, contributing to sagging opinion polls that dogged Anaya even while he recorded impressive gains for the state.

Tom Brown must have walked into the February 8th State Police Board meeting hoping that Anaya would get at least some of what he wanted in the way of personnel changes. But CdeBaca would offer none of what he said had been asked of him.

"On February 8, 1983, the day of the board meeting, I only promoted

Lieutenant Garcia to captain, which would be the next step in the chain of command. Chairman Brown was expecting me to make other demotions and promotions, which I didn't.

"After the board meeting, Lieutenant Garcia showed up at my office complaining. He reminded me that the governor had promised him the promotion to deputy chief and I told him he should be glad he got promoted to captain. He said, 'I'm calling the governor,' and I replied, 'Be my guest, you can use my telephone.' He dialed the direct line to the Governor's Mansion, which I, as chief, didn't have.

"Freddie spoke to the governor, 'Hey, my man, you promised me that I was going to get promoted to deputy chief and Chief CdeBaca handed me a bone.' I couldn't hear the governor's reply, but I said to Freddie, 'Let's go see the governor at the mansion and settle this.'

"When we arrived at the mansion, the first thing Freddie said to the governor was, 'You promised me I would get promoted to chief, and all I got handed was a bone.' The governor asked me how soon I could promote him. I answered, 'Why don't you look at his personnel file.' At this time, Freddie threatened to sue me, Captain Bob Carroll, agent Bob Ortiz and 'you too.' (referring to Anaya). He told the governor he wanted 'those reports expunged from my personnel file.'

"Governor Anaya did not reply. I looked at Governor Anaya and told him that those files could not be purged under any circumstances. I told them, 'This meeting is useless and I got up and left.'"

CdeBaca, Carrol and Ortiz were all somehow connected to the sensitive material in Garcia's personnel file that drew Garcia's ire at the meeting with Anaya, according to CdeBaca.

He said that Garcia in his remarks to Anaya repeatedly asserted that the governor had promised to eventually name him chief, that his promotions would not end as deputy chief.

Anaya said for this book that he resented having top-level appointments forced upon him but agreed to keep CdeBaca as State Police chief if he and Garcia could work together as the two top men at the agency. Anaya wanted Garcia as deputy chief despite CdeBaca's protestations. Anaya said he personally told CdeBaca that he could not stay when it became apparent that he and Garcia could not work together because of "considerable friction" between the two.

CdeBaca said Anaya never terminated him but all of it left him knowing what he had to do. "I went home that night and roughed out my letter of resignation," he said.

"Early the following morning, I called Tom Brown, chairman of the board, and asked him to meet me at the Village Inn for breakfast. I told him of my meeting with the governor the previous night and I handed Mr. Brown my resignation. He asked me not to resign. I told him I was spending my time with Governor Anaya discussing promotions and nothing was going to change unless I did what he wanted.

"I informed Mr. Brown that I was arranging for a press conference and was inviting the three major television stations. Mr. Brown begged me not to go through with the press conference. I said, 'What other choice do I have? The State Police employees have a right to know why I am resigning and so does the public.'

"That afternoon, I went through with the press conference. All three television stations were there. My family, loyal State Police officers and civilians were present. I could see tears in some.

"Here is an excerpt of what I said to the employees of the department and the citizens of the state: 'Governor Anaya has asked me time and time again to promote and demote certain State Police officers. I feel that I cannot compromise principles. To do so would be to tarnish the badge of my profession. The governor should not invoke politics into a professional organization. For me to comply with his demands would demoralize the department. He wants me to promote officers who are not deserving. I will not serve as a puppet and expect the employees to respect me. As I retire, I salute all the employees and thank them for their hard work and loyalty.'

"Thus my career with the New Mexico State Police Department came to an end. The State Police motto is, 'Pro Bono Publico,' (for the good of the public) and I hope I lived up to that motto."

Brown, an Artesia resident who lobbied at the state Capitol for 24 years, recalled the breakfast meeting with CdeBaca on February 9th. "I remember trying to talk him out of resigning," Brown said. But he said he recalled few other specifics about that meeting.

"I know that (CdeBaca) did not see eye to eye with the incoming governor," said Brown. Anaya and Garcia, on the other hand were close, he said. "I know that (Anaya) thought a lot of Freddie (but) Toney never put any pressure on me to promote him at all."

Brown said he had conversations with Garcia adding, though, that he did not recall Garcia saying that he wanted to be promoted to chief in any of those conversations.

CdeBaca said he found it peculiar that Brown and Garcia would be talking at all.

Garcia could not be reached to comment for this book.

CdeBaca retired with an annual salary of about $42,000. There were 381 commissioned officers on the force at the time.

His abrupt resignation sparked comment within the news media and from the general public. Robert E. Storey, reporter for *The Santa Fe New Mexican*, wrote, "In a few days after Governor Toney Anaya figures out what he's done, he's probably going to kick himself. By unceremoniously dumping New Mexico State Police Chief Richard CdeBaca, he's only multiplied his problems and not solved any. Eventually, he'll discover what those involved with the State Police knew—that CdeBaca was the right man at the right time for a very difficult position ... Anaya led with his political gut instead of his head."

District Attorney Eloy Martinez, who admitted he was not the most-impartial observer, expressed disappointment in a published report. "I think it is not in the best interest of the citizens of this state, or of the state's law enforcement, to have the whole issue come down the way it did. It is on the surface too political," he said.

One man wrote of CdeBaca in a letter to the editor: "Here is a man who ... started at the bottom of the ranks and earned his way up to the top by virtue of his hard work, dedication and accomplishments in every position that he has held. There is nothing but praise for Mr. CdeBaca."

Another letter to the editor read: 'The governor insists he is going to take politics out of the State Police and yet is considering appointing people to positions within the department who openly supported him during his campaign with no considerations for those people who have worked hard for many years to gain the rankings of sergeant, lieutenant, captain, major, deputy chief and, hopefully, someday, chief."

Before the controversy ignited by Martin Vigil's retirement as State Police chief, Santa Fe District Attorney Eloy Martinez (at lectern) shared a stage with (from left) then-Deputy State Police Chief Richard CdeBaca, Santa Fe City Police Deputy Chief Juan Garcia, Santa Fe County Sheriff Eddie Escudero, and Vigil.

CdeBaca said he also got support from Bruce King and others in government.

"Bruce King called me, expressing regrets over my resignation and so did several state senators and representatives. Private citizens called me supporting me for standing up to Anaya. Felix Rodriguez, who had been at the Penitentiary of New Mexico for many years, was quoted in the newspaper calling Anaya, 'a little dictator.'"

But it wasn't entirely rosy for CdeBaca. *Albuquerque Tribune* reporter Mark Hopwood wrote: "Don't shed a tear for former State Police Chief Richard CdeBaca. An honorable man and a good police officer, CdeBaca became a loser in a political game he helped initiate … The intention of CdeBaca's game was to keep a certain circle of State Police officers and hangers-on in control of the department while keeping an opposing group out of power."

Hopwood reported that several "challengers to the ruling clique" in the State Police were active in Anaya's gubernatorial campaign. The clique long headed by Martin Vigil initiated problems that spilled over into 1983 by "foisting one of their own on the winner of the election," he wrote.

Anaya repeatedly referred to cliques that had to be broken up and called CdeBaca "petty." Anaya, wrote Hopwood, claimed that Vigil, King and others "extracted commitments on who would be promoted in return for naming CdeBaca chief."

Robert Storey of *The New Mexican* wrote that Anaya wanted to stop what he perceived as favoritism in the reassignment of veteran officers to undesirable places each time a new chief came in. "The department is full of cliques and factions that are disrupting the law enforcement work," Anaya said then. "This kind of stuff has been going on for decades. The only thing that is different this time is they have a governor who isn't going to put up with it."

Storey wrote that Anaya accused CdeBaca of attempting to perpetuate the old ways. Anaya said he became convinced that CdeBaca was creating his own clique and was involved in favoritism.

The new governor predicted that the controversy would fade and that the State Police would emerge stronger because of a "core of dedicated professional law enforcement officers."

CdeBaca noted it in his records.

"Governor Anaya made the statement, 'I'm convinced more than ever that the state is better off with Richard CdeBaca out of the State Police.' He denied that he ordered Freddie Garcia promoted but acknowledged that after the election he discussed a deputy chief position with Garcia. His statement was published in *The New Mexican* on February 12, 1983.

"When I resigned, Deputy Chief Don Moberly, was named acting chief by the board. But in time, governor Anaya replaced him with Captain Maurice Cordova and Don Moberly was demoted and transferred. Major R.D. Thompson was demoted and transferred to Las Vegas. Captain Al Briggs was transferred from the Intelligence Division in Santa Fe to Las Cruces. Freddie Garcia was promoted to become a deputy chief as promised. Captain T.J. Chavez also was promoted to deputy chief. The two majors who were zone commanders both resigned.

"Chief Cordova demoted and promoted all those officers that Governor

Anaya had wanted me to do. After about two years, Chief Cordova and T.J. Chavez abruptly left the department. The State Police Board replaced Chief Cordova with Captain Maurice Payne."

Four chiefs of police served under Anaya: CdeBaca, Moberly (who was acting chief), Cordova and Payne. It not only was evidence of instability during a troubled time, CdeBaca said, it affected the quality of law enforcement within the State Police for years. "There was an exodus of officers," he said.

Demoted early in Anaya's administration, Moberly had been promoted to deputy chief by Vigil. CdeBaca, on his way out of headquarters, said he informally designated Moberly as acting chief. "I didn't do anything in writing. He was the only deputy who was serving at the time so I just told him that he was to step in and take over as acting chief."

Vacancies on the force totaled about 40 during Payne's tenure, CdeBaca said. He said Payne sacrificed the positions in return for money from the Legislature to give salary increases to remaining officers.

CdeBaca said he counseled Payne against giving up the positions. "I told him, 'Go and beg, plead as chief, humble yourself and ask those legislators as we have always done for more money, but don't give up those positions.' The up side of Chief Payne's action was that officers got paid for their overtime but it took years to rebuild the ranks within the department."

As for assertions by Anaya and others regarding cliques in the State Police, CdeBaca said Anaya might have mistaken loyalty for cliques. "What cliques was he alluding to? All of retired Chief Martin Vigil's staff was gone. Deputy Chief Bullock had been killed in a truck accident. Deputy Chief M.S. Chavez had been retired for seven months. Deputy Chief Steve Lagomarsino had been demoted the previous year and had retired. Major Hoover Wimberly retired rather than come back to work as directed by Chief Vigil. Major 'Red' Pack had died during a hunting accident.

"Only Deputy Chief Don Moberly remained from Chief Vigil's staff."

CdeBaca during interviews repeatedly bristled at the mention of "cliques." But he acknowledged that there were, indeed, factions within the State Police that sometimes were informally defined along ethnic lines. "I remember when I was a patrolman in Santa Fe, a white police officer told me, 'If my activity is low at the end of the month, I can just go pick up Mexicans on Agua Fria Street to raise my numbers.'"

Sometimes, he said, it was jealousies that led to divisive remarks. "My broad experience as an officer and the education that I pursued while with the department prepared me for the promotions that became available," he said. "Still, some officers called me *lambe*, or boot kisser, because of the ranks that I attained. And these were Hispanic officers. I'd tell them, 'You had the same opportunities I had. It has nothing to do with being a *lambe*,'" said CdeBaca, whose father was Hispanic, his mother an Anglo.

Other times, nasty remarks might have been rooted in more than jealousies, CdeBaca said. "After Maurice Cordova became chief and made changes, there were comments among State Police officers that 'the Mexican mafia' had taken over at headquarters," he said.

CdeBaca, who opened a Santa Fe mercantile store and developed a mobile home park after retiring, insisted that he does not hold personal animosity toward Anaya. "There was life for me after Toney Anaya. If I had remained as chief, I would have retired with a salary I couldn't live on, and I would have missed some great business opportunities. If I were to sit down with Toney Anaya for a cup of coffee, I would tell him, 'You came into my life at the right time.' Toney Anaya is not my enemy. Had he respected me for promoting Freddie Garcia one step at a time, Toney Anaya and I probably would have had a decent working relationship."

Still, there is a notation in CdeBaca's records that, arguably, hints of feelings a bit more hostile. CdeBaca, paraphrasing one of Anaya's own remarks, wrote:

"Governor Anaya left office with a very, very low popular rating. The State of New Mexico was better off without him."

And CdeBaca offered no bouquets for Martin Vigil's departing move, even when reminded that Vigil was suspected of willfully directing an effort to ensure that his protégé would succeed him as chief. "Martin Vigil didn't do me any favors," he said. "If he really was looking to help me, he would have retired one year earlier and given me a chance to present myself and my programs solidly before the new governor's term. As it turned out, I went in as chief with a wounded wing."

Some of the support expressed to CdeBaca following his departure, went beyond soothing words.

"Two weeks after my retirement, the mayor of Santa Fe, Louie Montano, offered me the job of chief of police, which I declined. I did agree to serve on the city's Public Safety Committee. Governor Garrey Carruthers, who succeeded Toney Anaya, appointed me to the Governor's Organized Crime Prevention Commission."

Out of the police force that he joined at the age of 23, CdeBaca said he considered himself to be in the prime of life.

"I was 49 years old when I retired from the State Police. I purchased Big Jo Lumber Company, which was an institution in downtown Santa Fe since 1927. I moved the business to Siler Road and we have been serving Santa Fe for more than 32 years. Several times we have received the City of Santa Fe Award for being the best small business."

"On November 26 of 1983, I married Juanita Lujan and together we managed the Mobile Home Park which I built. In 1989, we sold the mobile home park. The store continues to be very successful."

In 1990, following Republican Garrey Carruthers' four-year term as New Mexico governor, an old friend re-emerged high upon the state's political scene.

"In November of 1990, Bruce King was elected governor for his third term. When he was appointing people to serve on his cabinet, he offered me the position of secretary of the Department of Public Safety. I was honored he would offer it to me, but I wrote him a letter declining it and somehow the letter got published in the newspaper.

"In January of 1991, Governor King called me while we were vacationing in Arizona and asked me to come and see him at his office. The day I arrived at his office, there were two other men waiting to be interviewed for the position of Public Safety secretary. Molly Chavez escorted me to the governor's office. Governor King asked me, 'How soon can you report to work? The secretary, Neil Schiedel, is gone and the position is vacant.'

Alice King and husband, Gov. Bruce King, (both seated) visited with ranking members of their administration in December 1992. Pictured standing (left to right) are Mike Cerletti, Lt. Gov. Casey Luna, Bill Garcia, Richard CdeBaca, Kay Marr, Jerry Manzagol, Eloy Mondragon, Judy Basham, Dick Heim, Anita Lockwood, Patrick Baca, Laura Treat, Alan Morgan, Frank Dubois, and Wayne Powell.

"I reported to work the next day and was the last person to be appointed to Governor King's cabinet, and once again I would be in charge of the New Mexico State Police. The governor also named me the drug czar for New Mexico."

King also had his eye out for a federal post in which CdeBaca might serve as a new Democratic president prepared to enter the White House.

THE WHITE HOUSE

WASHINGTON

June 28, 1994

Mr. Richard C. de Baca
Cabinet Secretary
New Mexico Department of Public Safety
P.O. Box 1628
Santa Fe, New Mexico 87504-1628

Dear Richard:

Thank you for participating in the recent White House briefing on crime. I hope that you found the discussions to be informative and productive.

As my Administration works with Congress to develop an effective approach to preventing crime and reducing violence, I am grateful for your interest in this crucial endeavor. Your personal commitment can make a significant difference in the lives of your fellow Americans. With your help, we can give our citizens hope that their schools, neighborhoods, and communities will be safer places in the future.

I hope I can count on your support and continued involvement.

Sincerely,

Bill Clinton

A letter from President Clinton.

"On December 22, 1992, I received a letter from Governor King stating, 'I have recommended you to President-elect Clinton for appointment to a federal board, commission or a task force. President-elect Clinton needs dedicated, enthusiastic and creative individuals to help him during the next four years. Your high level of knowledge, skills and abilities will be an asset to him in this process.'

"I didn't expect anything to come of it, but I respected Governor King for the recommendation. I also knew that he and the president were good friends. On August 11th, Governor King announced that National Drug Czar Lee Brown had appointed me to serve on the Director's Panel on rural Drug Abuse and Trafficking. My contribution would include offering recommendations for the National Drug Control Strategy and advising Director Brown about emerging issues and trends in abuse and trafficking."

In his post as state Public Safety secretary, CdeBaca in 1992 hosted a press conference in Albuquerque in support of the national gun control measure known as the Brady Bill. Sarah Brady, who chaired the national effort, thanked CdeBaca in a letter that autumn. In October 1994, he was invited to the White House to witness then-President Bill Clinton sign a comprehensive crime bill. "While I was at the White House ceremony, I met Senator Ted Kennedy, among others, and I was surprised when he asked me for Emilio Naranjo, who he called the 'patrón' of Rio Arriba County," said CdeBaca.

CdeBaca considered his tenure as Public Safety secretary to have been successful. Soon after going in, he drew praise from legislators of both political parties for cutting back on the number of cars that his agency's employees drove home, and he pointed to other more-substantive accomplishments.

"Under my administration as Public Safety secretary, we developed a strong working relationship with the National Guard, and the guard became a strong advocate for the anti-drug D.A.R.E. program. It helped us numerous times with our drug interdiction efforts.

"We also worked closely with the Legislature and the governor to get an appropriation in the amount of $13 million for the expansion of the Law Enforcement Training Academy.

"Working with the Army Joint Task Force 6 based out of El Paso, we built a modern police firing range next to the penitentiary without any cost to taxpayers. A rappelling tower was constructed on State Police property used for training. No taxpayers' money was used for the project. It was built with donations.

"I convinced the Legislature to finally relieve the State Police of school bus inspections. That responsibility was transferred to the Motor Transportation Department. Under Governor King's administration, we not only filled the State Police ranks but we also brought manpower to an all-time high."

"The governor and the adjutant general of the National Guard awarded me with the highest civilian award, the New Mexico Medal of Merit. This was the most-prestigious award I received in all my years of public service. The declaration read in part: 'As the head of the Governor's lead agency in the War on Drugs, Mr. CdeBaca planned, supervised and improved joint operations between state, federal, and local law enforcement agencies and the military, enhanced information sharing and intelligence operations, and pioneered driving while intoxicated prevention and drug abuse youth education programs.'"

"During Governor King's last four years in office, he never asked me to promote or demote anyone. In fact, he never interfered with my job."

"In November of 1994, Governor King lost re-election to Gary Johnson. Gary Johnson was a newcomer to politics. He had never served in an elected capacity. Many political observers believed that Governor King lost the election to an unknown because of the adverse publicity he got on the land swap with the Bureau of Land Management. A lawsuit was filed by a rancher whose land bordered the BLM property. The Kings had plans to develop the land. A federal district judge termed the land swap a 'sweet deal.' The voters apparently looked at it the same way and voted against Governor King."

Gary Johnson, a private construction contractor, defeated King by more than 46,000 votes. Roberto Mondragon, who had served twice under King as lieutenant governor, ran as a Green Party candidate for governor that year, collecting nearly 48,000 votes.[1]

The controversial land swap alluded to by CdeBaca was aired before U.S. District Judge John Conway in February 1994 as interest in that year's gubernatorial race was picking up. King's family business in 1992 gave up 17,000 acres of ranch land in Cibola County in return for 800 acres managed by the BLM west of Santa Fe in what figured to become a lucrative real estate market, reported Mark Oswald, then of *The Santa Fe New Mexican*.

Conway said in court that the Kings seemingly "came out smelling like a rose" in the deal. He asked a BLM attorney why he should not suspect that the agency "gave away the farm."

CdeBaca, while discussing later his work as state Public Safety secretary, mentioned the property obtained by the Kings west of Santa Fe. The subject came up while CdeBaca told of his department's accomplishment in securing a new firing range for law enforcement.

CdeBaca said King called him into his Capitol office one day and told him that the value of the property that the King family had obtained in 1992 would continually be deflated because of the firing range used by State Police and others nearby.

"The firing range was adjacent to the Kings' property," CdeBaca said. "What other conclusion would you come to," he said when asked if he thought the firing range would devalue the King family acquisition.

CdeBaca said the governor asked him to go into another room of the Capitol to meet with his niece, Rhonda King, to further discuss the issue. In that room, Rhonda King opened papers to show the layout of the property, he said, adding that he got the impression that the governor was looking to make a case for having the firing range moved.

But CdeBaca said he already had begun steps to make such a move and that King apparently was not yet aware of it. "At the time, I was already pretty much settled on the establishment of the new firing range near the Penitentiary of New Mexico," he said. "We still had some hurdles to clear. For example, I was still working to obtain a lease from the rancher who had property that we would need to build that new firing range."

CdeBaca said he saw nothing unseemly in the meetings he had with Governor King and his niece.

Recruit school graduation in 1992 brought the newest members of the
New Mexico State Police into contact with Chief John Denko and state
Public Safety Secretary Richard CdeBaca.

King and CdeBaca, of course, would have numerous other conversations,
some that both men wish had never surfaced. "One state representative kept
calling me and insisted on knowing why her husband, who worked for the State
Police, was being transferred. I told her that I wasn't aware of any such plans.
Then she called to ask why her husband had not been promoted to lieutenant
instead of another officer who she criticized as unsuited to serve the Northern
New Mexico community where he was stationed. I told her that I didn't interfere
with the police chief's promotions.

"Finally, Governor King called me in to ask what was going on with the state representative and her husband. I told him that the legislator was trying to use the influence of her office to enhance her husband's career."

Days after Gary Johnson became governor in January 1995, CdeBaca had a talk with yet another person working in the governor's suite of offices. There had been a long string of such visits over the years. Remember, it was the chief of staff to Democratic Governor John Simms who in 1956 talked CdeBaca into joining the New Mexico State Police. Decades later, Johnson's chief of staff would ask him to remain on as Public Safety secretary, the position that oversees the State Police.

"Lou Gallegos asked me to stay as Public Safety secretary but I declined. He asked me to recommend someone for State Police chief from the ranks and I wrote a letter on behalf of Major Frank Taylor. He was appointed chief.

"That ended my paid public service career and I returned to work with my sons and my wife, Juanita."

But CdeBaca would continue contributing in other ways. In 2000, San Juan Pueblo Governor John Bird appointed the former State Police chief to the pueblo's gaming oversight commission. CdeBaca served as chairman during his one year on the panel.

In all, CdeBaca served more than 30 years with the New Mexico State Police or overseeing the agency. "I left an unblemished record. I never had a verbal or written reprimand," he said. "I was loyal to every chief and every governor that served in office. Toney Anaya was the exception."

"It was a very challenging career because you never really knew what was going to happen from one day to the next," said CdeBaca. "More than I might have imagined going in, there were tragedies and barbaric acts. You can never really get those things out of your mind, out of your system. I've probably had enough of that for one lifetime."

Going in as chief, CdeBaca inherited from Vigil more than a strife-worn department and some of his critics. He kept Vigil's secretary, a woman who had served Vigil for 12 years. "Juanita was very good at her work so I kept her as my secretary during my brief time as chief. After I left, we got married and she has become a wonderful partner during the second half of my life."

Years after CdeBaca and his mentor, Martin Vigil, had both left the chief's office, their paths would cross one last time. Controversy stirred by one man's passing of authority to the other was behind them when Vigil injured his head while tending to pet rabbits at his home in Española.

Vigil needed help walking during his recovery and CdeBaca several times volunteered assistance. "I'd hook his arm in mine and we'd walk around his yard," CdeBaca said. "I considered it nothing more than loyalty to an old friend and superior who I respected. Loyalty was drilled into me as an officer. Before that, it was taught to me as a young boy at home."

Critics wondered if CdeBaca didn't take his concept of loyalty too far. Early in February 1983, *Albuquerque Tribune* reporter Mark Hopwood reported that CdeBaca kept "a notebook of derogatory comments made by secretaries and clerks working in State Police headquarters."

CdeBaca said it was not true. "It was a ridiculous accusation. It would have been a waste of my time," he said.

Hopwood in the same newspaper column attributed to Anaya a story that the new governor purportedly said served as an example of the power that the Vigil clique retained. Anaya asserted, wrote Hopwood, that CdeBaca had ordered a mechanic at the State Police garage to work on Vigil's personal auto but not to report it on his work log. The incident purportedly occurred after Vigil had retired.

"A State Police mechanic did work on Martin Vigil's car and then kept it off the books. But it was unbeknownst to me," CdeBaca said. "It was Captain I.B. Picket who told me about it right after I had left the department. He told me that he was the one who allowed the mechanic to work on the windshield wiper of Martin Vigil's car.

"I have no idea how it all came about, but Captain Picket first informed me about it and then apologized to me. I told him it was water under the bridge and that it was best that everybody move on."

And so they did through some difficult times for the New Mexico State Police.

CdeBaca had seen long strings of chiefs, governors and newspaper head-lines stream through his career. He wrote too many tickets to count, completed more incident reports than he cares to remember. He saved lives, lost others and lived like a gypsy when others his age were setting down roots. Political games-manship was everywhere. CdeBaca was both propelled and stung by it. In all likelihood, he played the games as hard as anyone.

A State Police crime scene: Police work, like politics in government, will continue to fuel the daily news. Photo by Luis Sánchez Saturno, *The New Mexican*.

As chief, he drove what was perhaps his department's finest car but never forgot his first police unit that invariably spit out thick black smoke as it approached its top speed while violators sped away in better vehicles.

Other times when CdeBaca got to where he needed to be, he often did not like what he found, such as the day when he and his father-in-law were pulled away from a family dinner and soon found themselves collecting body parts off of a Southern New Mexico highway. CdeBaca probably was never able to come up with a satisfactory answer to his father-in-law's question that night, asked as the older man looked in disbelief at his blood-stained clothes and hands.

"Why would anyone in his right mind want to be a police officer? You almost have to be born into it," CdeBaca said. "I don't know that I would do it again ... I guess I probably would, though. I never could have accumulated so many experiences if I had become an accountant."

Conclusion

Richard CdeBaca did not climb to the top of the New Mexico State Police Department by being unprepared. But he admits he was not in a position to fully inform his superior one day when he was summoned by the chief, who wanted to be briefed on developments that at the time seemed like they might be from another world.

CdeBaca probably will always feel like he fell short of his own standards when in the mid-1970s he was unable to adequately brief Chief Martin Vigil about mysterious cattle mutilations occurring in Northern New Mexico.

CdeBaca was more accustomed to police work that could be reasonably explained even if not fully defended. Policemen like Captain E.A. "Tuffy" Tafoya in Gallup seasoned him for the rough and tumble world of a cop's daily routines.

Tafoya got his nickname after having arrested two men for minor offenses around the time that CdeBaca joined the force in the mid-1950s. As CdeBaca tells it, Tafoya had two offenders whom he had to transport to jail but only one set of handcuffs in a situation where he sensed that the two men were eager to break for freedom.

"Tafoya ended up cuffing the right hand of one of the men to the left hand of the other man," CdeBaca said. "He then directed one of the offenders to sit on one of the big front fenders that protruded out from the patrol car's hood and had the other offender sit on the front fender on the other side of the car. (Tafoya) then proceeded to drive the men to jail. The two men on top of the car must have known that if they tried to make a run for it, they'd probably get run over."

It was police work of another period, much like CdeBaca's lauded record of recovering stolen vehicles during the 1950s and 1960s while acting largely on hunches, not probable cause.

Told years later of Tafoya's nickname and how he purportedly came upon it, State Police spokesman Lieutenant Eric Garcia couldn't conceal a chuckle. "Absolutely not," he said when asked if police officers could get away with such conduct today, no matter the circumstances. "Today, an officer would get a good old-fashioned ass-chewing from the chief before facing department reprimands and civil sanctions," he said.

Whatever a State Police officer does "must be done so it doesn't bring disrepute upon the agency," said Garcia, who went on to become chief of the Española Police Department.

Disrepute is something that CdeBaca said he sought to avoid at each of his postings as a state policeman. Garcia said CdeBaca's approach to his work is reflected in how CdeBaca is remembered. "His reputation in the department is unquestionable," Garcia said. "He had such a quality history of working with veteran officers. They enjoyed his quality leadership and no-BS attitude: Let's get the job done; let's get it done right and as quickly as possible."

Proud of the reputation, CdeBaca can't help but regret that one job left undone is resolution of Northern New Mexico's mysterious cattle mutilations.

An estimated 60 cattle had been mutilated on ranches in Dulce and other parts of Rio Arriba County by spring 1979, according to news reports. There had been nearly 8,000 reported cases in multiple states, mostly in the West. With scalpel-like precision, sex organs, eyes, tongues, ears and rectums were removed. Few tracks and very little evidence, save for the carcasses, were left behind, the *Albuquerque Journal* reported from its Washington, D.C., bureau in March 1979. Repeatedly, the best livestock seemed to have been singled out, the *Journal* reported.

Because of ranchers' mounting financial losses, members of New Mexico's congressional delegation and others in the nation's capital as well as in Santa Fe began addressing the mutilations as a law enforcement issue.

Gabe Valdez, an honored New Mexico State Police officer stationed in Dulce, told me early on as I worked as a reporter for *The Santa Fe New Mexican*, that "aircraft unavailable to us" appeared to be involved in the mutilations, hinting strongly at extraterrestrial activity. Others, too, spoke openly of possible alien involvement.

Valdez had worked on 32 mutilation cases in New Mexico during three years leading into 1979 and was considered to be the state's principal source of information on the subject. By the late 1970s, he had concluded that the mutilations were tied not to aliens but to a top-secret U.S. operation.

Tunnels discovered in Dulce were found to be "connected to the cattle mutilations," he said at the writing of this book. He said he was confident that the research has been traced to its source thousands of miles away, although very little of what he suspected has been proven.

Retired since 1992, Valdez said he found that listening devices had been secretly placed on his phone and other parts of his home in Dulce prior to his moving to Albuquerque.

Valdez said that Vigil and his other superiors at State Police headquarters were supportive of his work with the cattle mutilations. "No doubt, it wasn't a routine investigation for the State Police," Valdez said. "I had burglaries, homicides and fatal accidents to investigate so I couldn't work on the mutilations full time. But my superiors gave me a free hand to do whatever I needed to do while investigating the mutilations. Neither Martin Vigil nor anyone else interfered with me. In fact, I went to Canada with the approval of the State Police to work on these cases with the Royal Canadian Mounted Police, and I also went to Colorado to help with lab work there."

Valdez died in his Albuquerque home in 2011 of an apparent heart attack.

New cases of livestock mutilations continue to be reported in New Mexico, Colorado and as far away as Argentina.

It's all baffling to CdeBaca. He had much to learn when at Martin Vigil's direction, he began inquiring deeper into New Mexico's cattle mutilations, and he admits that so much remains to be explained even today. He refers to the issue as yet another example of the extraordinary demands placed on law enforcement during his tenure with the State Police.

"You put on your uniform for the first time and, honestly, you don't know what to expect," he said. "It's probably truer today than ever because of what we've been through in recent times."

CdeBaca's first uniform was donned in 1956 and his first patrol car already had logged more than a few miles when he initially got behind the oversized wheel. The wide-eyed young cop was in for a heck of a ride.

NOTES

Chapter 1

1. "History of the New Mexico State Police," www.nmstatepolice (accessed July 17, 2009).
2. Ibid
3. Ibid

Chapter 3

1. New Mexico Secretary of State, Official Results of 1966 General Election, New Mexico State Capitol North, Santa Fe, New Mexico, November 23, 1966, n.p.
2. David Roybal, *Taking on Giants, Fabián Chávez Jr. and New Mexico Politics*, (Albuquerque: University of New Mexico Press, 2008), 176.
3. Ibid, 173.
4. Ibid, 173.
5. Ibid, 173.
6. Ibid, 174.
7. Ibid, 173.
8. Ibid, 173.
9. Ibid, 173.
10. Ibid, 173.
11. State Judicial System Study Committee, *The Courts in New Mexico, January 1961*, (Santa Fe: New Mexico Legislative Council Service, 1961) 10.
12. Ibid, 19.
13. David Roybal, *Taking on Giants, Fabián Chávez Jr. and New Mexico Politics*, (Albuquerque: University of New Mexico Press, 2008), 177.

Chapter 4

1. Rubén Sálaz Márquez, *The Santa Fe Ring, Land Grant History in American New Mexico,* (Albuquerque: Cosmic House, 2008), 141, 142.

Chapter 5

1. Richard Gardner, *¡Grito! Reies Tijerina and the New Mexico Land Grant War of 1967,* (New York: Harper & Row, 1971), 259.
2. Ibid, 120.

Chapter 6

1. Richard Gardner, *¡Grito! Reies Tijerina and the New Mexico Land Grant War of 1967,* (New York: Harper & Row, 1971) 267.
2. Ibid, 210.
3. Ibid, 249.
4. Ibid, 278, 279.
5. Ibid, 286-289.
6. Ibid, 289.
7. Ibid, 284.
8. Ibid, 289.
9. Ibid, 290.

Chapter 7

1. Arthur Kopecky, Leaving New Buffalo Commune, (Albuquerque: University of New Mexico Press, 2006) XIV.
2. Ibid.
3. Ibid.
4. Pam Hanna (Read), Infinite Points of Time: Morningstar Chronicles Part II (New Mexico), essay last updated July 17, 2009, n.p.
5. Ibid.
6. Arthur Kopecky, *New Buffalo, Journals from a Taos Commune,* (Albuquerque: University of New Mexico Press, 2004), Forward XIII.

Chapter 8

1. Jeff Bingaman, attorney general, *Report of the Attorney General, 1980 Riot at the Penitentiary of New Mexico, Part 2,* (Santa Fe: State of New Mexico, 1980), B-16, B-17.

2. Ibid, B-16.

3. Ibid, B-20, B-21.

4. Ibid, B-21.

5. Roger Morris, *The Devil's Butcher Shop, The New Mexico Prison Uprising*, (Albuquerque: University of New Mexico Press, 1983), 16, 17.

6. Ibid, 18, 19.

7. Ibid, 28.

8. Ibid, 43.

9. Ibid, 47.

10. Ibid, 15.

Chapter 10

1. Paula Moore, *Cricket in the Web*, (Albuquerque, University of New Mexico Press, 2008), 56-59.

Chapter 13

1. Paula Moore, *Cricket in the Web*, (Albuquerque: University of New Mexico Press, 2008), 41, 136, 144.

2. Ibid, 144.

3. Ibid, 128.

4. Ibid, 128, 130.

5. Ibid, 40.

6. Ibid, 169.

7. Roger Morris, *The Devil's Butcher Shop, The New Mexico Prison Uprising*, (Albuquerque: University of New Mexico Press, 1983), 49.

Chapter 17

1. *New Mexico Blue Book*, 2005-2006, (Santa Fe: Office of the Secretary of State, 2005), 105.